The Attack on Troy

The Attack on Troy

Rodney Castleden

Pen & Sword
MILITARY

First published in Great Britain in 2006 by
Pen & Sword Military Classics
an imprint of
Pen & Sword Books Ltd
47 Church Street
Barnsley
South Yorkshire
S70 2AS

ISBN 1-84415-175–1

Typeset in 11/13pt Plantin by Mac Style, Scarborough, N. Yorkshire
Printed and bound in England by CPI UK

Pen & Sword Books Ltd incorporates the Imprints of Pen & Sword Aviation,
Pen & Sword Maritime, Pen & Sword Military, Wharncliffe Local History, Pen
& Sword Select, Pen and Sword Military Classics and Leo Cooper.

For a complete list of Pen & Sword titles, please contact
Pen & Sword Books Limited
47 Church Street, Barnsley, South Yorkshire, S70 2AS, England
E-mail: enquiries@pen-and-sword.co.uk
Website: www.pen-and-sword.co.uk

Contents

To John Urmson

We could bring Troy's hallowed crown of towers
toppling down around us – you and I alone!
                              (*Iliad* 16. 118–19)

Illustrations

Plates
(between pages 86 and 87)

Acknowledgements

I first worked with Rupert Harding when he was at Sutton and we planned *Britain 3000 BC* together. I am grateful to him for proposing this project after his move to Pen & Sword; we started discussing it as I was putting the finishing touches to *Mycenaeans*, which includes a brief outline of some of my ideas about the historicity of the Trojan War. This new book has given me an opportunity to develop them more fully, and with unexpected results. A book exploring in detail the events of the Trojan War seemed a natural development from my earlier writings. *The Attack on Troy* has become the fifth book in an Aegean sequence which already includes *The Knossos Labyrinth*, *Minoans*, *Atlantis Destroyed* and *Mycenaeans*. Readers may like to refer back to the earlier books in the sequence, but in terms of their main ideas the individual books are self-sufficient.

It is quite possible that this Aegean sequence would never have begun but for a holiday visit to Crete, a long time ago, with the historian John Urmson. Visiting Knossos and other sites with John led to animated and stimulating discussions about the Minoans. John has always been a sensitive and thoughtful listener, a good sounding-board for new ideas, a mine of obscure information. His patience when collaborating with me on our joint project, the music drama *Winfrith*, will never be forgotten.

I owe a continuing debt to Sinclair Hood, a great scholar whose profound knowledge of the Aegean bronze age informs his views about the period in a unique way; it is always refreshing to contemplate his strongly held and often highly individual views. I also owe a great deal to the many scholars who have delved into the Homeric question. Inevitably, this book has as its focus the reconstruction of a narrative, and deals with the archaeological, geographical and geomorphological evidence for that narrative – as well as the more familiar documentary evidence. It draws repeatedly on the huge body of Homeric scholarship, though I am very aware that a book of this length cannot discuss all the many arguments and counter-arguments regarding Homer. In the interests of a balanced treatment, some of those discussions have been left to one side; they were nevertheless considered in the preparation of the text.

In the opening stages of the project I anticipated that the unavailability of published, official topographic maps of the Troad at 1:50,000 or 1:25,000 scales was going to be a major problem. In Britain high-quality maps have always been available at any scale I want, so that I can measure or calculate distances, areas, slopes, intervisibility, and so on. A geographical perspective on events was essential and I could not imagine working on a project like this without accurate maps. As it turned out, I was very lucky in having access to two resources. The first included the exceptionally high-quality nineteenth-century maps of Lieutenant Thomas Spratt (British Admiralty Chart No. 1608, 1840) and Emile Burnouf (1879), which showed the landscape as it was seen by Frank Calvert and Heinrich Schliemann; Schliemann himself used and annotated Spratt's map. The second included the several excellent new contour surveys made in the course of Professor Manfred Korfmann's Troia Project. I am very grateful for the painstaking survey work that went into the creation of those maps, which make all kinds of new insights possible.

Michael Wood's *In Search of the Trojan War* is a book I have gone back to again and again since it was first published, both before and after visiting many of the sites described in it, and I am more and more impressed each time I re-read it. It is a far better informed, far more penetrating and far more scholarly book than anyone could expect from a television tie-in, and this is apparent in the number of scholarly citations the book now gets. It is good to see work of this quality gaining recognition.

Thanks are due, once again, to the staff at the Sackler Library at Oxford, where most of the reading was done.

I used several translations of the *Iliad* while working on this book, especially those of Rieu and Butler, enjoying each for different reasons. The recent Penguin translation by Robert Fagles has a boldness and vigour that I like very much, and I found myself using that most. The line references in this book are to the lines in Fagles' translation; I apologize if this confuses or irritates readers who prefer another translation.

Chapter 1

Introduction

Agamemnon! Menelaus! All Argives geared for war!
May the gods who hold the halls of Olympus give you
Priam's city to plunder, then safe passage home.
(*Iliad* 1. 19–21)

The Greek attack on Troy is one of the great landmarks of proto-history, its story the stuff of great literature. The city of Troy itself is certainly a landmark in archaeology; a bill-board near the ruins credibly claims it as the place where 'the first chapter of modern archaeology was written.' Today, Troy is a shambles, a famous archaeological site infamously ravaged by insensitive and impatient excavators, a confusing jumble of artificial hills and ravines, ravaged walls and spoil-heaps, in which it is very hard to imagine, let alone see, 'turreted Ilion … replete with splendid houses'. It is also a very small site, and that is something that has been a continual worry to scholars. Why on earth would the Greeks have assembled such a huge fleet and so many warriors to take such a small and insignificant site? There is a mystery here.

The archaeologist who is co-ordinating the current campaign of excavation at Troy, Professor Manfred Korfmann, has said, 'When Homer created the first epic poem from the myths handed down to him, he changed the world. It was really because of him that these ruins were so long the symbol of rivalry between East and West.'[1] This implies that the place became important because Homer wrote about it. But if a poet wanted a location in which to set his epic story, why did he choose somewhere so insignificant – unless of course it really was the right location and the story was true?

Troy had humble beginnings. It started in 3600 BC as a small village on a low flat-topped hill. It was rebuilt after successive destructions in successively grander transformations, and was finally abandoned in AD 550. By then it was already a mythic city and had been rebuilt, just as Tintagel Castle was built, on the strength of its own myth.[2] It was a powerfully symbolic place. Xerxes sacrificed a thousand oxen at Troy before embarking on his campaign against

Greece. Alexander offered sacrifice at the Tomb of Achilles – and always slept with a copy of the *Iliad* under his pillow.

Since the time when it was finally abandoned it has continued to exist in the world's imagination. Troy is an immortal city with a human story immortalized by the poets and dramatists who wrote about it in antiquity; it was they who singled out and privileged the place. The ancient tale of Troy's downfall has been told and retold, again and again – by Homer, Virgil, Chaucer, Shakespeare, Yeats, Berlioz and Tippett. Wagner considered writing his own version of the *Iliad* – an opera called *Achilleus* – but unfortunately the project got no further than the idea. On a political level the story of Troy came to epitomize the continuing struggle between East and West, between Asia and Europe, between Turkey and Greece.

The real Troy, the bronze age city of stone and bricks of sun-dried mud, was destroyed repeatedly, but one destruction counted for more than any other, the destruction commemorated in the tale of the Trojan War, the sack of Troy that was the climax of the attacks by the Mycenaean Greeks in the late bronze age. In antiquity there was a tradition of another, earlier, destruction of Troy. We hear far less about this one. According to legend, the walls of the town were built by Poseidon and Apollo together with Aiakos from Aigina, and commissioned by the king of Troy, proud Laomedon, the father of Priam. King Laomedon cheated the gods out of the reward (of horses) he had promised them. In revenge, Poseidon released a monster to menace the city. It was Heracles who freed Troy from this danger, then he too was cheated by Laomedon; in response, Heracles (who was the king of Tiryns) sacked the city. This event is firmly embedded in Greek mythology and is referred to in the *Iliad*.[3] There may be distant memories here of damage to the city by tsunamis or earthquakes – the area is prone to both – and of earlier dealings with Mycenaeans, perhaps even an earlier attack by Mycenaeans.

The date of the Trojan War was much debated in antiquity. Herodotus gave 1250 BC, Eratosthenes of Alexandria 1184 BC, Doulis of Samos 1334 BC (the earliest date), while Ephorus gave 1134 BC (the latest date). These estimated dates were computed from genealogies and they incorporated estimates of generation length that may have been inaccurate; it is possible, for example, for a man to father a son at sixteen or eighty-six. The most precise attempt at a date is the one given on the Parian Marble. This gives the sack of Thebes as happening in 1251 BC, Homer as living in 907 BC and the sack of Troy as happening on 5 June 1209 BC. The surprising pseudo-precision derives from a surviving line from the *Little Iliad* – 'it was midnight and a bright moon was rising' – but bright moons do not necessarily have to be *full* moons, and the 5 June date was inferred from that assumption.

In terms of harmonizing with the archaeological evidence from Troy itself and from the Mycenaean centres, the date offered by Herodotus looks likely to be the closest. For the purposes of this book, the Trojan War is taken as a historical event; it will, I hope, become obvious during the course of the book why I believe it is legitimate – indeed inescapable – to regard the war as truly historical. It is also taken as happening in the years around 1250 BC. Modern archaeologists are not by any means agreed about the date of the Trojan War. Even in terms of the archaeological evidence from Troy itself there is room for disagreement; some archaeologists think the Troy VIh layer represents the Homeric sack of Troy, while others argue for the next layer up, the slightly later Troy VIIa, equivalent to Late Helladic IIIB in Greece. Sinclair Hood argues for a later date still, Troy VIIb 2, which is equivalent to Late Helladic IIIC in Greece.[4] Emily Vermeule thought the fall of Troy remembered in the *Iliad* might be a much earlier destruction in around 1400 BC, when Greek pottery dating to Late Helladic II–IIIA 1 was being imported to Troy.[5] The absolute calendar dating for these horizons is debatable, and that means that archaeologists are looking at a range of dates between 1400 and 1100 BC. My preferred date, 1250 BC, is right in the middle of this range.

One reason for preferring 1250 rather than a later date is the fact that the mainland 'palace' centres were destroyed in 1200 BC and I think it fair to assume that those destructions must have marked an end to foreign adventures. I remain persuaded that this is a strong argument, though Sinclair Hood argues that at least some of the mainland Greek centres were reoccupied in LH IIIC and that they could have been centres from which a Trojan War was mounted.[6] Several reasons for preferring a later date have been offered, including the following:

1) the Catalogue of Ships and the Catalogue of Trojans seem to belong to a later period;
2) the Greek lifestyle described in Homer seems (to some scholars) to post-date the ordered, palace-based bureaucratic society of the Mycenaeans;
3) it would involve a shorter time interval across which an oral tradition had to stretch.

On the other hand, there are counter-arguments to each of these points:

1) the relatively small number of glaring anachronisms in the two catalogues can be explained as later interpolations, acquired during the many retellings before the Epic Cycle was written down;
2) the bureaucracy that is seen in the archaeological evidence of the Mycenaean and Hittite tablets may be only one side of a society that had its 'heroic' side as well;
3) if a set of poems of the length and complexity of the Epic Cycle poems could be transmitted orally across three centuries, then it could just as easily be transmitted across five centuries.

As yet there is no proof that the Trojan War as described in Homer happened, but there is also no proof that it did not, and quite a lot of circumstantial evidence that it or something very like it did happen. Three strands – the contemporary documentary evidence for the period, the archaeology, and the existence of a complex and highly detailed Greek oral tradition – these three strands woven together suggest that a Trojan War is more likely to have happened than not, and more likely to have happened in the mid-thirteenth century than before or later.

The story of the Wooden Horse, that notoriously treacherous gift of the Greeks, is one of many problems we will encounter in accepting as historical fact the traditional story of the Trojan War. The reconstructed horse at Troy, with its conspicuous rows of windows, does little to convince us that it was ever true. Nor does the 12 tonne fibreglass horse – a different horse bearing a different message – on the seafront at Çanakkale. That one was a gift from Warner Bros, who apparently felt that a peace offering to the Turks was needed for not making the film *Troy* in Turkey. In spite of that, interest in the archaeological site continues to increase, and seven new hotels are planned for Çanakkale, the nearest modern town to ancient Troy.

Ovid once wrote, 'Whatever was is now.' As we shall see, many of the issues of long ago are still live, still affect people today. There is animosity between Greeks and Turks. The Turks still hate the nineteenth-century German archaeologist Heinrich Schliemann for stealing 'Priam's treasure' from Troy, and the Turkish government is still trying to negotiate the return of the treasure from the Pushkin Museum in Moscow; the Russians took it – the spoils of a much later war – when the Soviet army took Berlin in 1945. And the spoils of war are what the *Iliad* is about.

To see past these and many other ramifications to the core bronze age reality – to what really happened at Troy in 1250 BC – is surprisingly hard to do. But the evidence exists and we need to look steadily and objectively at it, strand by strand, to see just how much it proves. An imposing barrow overlooking a bronze age battlefield suggests a war grave, but does it have to be, and does it have to be contemporary with the bronze age battle?

> I've stood upon Achilles' tomb,
> And heard Troy doubted; time will doubt of Rome.[7]

Perhaps Byron was right to be scornful; as we shall see, the topography of the Troad, the bronze age geography of the place, carefully reconstructed, has much to tell us about the truth of Troy.

Chapter 2
The Evidence

Come, tell me the truth now, point by point ...
How are the other Trojans posted – guards, sleepers?
What plans are they mapping, what manoeuvres next?
(*Iliad* 10. 449; 474–5)

The sole sources of information for the Trojan War until the late nineteenth century were the poems deriving from the Epic Cycle (mainly the *Iliad* and to a much lesser extent the *Odyssey*, which have survived intact, but also the lost poems, the *Kypria, Aithiopis, Little Iliad, Ilioupersis, Nostoi* and *Telegoneia*, which survive only in summary) and a few other later Greek writings that were evidently based upon them. The Epic Cycle or 'Homeric' version is thought to be a version of the story written by and for Greek colonists in Anatolia; it seems there were sagas composed on the Greek mainland that dealt with the Trojan War too, non-Homeric sagas, and these date from earlier than 750 BC.[1] Even buried within the *Iliad* are references to other poems, now totally lost, that told missing parts of the story. These cross-references to other poems in the cycle were probably left in deliberately to remind listeners of poems they had heard on other occasions; in this way the bard could extend the imaginative experience of his audience endlessly outwards. There was uncertainty in ancient times as to whether this story was history, legend or poetry, and that uncertainty persists to the present day. By the early nineteenth century, most scholars had come to the conclusion that it was poetry, pure fiction, and had no basis in fact at all.

Then, out of the blue, Heinrich Schliemann's late nineteenth-century excavations at Troy and Mycenae seemed to provide archaeological proof that it was history after all. It was an intensely dramatic moment. Since then scholars have been engaged in a fierce debate about the extent to which archaeological evidence corroborates the Epic Cycle. The debate for the past hundred years has revolved mainly around *how much* of the Epic Cycle narrative is based on historical events.

Frank Calvert, who was the American vice-consul at Çanakkale, bought the eastern half of the Hisarlik tell and started excavating. He uncovered the remains of the Temple of Athena and the Hellenistic walls raised by Lysimachus (301–280 BC), the later city of Ilium's magnificent defences, which Schliemann's excavations would later destroy.

Schliemann's first excavations at Troy took place in 1870–3. He used between 80 and 160 workmen to drive great trenches through the Hisarlik mound, against the advice of Calvert, who had wanted a network of more modest trenches. Schliemann's brutal digging destroyed many of the remains of the beautiful city of Lysimachus, the later city in which he was not interested, but it also unknowingly destroyed much of the Homeric citadel too. By 1872, Calvert had withdrawn his permission for Schliemann to excavate his part of the mound, and it is not difficult to understand why. Schliemann was irritated by Calvert's refusal to co-operate. Then Calvert published an article in the *Levant Herald* (on 4 February 1873) in which he wrote damningly of Schliemann's evidence from the Troy excavations, 'a most important link is missing between 1800 and 700 BC, a gap of over a thousand years, including the date of the Trojan War.'

Schliemann was furious with Calvert. Schliemann was sure Troy II was right for Homer's Troy when he found 'Priam's Treasure' in its debris, though this is now known to date from 2200 BC, too early by a thousand years to have been the Troy of Priam. But Schliemann knew inwardly that he had not really solved the problem. By 1879 he was writing, 'I thought I had settled the Trojan question for ever ... but my doubts increased as time wore on.' Calvert had been right.

Schliemann's final campaign at Troy focused on the area outside the great ramp marking the entrance to the Troy II citadel. These excavations, which were directed by Wilhelm Dörpfeld, uncovered a large megaron (a substantial rectangular building with a large rectangular main chamber and a vestibule or porch) like the one at Tiryns. In it, he found Grey Minyan pottery belonging to Troy VI, together with Mycenaean pottery now familiar to Schliemann from his work on the other side of the Aegean at Mycenae and Tiryns. The discovery of Mycenaean connections for Troy VI both excited and shocked Schliemann; Troy VI was the Troy that had contact with Agamemnon's Mycenae and must therefore have been contemporary with it. Troy VI, not Troy II.

Schliemann died shortly after this devastating revelation, at Christmas 1890. Wilhelm Dörpfeld continued the archaeological excavation at Troy. The great landmark campaign came in 1893–4, when the walls of the Troy VI citadel were uncovered. Dörpfeld was profoundly impressed when he saw the great North-East Bastion and recognized from its ambitious and accomplished masonry that this must be the Troy of the Trojan War. Hosts of philhellenes and Homer scholars rushed to agree. One of them was Walter Leaf: in his book *Homer and*

History, he wrote, 'We shall therefore not hesitate, starting from the fact that the Trojan War was a real war fought out in the place, and at least generally in the manner, described in Homer, to draw the further conclusion that some at least of the heroes whom Homer names as having played a prominent part in that war were real persons named by Homer's names, who did actually fight in that war.'[2]

Unfortunately these enthusiastic conclusions did not flow from Dörpfeld's discoveries at all. They were even so a breakthrough in that, as normally reticent scholars were saying, the startling new revelations were uncovering a 'past in which we had ceased to believe'.[3]

In the 1930s, Carl Blegen took a new look at the sequence of building phases at Troy, and inferred that there had been no less than forty-seven different stages. He homed in on the Troy of the Trojan War, looking again at Troy VI. Blegen became convinced that the destruction at the end of Troy VI was caused by an earthquake, not by people. He looked next at the following phase, Troy VIIa. This was a phase of very modest rebuilding inside the citadel. A shanty town was built. Where once there had been large, elegant, free-standing buildings, now there were only gloomy shacks cringing against the circuit walls.

The walls of Troy reconstructed. This is how the North-East Bastion of Troy's citadel would have looked in 1250 BC. The Bay of Troy is on the right, the citadel in the centre, the town wall to the left. The upper part of the wall was made of mudbrick.

Blegen interpreted this as the townspeople of Troy sheltering within the walls, threatened by the prospect of a siege. The destruction of Troy VIIa by fire was a man-made destruction. The date was now becoming a problem, as the Mycenaeans could not have attacked Troy after their own citadels had fallen in 1200 BC. Blegen thought the VIIa phase was quite short, perhaps only one generation, and he proposed a date of 1240 BC, later revising it to 1270 BC.[4]

Carl Blegen's version of the fall of Troy was opinion-driven, and no more objective or authoritative than Wilhelm Dörpfeld's. Troy VI is likely to have made a worthier target of a Mycenaean expedition than Troy VIIa, and this is *archaeologically* corroborated – by the cessation of imports of Mycenaean pottery at the end of Troy VIh (the final phase of Troy VI) in 1250 BC.

During the course of the twentieth century, archaeology added gradually more and more information about the twelfth and thirteenth centuries BC in the Aegean. There were two landmark breakthroughs in particular – Carl Blegen's discovery of the cache of archive tablets at Pylos and the decipherment of Linear B by Michael Ventris.[5] We now know that the Mycenaeans spoke an early form of Greek, and we can reconstruct the Mycenaean society that organized the expedition against Troy.[6] Certainly some elements in the Homeric story are true: to take but one example, the seizure of women from across the Aegean, as recorded on Greek Linear B tablets.

New findings from archaeology at the turn of the twenty-first century have drawn attention to a location a short distance away, to the Bay of Beşika 8km to the south-west of Troy. Close to the shore at the northern end of this small bay were a settlement and a cemetery, and they both belonged to the Mycenaeans. It would be hard to exaggerate the importance of these finds; archaeological evidence for the location of the Greek camp has been found at last.[7]

Later we shall see that clay archive tablets found at the Hittite capital, Hattusa, can shed yet more light, from a different direction, on ancient Troy. They give evidence that there were repeated disturbances along the western coastline of Anatolia and in particular that the Mycenaeans were causing trouble there for perhaps a hundred years leading up to 1250 BC, and not just for the ten years allocated to the Trojan War by Homer.[8]

As well as the archaeological evidence, we now also have a substantial amount of modern geomorphological evidence to help us in reconstructing the Trojan War. It is now possible to reconstruct with some confidence the shape of the landscape round Troy in the late bronze age, including the location of the shoreline, which turns out to be crucial in a number of ways. Several boreholes have been drilled in recent years in the Plain of Troy and the Bay of Beşika, and they allow us to reconstruct fairly accurately both the coastline and the nature of the terrain behind it.[9]

Armed with all of these different lines of evidence it is now possible to make a better informed reconstruction than ever before of what really happened in the Troad in the thirteenth century BC.

Chapter 3
Troy

It was you, Hector, you and you alone
who shielded the gates and the long walls of Troy.
(*Iliad* 22. 595–6)

The city of Troy described in Homer was a real city that stood on the Turkish hill called Hisarlik. There can be little doubt of that any more. Even the earliest hopeful travellers visiting the site commented that the view from the summit plateau, where the citadel had stood, was exactly as Homer described it. There is one detail in particular which has struck everyone. From the citadel it is possible to see the island of Samothrace peeping above the hills of the small island of Imbros, 80km (50 miles) away. Homer evidently had in mind either this spot or one close at hand.

In the *Iliad*, Hector talks of fighting on a battlefield between Ilios (an alternative name for Troy) and the Hellespont and giving back a Greek warrior's body to be buried in a mound beside the Hellespont.[1] This shows that Troy was close to the Hellespont. Poseidon looks from the highest peak of Samothrace (1600m high) towards the Greek ships, Priam's city and Mount Ida, with the clear implication that the Greek camp, Troy and Mount Ida were all visible from the highest point on Samothrace.[2] Poseidon dives into the sea, sets off towards the Greek ships and stables his horses in a sea grotto between Imbros and Tenedos before continuing to the Greek ships. It is clear that all of these features are conceived as lying approximately in a straight line. Troy was therefore not only near the Hellespont but on an approximately straight line connecting Mount Ida, Imbros, the Greek camp and the peak of Samothrace. The only major bronze age city that fits the description is the one found at Hisarlik.

The peaks of Samothrace and Mount Ida are both visible from Hisarlik; Hisarlik is in the plain; Hisarlik could be reached within an hour or two from the site believed to be that of the Greek camp.[3]

When Alexander the Great visited Troy to pay homage to the heroes in 334 BC, it was to Hisarlik that he came – and nowhere else. The Ilians who lived there showed Alexander their Temple of Athena, and in it some of the weapons and armour that had been used 900 years before in the Trojan War, including a wonderful relic that they said was the shield of the hero Achilles himself. Alexander was in no doubt whatsoever about the identity of the site, and nor were the Ilians who curated it. It was Alexander's idea to enlarge and embellish Ilium to what he imagined had been its former grandeur. From 301 BC onwards, he was able to do this, and it was he who ordered the rebuilding of Troy. The academic debate about the location of Troy only started in AD 160 with Demetrius of Scepsis, and it was finally settled by the discovery in 1893 of the remains of a late bronze age fortress within the Hisarlik mound, a fortress that was contemporary with the great strongholds of Mycenaean Greece, and overlying the smaller, older acropolis identified by Schliemann in 1872.

Troy stood in the north-westernmost corner of Anatolia, or what is now Turkey, on the western fringe of the Hittite Empire. The city was built on a low, flat-topped hill overlooking a substantial bay that opened onto the entrance to the Hellespont to the north. Powerful sea currents have always swept through this 2km wide channel separating Europe from Asia – and powerful economic and political currents too. The channel has from the bronze

The Troad, the bronze age kingdom of Wilusa: physical geography.

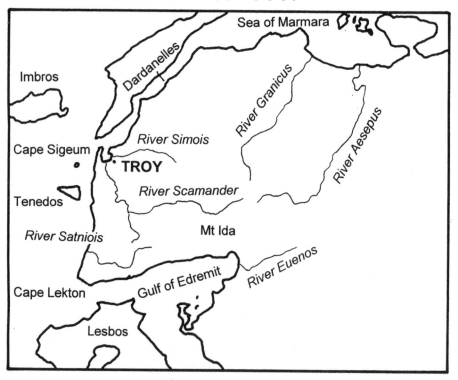

age onwards been a major international thoroughfare for ships trading between the Black Sea and the Mediterranean. Troy occupied a key position, dominating the harbour that opened like a sentry box onto the Hellespont. That is what made Troy so desirable, both to the Trojans and to the Greeks who came to plunder their city and, perhaps, take it from them.

There were major east–west land routes converging on the Hellespont, where people could cross from Asia into Europe. There was a also a major land route through western Anatolia leading from the Mycenaean colonies in the south-west to the shortest crossing into Europe; that too passed the city of Troy.

For long periods during the summer, the sailing season, a strong north-east wind blows across the southern entrance to the Hellespont. This head-wind was impossible for the square-rigged shallow-draft vessels of those times to cope with. Vessels like these had to sail before the wind. They might at a pinch be rowed, but not against both winds and currents in the Hellespont.[4] This meant that ships must often have had to put into the last harbour before the Hellespont, which was the Bay of Beşika, Cradle Bay. This break in the cliff coastline is now hardly noticeable because it is almost entirely blocked by silt and coastal sand dunes, but in the late bronze age it was a small semicircular harbour, making a welcome refuge for those waiting for the wind to change so that they could pass through to the Black Sea.[5] This small harbour would have been supervised by the Trojans, and doubtless harbour dues were collected from the ships' captains to fill Troy's coffers.

The Bay of Troy was doubtless used in conjunction with the Bay of Beşika. Square-rigged shallow-drafted ships could only sail before the wind and there was always a danger of ships being trapped in a harbour by days or even weeks of wind blowing in through the harbour entrance. Many bronze age ports had two harbours, facing in different directions; Amnisos, the port of Knossos, is another example. Possibly the Trojans used the Bay of Troy and the Bay of Beşika in this way.

Troy was a wool-producing kingdom, probably exporting fleeces, wool, yarn and textiles. The Plain of Troy would have been suitable for horse rearing, as was the Plain of Argos.[6] Homer says the Trojans were horse-breeders, just like the Mycenaeans, and numerous horse bones have been found at Troy, suggesting that horses really were part of the Trojan economy, as Homer said.[7]

The Bay of Troy probably served as a harbour for a fishing fleet. Shoals of mackerel and tunny came through the Hellespont every autumn, and there were probably shellfish, including oysters, in the bay itself.

The Trojans must have had their own fleet, even though there is no archaeological or documentary evidence of it, if only to act as a coastguard. It is likely that the Trojans used ships for trade. It is also likely that they used ships to raid other coastal settlements, just as they in their turn were raided by the Mycenaeans. The events of the Epic Cycle in effect imply that the Trojans

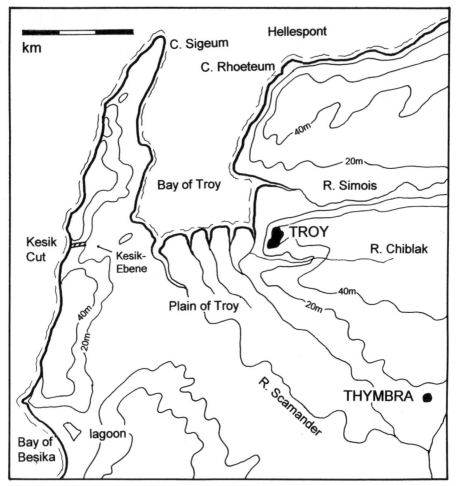

The Plain of Troy as it was in 1250 BC.

pillaged mainland Greek centres in the same way that the Mycenaeans pillaged Troy. The Mycenaean attack on Troy was after all a 'tit-for-tat' attack, in retaliation for Paris's abduction of a Mycenaean princess from Therapne in Laconia. The Trojans would have needed warships to protect their mercantile interests, defend themselves against pirates, and plunder other coastal towns. On the other hand, there was no Hittite Grand Fleet; the Hittites were not the great seafarers that their neighbours the Mycenaeans were; they were fundamentally a land power. On balance, the Trojans must have had ships but their fleet is likely to have been small.

What was Troy called? Place names can persist over surprisingly long periods. The obscure village of Gnossu in Crete turned out to be the site of the classical city of Knossos, which in turn stood on the ruins of the Minoan city named in the bronze age tablets as 'Ko-no-so', which was probably pronounced

'Konossos', much as we pronounce the place name today. Was Troy perhaps called something like Troia in antiquity? Homer uses Troia and Wilios; Hittite tablets of around 1420 BC refer to a city of Taruisa in a country called Wilusa located in north-west Anatolia; a Pylos tablet mentions 'To-ro-ja', a Trojan woman. Wilios (the Homeric Greek name) or Wilusa (the Hittite name, probably pronounced 'Wiloosha') was the name of the state. In line with the contemporary practice elsewhere in Anatolia, the capital city may have been known by the same name. Homer uses 'Ilios' (= Wilios) 106 times in the *Iliad*. The name 'Troia' is used 53 times. It is not clear what significance the two names had, but there is a genuine memory here of a place known by two names. Perhaps, as others have suggested, the citadel had a name of its own. Homer implies this by referring to a special part of Troy which he called the Pergamos, which must from the context have been the citadel.

It was recognized in late antiquity, by Strabo, that the Plain of Troy must once have been a bay and that it had been filled in by deposition from the rivers emptying into it, the Simois and the Scamander.[8] Schliemann did not want to believe that, because replacing the plain with a bay left nowhere for the fighting to take place. No plain, no battlefield. No battlefield, no Trojan War. Schliemann's collaborators, Rudolf Virchow and Emile Burnouf, sank shafts into the Plain of Troy and obliged Schliemann by concluding that the sea had never occupied the plain, though there had been a lake in the northern part of it. This wishful thinking was overturned by cores taken in 1977, which produced seashells showing that there had indeed been a large bay of the sea occupying the northern part of the Plain of Troy, its shore very close to Hisarlik at the time of the Trojan War.[9]

When the sea first rose to something close to its present level, in 5000–4000 BC, Troy stood on a headland jutting into the eastern side of a large bay, the Bay of Troy. The water was as much as 10m deep in the small inlet immediately to the south-west of Hisarlik, and which is now the silted Chiblak valley.[10] By 1250 BC the Chiblak valley and the whole of the southern half of the Bay of Troy had been filled in with silt deposited by the distributaries of the River Scamander (now called the Kalafati Azmagi). At the time of the Trojan War, Troy stood close to the south-eastern corner of the bay, and the sea level was 2m lower than today. In simple terms, of what is now the Plain of Troy, the northern half was a shallow bay and the southern half was a level alluvial plain – and that was where the battles between Greeks and Trojans were fought. Troy was no more than a kilometre from the sea, exactly as Strabo estimated, and there was still a substantial Plain of Troy to the south.[11] Allowing for the existence of a substantial bay *does* leave space for a battlefield after all.

The Bay of Beşika to the south-west of the Bay of Troy has also been at least half filled in, not by rivers but by the processes of coastal deposition. In 4000 BC only a narrow neck of land separated the two bays, but it nevertheless consisted of a barrier of solid rock rising to a height of 8m above present sea level, meaning that there was never any sea passage connecting the two bays.[12]

Since long before it was rediscovered as the site of ancient Troy, the low hill on which the city stood was known as Hisarlik – 'the place of the fort'. It is a small site, its originally level top wrecked by Schliemann's and Dörpfeld's savage late nineteenth-century excavations and turned, by their workmen, into a maze of gullies and hillocks. We know from sketches made by Dörpfeld towards the end of the nineteenth century and Maclaren in 1847 that Hisarlik had a smooth flat top. A low hill a mere 200m across, Troy is a very insignificant-looking site, whereas the story of Troy seems to have been painted on a colossal canvas. In later antiquity, Troy had become a sacred city, a city of noble dreams, a fable, the equivalent of Jerusalem in the medieval European mind.

The idea that Hisarlik was the site of Troy came from Dr Clarke, who visited the site in 1801, though his discovery was dismissed by others at the time. The claim was repeated in 1822 by the Scottish traveller Charles Maclaren. Calvert realized in 1853 that Hisarlik was a tell, a hill whose height had been raised by the debris of successive settlements built upon it. It was Calvert who persuaded Schliemann in 1868 that this was so, immediately following Schliemann's visit to Bunarbashi, another site to the south, which Schliemann had until then believed to be the site of Troy.

Hisarlik is a small plateau terminating in a steep drop down to the west, to the Plain of the Scamander, and a very steep drop down to the north, onto the Plain of the Simois, a river today called the Dumrek Su. Today, Hisarlik looks out to the north-west across a flat alluvial plain, land that in the late bronze age was a broad shallow bay 3km across, as Robert Wood rightly suggested in 1769. (It was Robert Wood who also proposed that the *Iliad* had initially been

The 'Ten Cities' of Troy

Phase of Troy's history	Calendar date
The founding of Troy	3600 BC
Troy 0	3600–3000 BC
Troy I	2900–2600 BC
Troy II	2600–2450 BC
Troy III	2390–2200 BC
Troy IV	2200–2000 BC
Troy V	2000–1870 BC
Troy VI	1700–1250 BC (the city of the Trojan War)
Destruction by the Greeks	1250 BC
Troy VII	1250–1020 BC
Troy VIII	800–85 BC
Troy IX	85 BC–AD 550
The abandonment of Troy	AD 550

transmitted by memorized songs – not written down.) The wide shallow bay would have allowed ships to sail in to within a kilometre of the walls of Troy. The bay in which Schliemann had not wanted to believe is mentioned in Homer; the River Scamander 'comes down to the broad bay of the sea'.[13]

Like other ancient cities, Troy was built and rebuilt several times, the mudbrick remains of each layer building the mound higher each time. The natural hill was 25m high. The summit of the hill at the time of the Trojan War was 40m high; almost half the height of the hill was the remains of earlier settlements. The first Troy, Troy 0, was founded in 3600 BC. It was a village only 90m across. The nine main layers, the nine 'cities', Troy I–IX, with their forty-seven subdivisions, represent the development of the village into a walled urban acropolis over a period of four thousand years, from 3600 BC until its final abandonment in AD 550.

The Citadel of Troy

The Troy that was attacked by the Greeks, Troy VI, flourished between 1700 and 1250 BC. In its day, this was by far the biggest and most important citadel in the whole of western Anatolia.[14] Within this long period, lasting 450 years, there were eight subsidiary phases, which archaeologists call Troy VIa–VIh, representing continuous cultural development and growth.

Troy VI was a more glamorous city than any of its predecessors. Its fortifications were built in a spectacular new style entirely different from anything the Mycenaeans had seen. The Mycenaeans had citadel walls, but they were nowhere like the quality of the walls of Troy in architectural refinement and sophistication. The Hittites had walled citadels too, but not quite like this; the Trojans were building in an eclectic style of their own.

The Trojan citadel was surrounded by a stone circuit wall 550m long, 5m thick and 6m high; it was built of closely fitting limestone blocks and had a vertical inner face but a sloping, or 'battered', outer face to give it greater structural strength. The batter, or inward slope, was a feature of earlier phases at Troy, though interestingly not of other sites in western Anatolia. The blocks were well fitted together, without mortar. The vertical joints in successive courses were carefully alternated to give maximum strength, just as in modern brickwork. Once the walls were built they were given a final dressing to ensure a smooth overall finish. This was not just for the sake of appearance, but to make the walls harder to climb.[15]

This very solid stone structure was surmounted by a superstructure, a vertical mudbrick wall that rose another 3 or 4m, making the wall an imposing 9 or 10m high in all. When excavated, fragments of the mudbrick superstructure were found still in position on the north-east side of the circuit, though they have subsequently been weathered away. At the very top, the wall thinned to about a metre to create a parodos or wall-walk 2–3m wide on the inside. This walkway was perched 2m or so above the general ground level

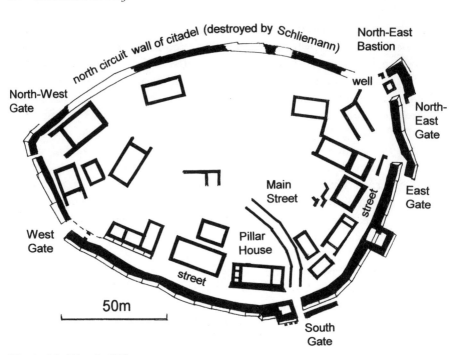

The citadel of Troy in 1250 BC.

inside the citadel, and was probably reached by stairways made of stone or mudbrick.

The use of sun-dried mudbricks for wall-building had a long history in the Near East, including Egypt. The mudbricks were strengthened by adding chopped straw and sometimes animal hair. Finished walls were often dressed with a coating of clay smoothed over them, partly to make the walls look smarter, partly to reduce water penetration. Mudbrick walls were less resistant to a determined attack than stone walls, and could be holed or undermined easily by enemy sappers, if they could reach the base of the brickwork. Siege scenes from Assyria and Egypt often show sappers using sticks and picks to make holes in mudbrick ramparts. The mudbrick walls were, even so, surprisingly good at absorbing the energy of a catapult shot.[16]

In the phase following the fateful attack, the phase known as Troy VIIa, the mudbrick wall was replaced, everywhere except in Tower G on the north-east side, by a thin stone wall 2m thick that was at least 2m high. It may be that this change of material was made as a result of the way the Mycenaean siege engines had been able to demolish the mudbrick walls. Behind this vertical upper wall there was the parapet that served as a walkway and fighting platform for the citadel's defenders. It may have been roofed to give some protection from arrows, spears and other missiles coming over the wall.[17]

The massive masonry of the lower wall was of a higher quality than before. The well-cut limestone blocks were laid in courses, the ashlar blocks not just fitting well on the outer face but right through the wall. The cyclopean masonry the Mycenaeans were building at that time was composed of two megalithic skins separated by a rubble fill. The Trojan masonry was much more sophisticated; it was well-jointed, with headers tying the outer face to the interior of the wall, and solid ashlar masonry right through. Where the wall is exposed once more to the light of day, it looks as good as the day when it was newly built. The wall was embellished with carefully designed offsets every 9m. The purpose of the offsets has been much debated. They often mark a slight change in the direction of the wall, and are therefore a clever way of avoiding the structural (and strategic) weaknesses associated with corners. There are, on the other hand, far more offsets than are needed to achieve a polygonal plan, and it is more likely that they were inserted for aesthetic reasons.

The South Gate of the citadel as it looked in 1250 BC (Troy VI). The massive tower with its thick walls was built to defend the gate and impress those approaching it. Note the six monolithic memorials at the base of the tower.

In Troy VI, the entire circuit wall of the citadel was rebuilt in this accomplished and grandiose style, with the exception of one short section on the west side. For some reason this section was not rebuilt. Perhaps it was regarded as being well enough defended by the steep slope up from the plain. More likely the rebuilding of the fortifications was a continuing process and the attack by the Mycenaeans came at a moment when the current rebuilding was not quite finished. Different sections of the citadel wall can be dated. The western section was built before Troy VIf; the eastern section was built during Troy VIf; several sections on the north-east, south and north-west were built in the following phase, Troy VIg.

Towers were built at irregular intervals round the citadel wall. At Hattusa, the Hittite capital, the citadel wall was lavished with towers, twenty in all, and they were evenly spaced. At provincial Troy, perhaps understandably, they were used more economically, probably no more than eight altogether, and placed beside gates to supervise and protect them. The projecting towers enabled the defenders to direct enfilading fire on attackers. Attack was likely to focus on gates, and some towers were built next to gates in order to defend them. In some places, where there were no towers, the walls were made to overlap in such a way as to expose the attackers to counter-attack from both left and right.

The advantage of placing towers at intervals along the wall was apparent to the Trojans, though they did not build them regularly at equidistant intervals. Towers H and I, added on the east and south in Troy VIh, were perhaps bigger and more impressive than they needed to be. Tower H is over 11m wide at its base and it projects 9m outwards from the curtain wall, twice as far as strictly necessary. Its function, narrowly viewed, was to protect the East Gate, Gate S, but its great size suggests that it had an aesthetic function, to convey an impression of strength and so intimidate those approaching the gate.[18] This is actually rather similar to the architectural principles at work in a Mycenaean citadel; at the Lion Gate at Mycenae, there is a similarly dual-purpose projecting bastion, a mass of masonry to intimidate the visitor.[19]

The building and rebuilding of fortifications at Troy went on more or less non-stop through the middle and late bronze age. The Trojan kings used the work on the fortifications as a conspicuous work-consuming project, one that would never end, rather like the pharaohs and the endless work they commissioned on their pyramids. It was, I think, probably by chance that one stretch of citadel wall on the west was left only half the thickness of the rest of the wall, and was poorly built of smaller stones. Here the defences of Troy were conspicuously at their weakest; startlingly, Homer actually mentions that there was one weak section of wall, 'by the fig tree where the city is openest to attack and where the wall may be mounted'.[20] The west citadel wall is of course the section that was most exposed, because it had only a few buildings of the town in front of it and the town wall with a gate only 60m in front. This is one

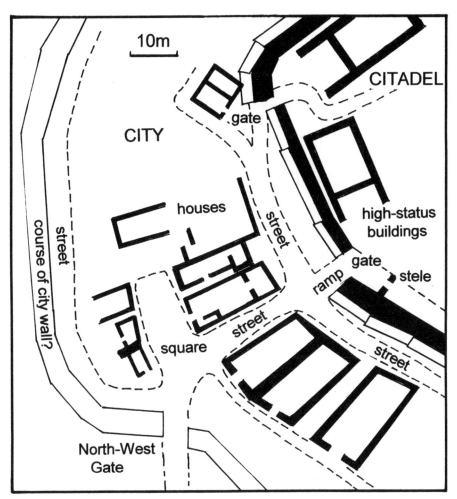

10m

CITADEL

CITY

gate

houses

street

course of city wall?

street

high-status
buildings

gate

stele

ramp

street

square

street

North-West
Gate

The weak west wall of the citadel. Recent archaeological work shows that it was not exposed to a direct attack from the west because there were houses in front of it and (probably) a town wall 60m away to protect it.

of those highly significant moments where a line in Homer and the detailed archaeology of Troy exactly match.

The 'well-built', 'finely towered' citadel of Troy had five gates and posterns (that have survived). The main gate of the citadel was Gate T, on the south side, and this was the entrance from the city. Gate T was flanked by a huge square stone tower 15m high and jutting out 9m from the citadel wall. The tower had six monolithic stelae lined up in front of it. Carl Blegen thought they must be plinths for statues of the gods of Troy but there is no reason to think this.[21] Certainly the stones had some profound ritual significance; they were probably idols in themselves, representing deities, or monuments to heroes or heroic events, rather like war memorials.

Inside the South Gate, a wide formal paved street with a central drain curved up to the summit, where there was some prestigious building. On each side rose imposing, high status buildings of unknown purpose. These stately buildings were trapezoid in plan, with their shorter sides facing the summit and their longer sides facing the fortification wall. House E had a steep retaining wall made of well-cut stone. House F had recesses for wooden beams and twelve stone bases on the floor to carry timber columns. House M had an L-shaped plan and stood on a carefully built retaining wall 27m long; like the circuit wall this had offsets – four of them – and they were not there to create a polygonal plan, but for visual effect. House M was built like a miniature fortress.

It is generally assumed that the royal residence, the palace where the king of Troy lived, stood on the summit. House M looks as if it might have been a royal house, and it might have been the house of King Priam. Some of the high status buildings in the citadel could be temples, and it may well have been a temple or temple complex that stood on the summit at Hisarlik. Most of the remains of the late bronze age summit building were removed when the later Temple of Athena was built or rebuilt there early in the third century BC (Troy VIII); that may indicate that the site was sacred rather than secular in the earlier period too.[22]

Temples at the heart of Troy? The location of the temples in later phases suggests that earlier temples were in the same area – on the summit.

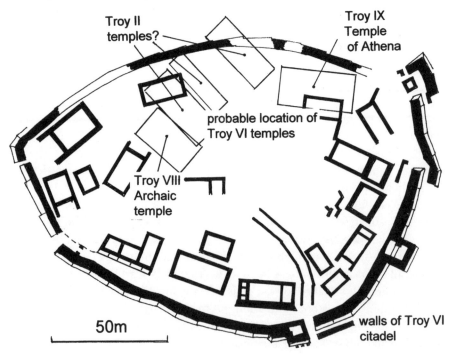

In 1250 BC, Troy VI was destroyed. Wilhelm Dörpfeld thought this destruction was the result of people attacking the site; he saw evidence of 'a great fire' at various points. Manfred Korfmann more recently found further evidence of an attack in a thick layer of charcoal dating to 1250 BC, along with slingshots, bronze spear points and arrowheads within the debris, some even lodged within the circuit wall.[23] This looks very much like hard archaeological evidence of the Greek attack on Troy.

But Carl Blegen believed that Troy VI was destroyed by an earthquake. The masonry of the citadel's circuit wall is founded on a cushion of earth, which acted as a shock absorber. The tower wall is founded directly on bedrock, and that is cracked; that is why Blegen argued for an earthquake. In some places there are large vertical cracks in the wall, which he attributed to earthquake damage. The thin-walled mudbrick superstructure of the citadel wall fell in several places, and some of the high status buildings were ruined. Even so, the main wall of the citadel remained standing; Denys Page is wrong to say that 'nothing was left standing intact, not even the circle of great wall and towers'.[24]

The citizens of such a rich and powerful city should have been able to repair the moderate earthquake damage (if indeed it *was* earthquake damage), yet no repairs were made. It looks as if the decision-making élite responsible for maintaining Troy VI was just not there any more.[25] A compromise explanation is possible – that there was an earthquake, and the Greeks were able to attack during the confusion, exploiting the structural damage. Even so, the toppling of the ramparts is equally likely to have been the result of the action of siege engines during the attack and slighting following the successful capture of the fortress; both techniques were in use in the following decades in Assyria. The toppling of the upper walls would have been sufficient to leave the defenders in the citadel defenceless; the toppled debris would also have blocked streets and partially buried the lower walls; the general mess resulting would effectively have rendered the citadel useless. In the circumstances, demolishing the solid masonry of the lower walls – a huge undertaking – was unnecessary.

On balance, the destruction of Troy in 1250 BC is far more likely to have been caused by human hand, and the damage visible in the archaeology is consistent with the Epic Cycle story of the sack of Troy by the Greeks.

The City of Troy

A problem in matching the site excavated at Hisarlik with the story told in the *Iliad* has always been the smallness of Troy in relation to the colossal force the Greeks ranged against it. The walled citadel is only 200m across. Many have suspected that there must have been a town outside the walled enclosure, standing on the gentle slopes to the east and south. The classical town of Ilion spread across these slopes, across two spurs and the intervening saddle, and it seemed likely that a bronze age town occupied the same area.

In 1988 Manfred Korfmann launched a new attempt to find the bronze age town. Since then he has successfully proved the existence of such a town on the western of the two spurs, extending southwards from the South Gate of the citadel for about 450m, at which point there was a major line of defence, a ditch about 2m deep that was followed for a distance of about 200m along the southern edge of the city. Pits and trenches in this area are believed to represent traces of the homes of the ordinary Trojans who once lived in this crowded city. The settlement as a whole covered an area of 270,000 square metres. Thanks to Korfmann's work, late bronze age Troy is seen to be *thirteen* times larger than previously thought, with a population of up to 10,000. This made it one of the biggest cities of its day in Anatolia or the Aegean region, and most certainly a worthy target for a Mycenaean invasion.

The nature of the ditch is intriguing. Korfmann thinks the steep-sided 2m wide ditch would in itself have made an excellent defence against chariots. He thinks that there might have been a wall or palisade on its inner side as well.

The city of Troy in 1250 BC. AA = suggested street, following the line of a modern track across the site. BB = suggested main street leading from the main gate of the citadel to the South Gate in the Town Wall.

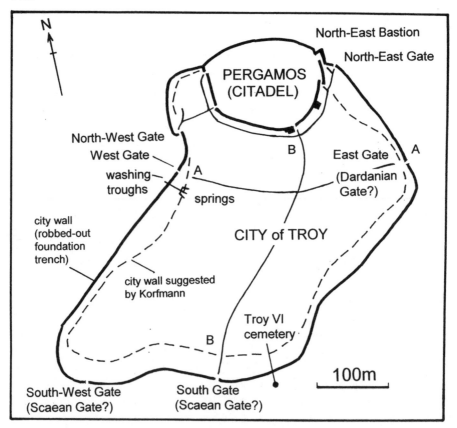

Korfmann has mapped the course of the ditch, which ran in a large irregular loop from the south-west side of the citadel southwards, then east to the remains he excavated, then northwards to return to the citadel wall on the east side. Unfortunately his plans vary somewhat from publication to publication. The town's West Gate is in survey square v11 in one map and w10 in another;[26] the East Gate is in P10 and Q10 in one map and Q13 in another. These variations suggest that there is a certain amount of guesswork in the reconstruction. Korfmann may, even so, be right to assume that the bronze age access routes from east and west closely followed the line of the modern track across the site.

Others see the bounding ditch Korfmann discovered as the foundation trench of a wall like the citadel wall, but thoroughly robbed for building stone in later centuries when the Hellenistic town was built. Close to the citadel, the chances that a fragment of wall survives are better. The Hellenistic builders were keen to conserve and build up existing deposits there in order to create a sound building platform for their new temples. Following this line of thought, Korfmann reasoned that the angle of the south-east corner of the North-East Bastion was the likeliest place for a piece of city wall running up to the citadel to survive; a wall here would have been necessary to stop the enemy from reaching the bronze age city's water supply. Korfmann's reasoning was vindicated when a short length of what seems to be a part of the city wall with the blocks of stone still in position was found just beside the citadel's north-east corner. It comes to an abrupt end after only 8m, and the break at this point is assumed to be one side of a gate. The town wall remnant is only 2m thick, half the thickness of the circuit wall surrounding the citadel, but that may simply reflect the lowly status of the townspeople compared with the status of those accommodated in the citadel. Really, more evidence of the town wall is needed, but it must be remembered that Troy is a large site and to date only 5 per cent of its area has been excavated.

Korfmann believes that the town wall existed independently of the boundary ditch. His reconstructions show this wall running just inside the ditch to west and east, but quite a long way north of it along the southern

The Nine Cities of Troy. A schematic cross-section of the citadel.

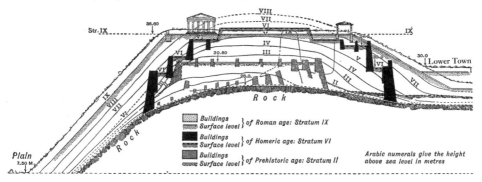

boundary. The position of this southern stretch of wall he infers from a step up in the terrain about 70m to the north of the inner palisade.[27] This is not good evidence. It may be simpler, provisionally, to treat the ditch as a quarried-out wall; such an interpretation is supported by solid archaeological evidence and creates fewer problems.

This fortified walled town with its citadel brings Troy firmly into line with the standard architecture of Near Eastern urban centres of the third and second millennia BC. The citadel now emerges as a special inner sanctum, where the king lived in a palace, where other high-ranking officials also lived, and where the city's holiest temples and shrines were built.

It is obvious now that the gates referred to in the *Iliad* were not the gates in the wall of the citadel, but the gates in the *city* wall. The Scaean Gate was evidently the one that led out of the city onto the main field of battle, which lay to the south-west; since the town was built on a site that sloped gently down towards the south, the Scaean Gate could have been on the south or south-west section of the city wall. The Dardanian Gate had a special function, which was opposite to that of the Scaean Gate: it was a rear gate that could be used for sorties – and for escape. It was in some way protected by the city's hinterland.[28] That strongly implies that it was on the side of the city facing away from the plain, well hidden from the view of the Greeks, and therefore must have been on the east side of the city. The name, Dardanian Gate, tells us that it opened onto the road to Dardania, which presumably followed the side of the Scamander valley to the south-east.

About 6km along this road, the traveller bound for Dardania descended onto the plain to cross the River Thymbrius before continuing inland up the Scamander valley. Here, on the tip of a spur very close to the confluence of the Thymbrius and the Scamander, was the bronze age town of Thymbra. Part of the site, known as Akshi Kioi, was excavated by Frank Calvert between 1857 and 1879. His focus of interest was the tell called Hanai Tepeh, which was probably the bronze age town's citadel. Calvert noted that the houses at Thymbra, like those at Troy, lacked doors or windows on the ground floor, speculating that they had upper storeys and were entered by ladder from the roof. Schliemann commented that the Thymbrian pottery was different from the pottery found at Troy and that it was surprising to find such a large cultural difference between two contemporary towns only 6km apart.[29] Even so, Calvert had discovered the Thymbra referred to as an inland location in Dolon's description of the encampment of the Trojan troops.[30] It played its part in the palaeogeography of the Epic Cycle poetic drama, and here it was, an archaeological reality on the edge of the modern map of the Plain of Troy.

Now, at last, we see the city of Troy emerging as a great metropolis that was a sufficiently important target for a Greek attack, and with significant details of its geography and architecture falling consistently into place in relation to the narrative in the *Iliad*.

Chapter 4

The Greeks

I have no taste for food – what I really crave
is slaughter and blood and the choking groans of men!
(*Iliad* 19. 254–5)

The Mycenaean Civilization

The poets of the Epic Cycle called the bronze age Greeks Achaeans, Danaans or Argives. We call them Mycenaeans – but that name is a modern invention. Some Mycenaeans, like King Agamemnon, came from the city of Mycenae and were Mycenaeans in both ancient and modern senses, but others came from other bronze age cities. Nestor, for instance, was born at Gerenia and had his capital at Pylos.

The Epic Cycle poems, written down from the eighth century BC onwards, have left us tantalizing fragments of an epic vision of the bronze age Greeks, the Greeks of five or six hundred years before, in a mix of bronze age proto-history and fictional embellishment that is very hard to disentangle. The Mycenaean heroes of Homer and the events surrounding them were generally accepted as historical until modern times. Ironically, it was only in the nineteenth century that scholars began seriously to question Homer's historicity, and it became orthodox to dismiss the poems as legend.

It was in the midst of this nineteenth-century climate of scepticism that Heinrich Schliemann set out to prove the historical accuracy of the *Iliad* by identifying the places described by Homer. His first major achievement was to uncover the site of Troy, which most scholars believe he did at Hisarlik in north-west Anatolia, though he misidentified the archaeological layer.

The Mycenaean élites were wealthy even in the early Mycenaean period. The rich objects Schliemann found in the shaft graves with their war-chariot scenes imply that their owners were rich, powerful and warlike. Yet at that stage the power was local. It was only later that the rulers of the Mycenaean kingdoms reached out and built far-reaching economic links across the Aegean. By 1400 BC the Minoans had lost their economic hold over the Aegean, shouldered aside by the Mycenaeans. Another three hundred years, and the Mycenaean civilization itself would be swept away.

The kings of the Mycenaean city-states ruled from centres that at first were unremarkable. It was only in the later Mycenaean period that they were developed into spectacular showpieces. The citadels were the hallmark of the Mycenaean civilization and it is easy to forget that they are alien to Greece. They combine two distinctive imported architectural ideas: the Minoan temple-palace concept and the awe-inspiring Hittite fortifications. Together they made a distinctively Mycenaean citadel, the forerunner of all later European castles.

Homer says the kings owed allegiance to a high king, Agamemnon, and there is some documentary evidence from a Hittite inscription that the Hittite Great King (a high king ruling most of Anatolia) was ready to address a Greek king as his equal. The king of 'Ahhiyawa' (the Hittite version of the name) is thought by many scholars to have been the king of 'Achaea' (the classical Greek version) – and according to Homer Agamemnon was king of the Achaeans.

The best literary source for the political geography of Greece is the Catalogue of Ships, which lists the contingents in the Greek combined expeditionary fleet.[1] This tells us not only how many ships were contributed by each kingdom, but which towns the men came from. It is still possible to identify two-thirds of the towns Homer listed, and nearly all are known from archaeological evidence to have been important Mycenaean sites. The Catalogue of Ships sketches a geography that is startlingly close to what we now know from archaeological evidence to have been the heartland of the Mycenaean civilization. One stumbling block with the Catalogue is that it parades an almost incredibly large military force. On the other hand, only a quarter of a century earlier, huge forces were assembled for the Battle of Kadesh. Ramesses II writes in a contemporary inscription that the Hittite Great King brought to Syria warriors from eighteen vassal and allied states, which provided 3,700 chariots and 37,000 infantry. The allied and vassal states included kingdoms in far-off western Anatolia too – including Dardania.[2] Maybe we should take the scale of the Catalogue of Ships, and the Catalogue of Trojans too, at something close to their face value, rather than dismissing the numbers out of hand.

The Mycenaeans traded long distances mainly by sea. In the island-studded Aegean, land was seldom out of sight, so it was easy to navigate safely to the east of Greece. Towards the end of the fourteenth century, political links with Egypt and the Levant were developed, and by the thirteenth century the Mycenaeans had gained control of all the longer eastern trade routes; there was a marked increase in the number of oriental objects and raw materials arriving in Greece.

The earliest representation of a Mycenaean ship is on a vase fragment from Iolkos in Thessaly. The Iolkos ship had its keel extended to make either a ram

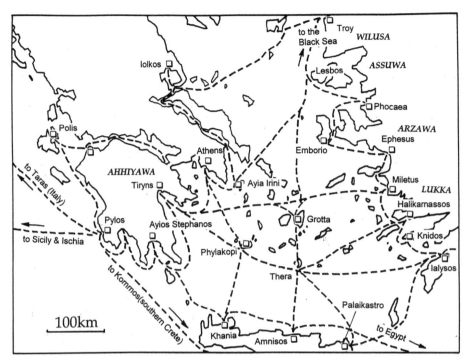

Trade routes in the Aegean in the late bronze age.

or a landing gangway. It also had many pairs of oars and, just like other ships of this period, a big oar-rudder at the upcurved stern. Images on seal-stones show a captain's cabin in the stern and a big square sail mounted on a single mast. The ships were shallow-draught vessels and could be beached in sandy bays. Homer describes them as being dragged up onto the beach and held upright with props or blocks.[3] He also describes the ships as 'black'; possibly they were commonly painted black or had their hulls waterproofed with pitch. Other hues were possible: Odysseus refers to crimson-painted ships.[4] The Thera frescoes, dating to around 1550 BC, show that there were several different types of ship in existence in the Aegean.[5]

A painting on the side of a clay box from a twelfth-century *tholos* tomb at Tragana depicts a ship from the period immediately after the collapse of the Mycenaean civilization. It shows what a large Mycenaean vessel would have looked like. The rigging is carefully painted in, including the stays for the single central mast. The stern has a high stern-post terminating in a fish-tail or possibly an animal head. Also at the stern are a large steering oar and a square cabin. At the prow there is another cabin and an elaborate forecastle with a banner mounted on top. A raised gangway runs the length of the ship, to allow deck-hands to move up and down the ship without interfering with the oarsmen. It may also have been a safety measure. If the rowers were slaves, galley-slaves in fact, the ship's officers would have been able to supervise them more safely from above; there must always have been a risk of mutiny. A single sail billows in the wind, and the ship's wake zig-zags away from the stern.[6]

One of the reasons why the Mycenaeans reached out to other lands was greed; the other was the poverty of their own land. Greece was always poor in resources. Its potential for wealth lay in the ingenuity, ability and single-mindedness of its people. Exactly how the Mycenaean rulers became so rich is something of a mystery. There was a ready-made market for wool and woollen cloth in the cold winter regions of central Europe lying just to the north of Greece, so it may be that Mycenaean wealth was built, like Crete's, on wool. It may also have been built in part on the slave trade. We know from the Pylos tablets that large numbers of slaves were systematically captured from the Anatolian coast; some were taken home, others were sold in the Aegean.

The Mycenaeans took over a well-developed Minoan trading operation at a time when the Minoan civilization underwent a weakening crisis. The result was the creation of a vigorous and well-organized trading empire similar in geographical reach to the Minoan empire it replaced. The Mycenaeans started to develop trading operations in the Aegean region in around 1500, the expansion phase lasting from 1450 BC until the fall of Knossos in 1380 BC.

In the fifty years after 1380 BC there was a dramatic increase in the number of Mycenaean sites round the Aegean. By 1330 BC, when the trading empire reached its fullest extent, there were twenty-four sites on the island of Rhodes alone.[7] The Mycenaean heartlands consisted of the Mycenaean territories, the kingdoms of the Peloponnese and the southern part of central Greece. Beyond this core was a region that was strongly acculturated with Mycenaean elements and was probably subject to colonization; this consisted of all the islands of the south and central Aegean, including Crete, and the south-west coastline of Anatolia. Further out still, there were areas where there was trading but only limited diffusion of Mycenaean culture; north-west Greece, south-east Italy, eastern Sicily, Tuscany, Sardinia, Cyprus, the Levant and the Nile Delta. The north-eastern Aegean was dominated by Troy. Scattered through the trading empire were trading posts, some of them home to sufficient numbers of ex-patriot Mycenaeans for them to be regarded as colony-communities.[8]

The Mycenaeans established a string of colonies along the west coast of Anatolia,[9] at Ephesus, Iasos and Miletus, but they had little effect on the interior. No doubt the Hittite rulers resented the Mycenaean interference and took action to prevent any further encroachment.[10] The Hittites regarded the Mycenaean colonies as a thorn in their side.

By the mid-thirteenth century, the time of the Trojan War, the Mycenaeans had gained control of the eastern trade routes. They had seriously impinged on Hittite territorial interests in at least four locations: the Lukka Lands, the Land of the Seha River, the Land of Zippasla in Arzawa, and Alasiya (Cyprus).[11]

The Kingdoms and Cities of Mycenaean Greece

Three sources enable us to assemble a picture of the political geography of the Mycenaean heartland: the Catalogue of Ships in the *Iliad*, other references in the Epic Cycle poems, and archaeological evidence. The physical geography of southern Greece divides it into clear-cut natural regions. High ranges separated Messenia from Laconia and Laconia from Argolis.

Argolis was the most powerful of the Mycenaean states. The sea bounded this great kingdom to the south and east, and it is surprising that there should be any doubt about the position of the boundary to the north. Immediately north of the capital, Mycenae, a high east–west ridge makes a natural divide between Argolis and Achaea, and relatively few Mycenaean sites are found in the area; it is likely that this no man's land was the political boundary for much of the bronze age. It is only the Catalogue of Ships that throws doubt. Instead of listing Mycenae with the other Argive cities – Argos, Tiryns, Asine, Mases, Hermione, Troizen and Epidauros – Homer lists it with Corinth, Sicyon, Pellene, Cleonae and Aegion, strongly implying that it was part of Achaea. Homer has Agamemnon remind us that his home is in Argos, yet he has the high king leading the armies of Achaea to Troy rather than those of his native Argolis. One possibility is that this was an expedient measure, reflecting the political tensions of the moment, rather than a long-term situation. Perhaps there was no one suitable to lead the Achaean forces; perhaps there were rival claimants for its leadership and they threatened the safety of the expedition; perhaps it was a show of solidarity with neighbours, like the provision of ships for the Arcadian troops; perhaps it had something to do with Agamemnon's wish to give the trusted and able commander Diomedes a high-profile role by giving him the command of the Argive troops.

Mycenae's power base seems to have been in the hills, the marginal lands, rather than in the Argive Plain. The location of the Mycenaean centres is at first sight curious. They are not in the centre of fertile plains, the logical place if agricultural production was the main preoccupation. The favoured sites are those with steep-sided hills, easily defended acropolis sites, and these are more often found where the hill country rises sharply from the alluvium round the edge of the plain. Tiryns, like Athens, is unusual in being an acropolis site surrounded by a level plain, but it does at least have steep craggy slopes rising abruptly from the plain.

The citadel of Mycenae strikes the modern visitor as an isolated stronghold in a wilderness, but in its heyday it was the focus of an inhabited landscape. There was a city beside it. Only an élite group, the rulers, priests and priestesses and their servants, lived in the citadel. The rest of the community lived in a town to the west. Within the citadel, the temple was deliberately placed on the highest part of the site.[12]

No longer actually on the coast, but still close to the Bay of Argos, is Tiryns, a great strong-walled fortress built on a low rocky hill rising out of the flat

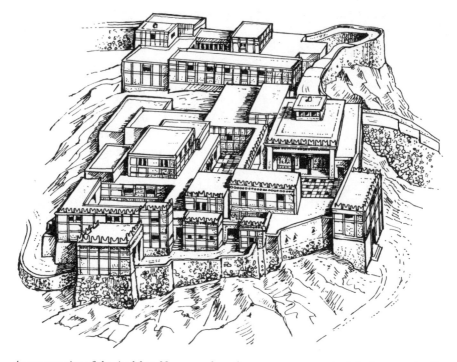

A reconstruction of the citadel at Mycenae, where Agamemnon was assassinated after returning from Troy.

lowland. Tiryns commanded the bay and the southern part of the plain. The visible remains are those of the thirteenth-century fortress, Homer's 'Tiryns of the mighty walls'. In legend, it was the first to be built, by the Cyclopes. It is thought that towers rose from the south–east and south–west corners of the fortress, to ensure that nothing happening out in the Bay of Argos escaped the notice of the lord of Tiryns. Across the Argive Plain, on rising ground at its western edge and commanding the whole plain, stands the unimpressive modern town of Argos. Argos was not to become the capital of Argolis until the Mycenaean period was over. Opposite Argos, dominating the eastern edge of the Argive Plain, is Midea, which was the third fortress of the Argolid, after Mycenae and Tiryns, and built on a high conical hill about halfway between them.

North-west of Argolis lay the kingdom of Achaea, stretching along the fertile lowland flanking the southern shore of the Gulf of Corinth. West of Argolis, beyond the Taygetus, lay Laconia, which would later become Sparta. As yet, the capital of this shadowy bronze age kingdom remains uncertain, but it is thought that the early buildings at the Menelaion on the hill at Therapne two miles east-south-east of Sparta may represent remains of Laconia's bronze age political centre, where Menelaus and Helen had their palace, 'lovely Lacedaemon'. An alternative site for the palace of Menelaus has recently been

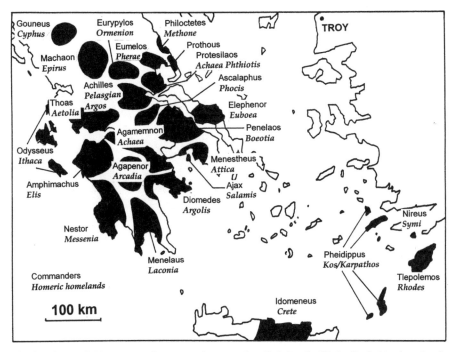

The kingdoms of Mycenaean Greece as they are described in the Iliad. *Each kingdom in the confederation sent a contingent of ships and troops on the expedition to Troy.*

uncovered at Pellana, 25km north of Sparta, and the academic dispute about which of the two sites was the true capital of Laconia has yet to be resolved.

Elis in the north-west Peloponnese was another kingdom, with its capital at Dymaia. In the centre of the Peloponnese lay land-locked Arcadia, with a fertile plain perched 600m above sea level as its focus.

Another swathe of Mycenaean kingdoms lay to the north of the Gulf of Corinth. In the west lay the land of the Aetolians; offshore lay the island group of Zakynthos, Cephallenia and Ithaca, where according to Homer Odysseus was king. To the east, stretching from the Gulf of Corinth to the Gulf of Euboea, lay Boeotia, with its rival cities of Thebes and Orchomenos. East of Boeotia lay the island of Euboea, listed as a separate territory in the Catalogue of Ships but possibly under the sway of Boeotia. To the south-east was the still insignificant city-state of Athens. The Athenian Acropolis, though repeatedly rebuilt in classical times, began as a bronze age citadel of the same type as Mycenae or Troy. Just like the citadels of Mycenae and Tiryns, the Acropolis at Athens was strongly refortified in about 1250 BC.

In Thessaly, to the north, lay a further group of Mycenaean kingdoms including Iolkos and Trikka. From the southern slopes of Mount Olympus south to Cape Tainaron, a tract of Greece about 400km by 200km was dominated by Mycenaean dynasts ruling upwards of twenty small kingdoms.

People and Society

Then just as today, there were quite large variations in stature from person to person. Surprisingly, Agamemnon is likely to have been only half a centimetre shorter than a modern Greek.[13] The skeletons of the aristocrats buried just outside the citadel at Mycenae were nevertheless about 6cm taller than the ordinary people of their time, and this is probably related to major differences in diet.[14]

Life expectancy was low. Men on average died at the age of thirty-five, women at thirty, and few people reached the age of fifty. This was normal for the population of Europe as a whole right through to the Middle Ages. With poor medical care and poor hygiene, people tended to die young. There were no antibiotics and many infections were life-threatening. Princes and kings had a better diet and better living conditions generally, but many of them died violently, some in battle and some, like Agamemnon, in palace coups. It is likely that infant mortality was high and that many women died in childbirth or shortly afterwards.[15]

The men in Grave Circle B were big, strong, powerfully built, and gave every appearance of being warriors. One had a left shoulder blade that showed signs of over-use, which could well have been due to the strain of carrying a heavy shield. The same man had received blows to his skull inflicted by a right-handed opponent.

When the face of another man was reconstructed from his skull, it was found to bear no resemblance to the face on the gold mask that had covered it when he was buried, proving conclusively – and rather disappointingly – that the gold funerary masks were not intended to be portraits.[16]

The king as head of state had divine ancestry and a special bond with a particular deity. He and his family lived sequestered in the citadel. He was rarely seen by the general populace, perhaps only glimpsed during formal processions and religious festivals or when going off in great style in his chariot to lead his warriors to war. Second in power and status to the king was the leader of the people, who may have been the commander-in-chief of the army. The king surrounded himself with an élite group of followers or companions, the equivalent of the dukes and barons of the medieval European courts; they had to be ready to do battle on the king's behalf and when off-duty functioned as his friends and table-companions. These were the chariot-riding warrior-aristocrats who featured so prominently in Homer. The priests were an important high status group within Mycenaean society. They were paid for their work and they were also land-owners and slave-owners. Priestesses too held very high rank.

The great bulk of ordinary people, the producers of the wealth, appear very seldom in either the archive tablets or the epic poems. They led unhistoric lives, lie in unvisited tombs. They nevertheless had some power. They were the *damos*, and they could, collectively, challenge the actions of their social superiors. Then there were the slaves.

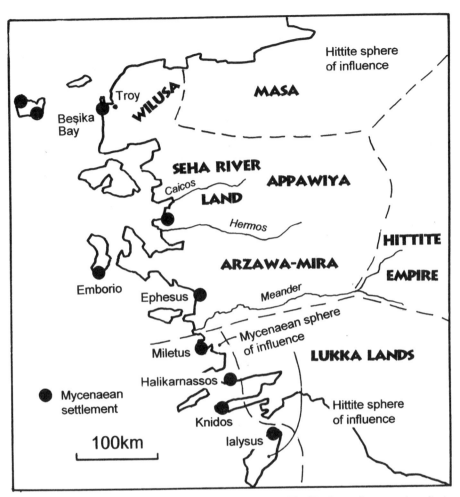

The disputed lands, where Mycenaeans clashed with Hittites. The kingdoms of western Anatolia in 1250 BC.

The Mycenaeans probably acquired their slaves routinely during warfare. Both slavery and the slave trade were endemic in the ancient world. When the Mycenaeans raided islands in the eastern Aegean or towns along the Anatolian coast, they routinely took slaves. Groups of slave women at Pylos were engaged as bath attendants, corn-grinders, bread-makers, flax-workers, spinners. Some were listed according to their place of origin. The conclusion is inescapable. These women had been captured mainly on the western Anatolian coast, rounded up and transported back to Greece to provide cheap labour. The men may have been killed to pre-empt any possible slave revolt; possibly they were instead deployed in the building of the massive fortifications at Tiryns or Mycenae.

Hittite sources show that by 1250 BC large numbers of Anatolians were living in Greece. Hattusilis III wrote a letter to 'the king of Ahhiyawa', which implies that one man was in some sense in overall charge in Greece. The Hittite king complained of the resettlement in Ahhiyawa of seven thousand of his western Anatolian subjects. Anatolia was already seriously underpopulated, so he was understandably angry about these abductions. The Mycenaeans' records confirm that they were indeed abducting large numbers of women from western Anatolia. If the same region was supplying men for wall-building at Mycenae and Tiryns, which were refortified at just this time, it would fit neatly with Strabo's story that the walls of Tiryns were built by giants from 'Lycia'; the Lycia of Strabo's time was the Lukka Lands of the late bronze age, in south–west Anatolia.[17]

Chapter 5

The Trojans

I would die of shame to face the men of Troy
and the Trojan women trailing their long robes
if I were to shrink from battle now, a coward.
                                        (*Iliad* 6. 523–5)

The Hittite Civilization

The city of Troy and its kingdom, Wilusa, lay on the north-western **edge** of
the huge Hittite Empire, which sprawled across most of what is now Turkey.
The Hittite civilization had many similarities and parallels with the
Mycenaean civilization, and some of the apparent differences are really
only apparent, and can be explained by differences in archaeological
survival. There are, for example, far more Hittite archive tablets, which tell
us in detail about such things as religious festivals. There were as many as
165 of these festivals in the Hittite calendar, lasting from a few hours to
several days. We have documentary evidence of these for the Hittites, not
for the Mycenaeans, though it can reasonably be assumed that very similar
festivals took place in Greece: the names of some of the Greek festivals are
documented.[1]

The Hittite Great King lived a life apart from his subjects, cloistered in his
citadel at Hattusa with his family, the Great Family, his bodyguard and his
courtiers and servants, co-ordinated by a chamberlain called the Chief of the
Wine Stewards. Kings were judges, supreme military commanders and priests.
In their role as priests, they wore a distinctive costume. It consisted of an ankle-
length robe, over it an elaborate shawl draped under one arm and over the
other, with one end hanging down in front. The king wore a skullcap and
carried a long ceremonial crook, something like a modern bishop's crozier but
with the large hook held low.[2]

The queen was a surprisingly strong and independent character, not always
amiable, and sometimes downright unmanageable: certainly a power in her own
right.[3] One fragmentary tablet refers to a Hittite queen who had been exiled to

Ahhiyawa. This implies that very close diplomatic relations existed between a Mycenaean king and a Hittite king.

In Anatolia as in Greece a citadel mentality had set in by the time of the Trojan War, which was a time of psychological confrontation not unlike the Cold War. The empire was huge and a considerable amount of power was delegated to district governors known as Lords of the Watch Tower. It was their job to collect taxes, to see that towns and citadels under their control were securely locked at night, and to maintain the fabric of buildings and roads. There were also regional military commanders, called Overseers of the Military Heralds, responsible for military defence.[4] Although this kind of detail is not known for the Mycenaeans, it is easy to imagine that they had similar socio-political and military responsibility structures.

Of the ordinary people, much less is known, except that they lived under the Laws. These listed punishments for specific offences such as murder, manslaughter, assault, abduction, theft, sorcery and forbidden sexual acts. One oddity of the Laws is that if a murderer was not identifiable, the owner of the property on which the murder took place became liable for compensation to the victim's family. The local courts were crowded out with people seeking justice for a wide range of wrongs. One family wanted the dowry back when a reluctant bride ran off on her wedding day. A farm worker wanted compensation for a working dog killed by an angry neighbour when the dog savaged his ducks.[5]

There was a surprising leniency about some of the laws. Murder, for instance, was not automatically punished by death; it was open to the victim's family members to name the punishment, and it seems they normally opted for financial compensation. The Hittite Great King, who at the time of the Trojan War was Hattusilis III, was ready to accept and reinforce local customs. In this way, Wilusa and the other kingdoms of the Arzawa Lands in the far west were allowed to keep their distinctive character.[6]

The Law Code even stipulates the prices of livestock and certain key commodities. The currency was in silver bars or rings, measured in two units by weight, the shekel and the mina. The shekel seems to have been 8.4g in weight. The prices laid down in the Law Code are almost certainly the prices that would have prevailed at Troy, as fixed throughout the Hittite empire; the Hittite Great Kings believed in recommended retail prices.[7]

Slaves constituted a large proportion of the population. Many were 'booty-people', taken as the spoils of war, and drafted into the army or temple service; some were used for farm work or sent off to colonize sparsely populated areas. There were also debt-slaves, people who were consigned to a period of slavery as a punishment for debt, but they could regain their freedom. Slaves were on the whole treated with respect, but a slave-owner could deal with his slaves as severely as he liked.[8]

Scribes were essential for administration in a world where only a small number of people could read or write. These were hard skills to acquire, because the hieroglyphic Hittite script had over 300 signs to learn. Scribes had to be trusted to write down accurately what was said, and inevitably they became powerful and important people in their own right, rising through the ranks of diplomats and ambassadors to the highest levels of Hittite society.

Many languages and dialects were spoken in Anatolia, but the scribes of the Great Kings used only two of these for their official documents – Hittite and Akkadian. Occasional tablets in other languages have been found. In the Arzawa Lands of the west, and therefore in Wilusa too, the local language was Luwian, which is closely related to Hittite, and there can be no doubt that the Wilusans and the Hittite Great Kings could understand one another.[9] A bronze seal was found at Troy with the name of one scribe on one side and that of another on the back – in the Luwian script.[10]

Most people were involved in agricultural production. Farmers produced cereals, vegetables and fruit. Herders up on the mountains produced the wool that was vital to the Hittite economy. The Epic Cycle poems tell us that the Dardanians, the people of Aeneas, were keepers of flocks on Mount Ida. Wars took people off the land. Armies were swelled with farm-worker conscripts; no farm work could take place on a battlefield, and the fertile Plain of Troy went out of production for the duration of the Trojan War, however long that was. Conquest and victory became all the more important, as only the spoils of war could make up the deficit of labour and produce.[11]

The Hittites practised a polytheistic and animistic religion, in which every part of the landscape, every stream, rock and tree, had a god or spirit residing in it. There are hints of this in Book 21 of the *Iliad*, where we hear of the Scamander speaking to Achilles: the river is a god. Three major deities were the Storm-god, the Sun-god and the goddess Ishtar. It is difficult to tell whether the Hittite gods and goddesses were regarded as in any way equivalent to Mycenaean gods. Probably they were not, as gods were treated as very individual: there were even Storm-gods specific to certain places. The Hittite archives record that when the Hittite Great King was ill, the Mycenaean Great King arranged for certain Mycenaean gods to be transported to Hattusa to make his royal brother well; the idols themselves must have been regarded as not just representing but containing the deities.

The Hittites made life-sized statues of their gods. A statue of a living king was promised to one of the temples; it would be made of silver, 'as tall as Hattusilis himself, with head and hands and feet of gold.' Some statues were described as seated, so they were very like the enthroned gods and goddesses that sat in the later classical Greek temples; there is also an indirect reference in the *Iliad* to a seated statue of Athena in the temple in the citadel at Troy itself; Hecuba chooses a dress to lay *on the knees* of the goddess's cult statue.[12] Although some have assumed that this reference to a lifelike enthroned goddess was an anachronism, an importation from a later period, the Hittite sources show that such statues were made in the late bronze age.

The Hittite archives include fragments of the texts of religious dramas dating from the time of the Trojan War. *The Vanishing God* has parts for actors playing the roles of gods, as well as a narrator and stage directions. There was an epic song cycle about Kumarbi, the father of the gods. Enough of it survives to show that it was a long poem, epic in scale, dealing with the creation myth, and using the 'Homeric' device of repeating phrases and lines to create an effect of great weight and dignity.[13] Fragments of many other epic poems have been found.[14] What we are seeing here is a civilization with all the skills at its disposal to record the events of a disruptive Mycenaean expedition against the western fringes of the empire; it could, moreover, have taken those events and turned them into an epic narrative drama on the scale of Homer. The Hittites, and therefore maybe the Mycenaeans, about whose literature we unfortunately (and ironically) know nothing, may well have developed their own early versions of what we now know as 'Homer'.

Troy was on the north-western edge of this Hittite world, a part of the Hittite civilization, rather than apart from it, as well as borrowing features from the Mycenaean civilization too. Trojan architecture had superficial points in common with both Mycenaean and Hittite architecture, but there were significant differences too. Mycenaean fortification walls were built in polygonal or cyclopean style, with the stones carefully fitted together to make a well-made surface to the wall, but the surface match did not extend into the wall's interior, which were rubble-filled. The Trojan citadel wall had masonry that fitted all the way through. The walls of Mycenae were built with sheer vertical faces; the walls of Troy were built with a distinct batter. Yet Troy had links with Mycenae in personal names and pottery styles.

During the development of Troy VI, trade between Troy and the Mycenaean centres in Greece gradually developed, generating a new 'High Troia Culture'. From Troy VIa though to Troy VIh, steadily greater quantities of Mycenaean pottery were in use at Troy.

The pattern of presence (and absence) of different styles of Mycenaean pottery at Troy usefully ties the chronologies of the two cultures together. It also proves that Mycenae 'dissociated' itself from Troy in Late Helladic IIIC, after Troy was destroyed in LH IIIB.

Five sword pommels made of white marble or alabaster from Troy VI are either Trojan imitations of Mycenaean swords or the remains of actual Mycenaean swords. There are also beads of glass paste, which show Mycenaean influence again. Ivory appears in Troy VI, possibly imported through the Mycenaean trading network. The first horse bones appear at Troy in Troy VI, though at Lerna they appear as early as the Early Helladic III phase, showing that the horse appeared in Argolis before it appeared at Troy, which is surprising. There is a major change between Troy V and Troy VI, and one of the most conspicuous features of Troy VI is the increasing influence of the Mycenaeans.

Greek pottery found at Troy

Style of pottery	Phase of Troy	Amount found
Late Helladic I	VId	small amount
Late Helladic II	VIe	small amount
Late Helladic II	VIf	increasing
Late Helladic III A	VIg	increasing
Late Helladic III A–B	VIh	large amount
Late Helladic III C	VIIa	none

Troy was falling more and more into the orbit of Mycenae as the Mycenaeans' outreach grew steadily more ambitious and rapacious. The natural culmination of this process was for the Mycenaeans to attack, whether to take the city over as a colony, or to knock it down as a perceived rival, or simply to plunder. After 1250 BC, significantly, there was no more Mycenaean pottery at Troy.

Troy's remarkable position at the crossroads between North and South, Black Sea and Mediterranean, East and West, Hittite and Mycenaean, made it an eclectic, international city. Troy was the Singapore of the late bronze age.

The Kingdoms and Cities of Wilusa

The high status architecture of Troy VI shows that Troy was the capital of Wilusa, the name given to the Troad kingdom in the Hittite archive tablets at Hattusa. Wilusa occupied the large Anatolian peninsula that formed the south-eastern coast of the Hellespont and Sea of Marmara. Wilusa is mentioned by King Muwatallis in a Hittite treaty of 1280 BC as being a friendly close neighbour of the Hittite Empire. To the south and south-east of Wilusa lay Arzawa, a large kingdom that was conquered about twenty years earlier by Mursilis II (1318–1290) and broken up into several separate states: Mira, Kuwaliya, Seha, Appawiya and Haballa. These later formed into a federation of Arzawa states. Wilusa seems to have been independent of Arzawa. Muwatallis was keen to emphasize the close ties of friendship that had existed between Wilusa and Hattusa for centuries.[15] Wilusa had obvious natural boundaries – the Hellespont to the north, the Aegean to the west, the Gulf of Edremit and the valley of the River Euenos to the south.[16] Probably the kingdom of Wilusa extended to the east as far as the River Aesepus or Makestos (the modern Simav Cayi), and to the east of that lay the kingdom of Masa.

There is a general convergence among leading Aegean scholars on the idea that the Troad was Wilusa.[17] Useful additional evidence emerged when in 1997 a spring cave was excavated at Troy with three arms for guiding water into a subterranean reservoir that ran a long way back into the hill under the city. The access to the spring cave consisted of a large passage tunnelled 18m into the hillside, where it divided into three branches, with a small spring at the head of each. Roman basins found outside show that the underground springs were in use in the Roman period, and the passage may have been enlarged at that time, but it is likely that the springs were in use in the bronze age too, supplying water to the Trojan women's washing troughs immediately outside the western wall of the city.[18] Radiometric studies indicate that the subterranean reservoir was dug in the early third millennium, well before the time of the Trojan War. In Clause 20 of the Alaksandu Treaty of 1280 BC, the chief gods of Hatti and Wilusa are invoked as witnesses to the oaths of friendship; the divinity of the land of Wilusa is invoked as 'the way into the underworld of the land of Wilusa'. The subterranean springs, with their passage into the underworld beneath the city of Troy itself, were evidently regarded as a holy place.

Wilusa, the kingdom of Troy, was a medium-sized Anatolian state. Taking the valleys of the Euenos and Aesepus as its landward boundaries, it covered a land area of 15,000 square kilometres.

The combined evidence of archaeology, physical geography and the Catalogue of Trojans in the *Iliad* can show us the political geography of Wilusa. Within Wilusa, there were at least eight different tribes, each with their own territories and kings. The Trojans themselves lived in the lower Scamander valley, the Plain of Troy and the surrounding hills, with coastlines on both the Aegean to the west and the south-western end of the Hellespont to

The tribes of Wilusa.

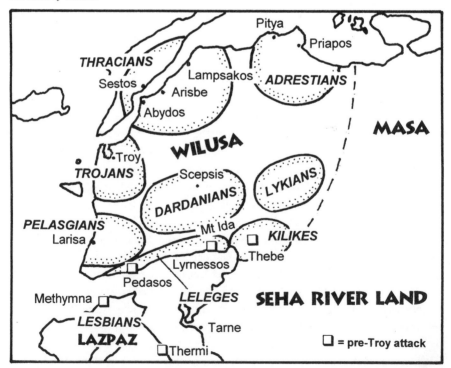

the north. Troy was evidently a very high status city, certainly the main settlement of the kingdom of Troy, and the leading city of Wilusa as a whole. Under attack from a Mycenaean fleet, it could probably count on the support of towns all over the Troad. If its influence was yet wider, it may be that it could call on allies further afield, possibly the neighbouring Arzawa states.[19] In addition to the explicit catalogues of allies in the *Iliad*, there are hints in the Hittite archives that very large confederations were created to deal with emergencies of this kind.

The Trojans' immediate neighbours to the south-east were the Dardanians, whose territory occupied the agriculturally rich upper Scamander valley and the pastures of the broad northern flank of the Mount Ida ridge. Linked to the lower Scamander valley and the Plain of Troy by the gorge of the Bally Dagh, Dardania was always closely linked economically and politically to Troy. It is not surprising that the Dardanians were regarded as the Trojans' principal ally.[20]

To the north-east of the Trojans were the Thracians, who seem to have occupied towns on both sides of the Hellespont: Sestos on the north-west and Abydos, Arisbe and Lampsakos on the south-east shore. In the lower basin of the River Granicus, opening into the Sea of Marmara, was the kingdom of the Adrestians, who had towns at Pitya and Priapos on the coast. To the south of the Adrestians, living far inland in the upper catchment area of the River Aesepus, were the Lykians.

Along the southern edge of Wilusa there were three kingdoms, of the Pelasgians, Leleges and Kilikes. The Pelasgians had a territory in the lower valley of the River Satnioeis, with a western coastline on the Aegean. At its mid-point, the Satnioeis passed very close to the Gulf of Edremit; there the ridge bounding its valley to the south fell away to make a pass through to the Gulf coast. This was a major route centre, the site of the fortress of Pedasos, which was one of the major towns of the Leleges. They lived in a narrow coastal strip along the northern shore of the Gulf of Edremit. At the head of the Gulf was an alluvial plain, not unlike the Plain of Argos, and with a fortified town on a hill at its inland edge – Thebe. This plain and its hilly hinterland was the territory of the Kilikes or Cilicians. I assume that the southern shore of the Gulf of Edremit belonged to the neighbouring state, the Land of the Seha River.

Each of the eight kingdoms of Wilusa had its own king or chief, but none of the other settlements reached the size or sophistication of Troy, so it is assumed that Troy was the capital of Wilusa as a whole and that the king of Troy was also the over-king of Wilusa. What physical geography and archaeology suggest is confirmed by Homer, who says that Priam ruled the whole of the Troad, the area bounded by 'Lesbos, Phrygia and the Hellespont'.[21] Phrygia was a post-bronze age kingdom apparently corresponding to part of bronze age Masa.

   The Trojans of the time of the Trojan War were not the same as the Trojans of earlier periods, culturally at least. The Trojans of Troy VI were eclectic and ingenious military engineers; they were vigorous, outgoing, well-resourced, rich. They were ready to draw ideas in from Hittite Anatolia to the east and Mycenaean Greece to the west, and the resulting mixture of ideas was their great strength. They were probably predatory, making a good living by extortion, but they also traded legitimately in chariot horses and wool. The Trojans were like the Mycenaeans in being interested in building and refining the strongest and most efficient fortifications they could design. It is thought that the earliest chariot warfare took place in Anatolia, and it may well have been chariot warfare, and the culture that went with that way of fighting, that led to the establishment of Troy VI.[22] Whether these chariot-driving 'new Trojans' were ethnically different from the Trojans of Troy I–V has not been established. The new Trojans in any case grew in strength. They came to dominate Wilusa and attract the attention of both the Hittite and Mycenaean high kings.[23]

Chapter 6

The Expedition Begins

… But now
the war, the deafening crash of battle, blazed.
(Iliad 12. 43–4)

Prelude to the Trojan War

The run-up to the Trojan War was described and to an extent explained in antiquity. These ancient views of the prelude to war were expressed in two of the poems of the Epic Cycle, the *Kypria* and the *Iliad*.

The *Kypria* is a lost epic poem and now exists only in the form of a summary written by Proklos.[1] The Proklan summary shows the *Kypria* as a preamble to the *Iliad*, though modern scholars believe that the two poems originally overlapped and some believe that the *Kypria* originally covered the entire story. Nevertheless, what we have is the Proklan summary, which tells us that the Trojans, led by Alexandros (Paris), mounted a deceitful attack on the Mycenaean kingdom of Lacedaemon (Laconia). Alexandros was excited by the idea of abducting and marrying Helen, the wife of Menelaus, king of Lacedaemon. He sailed from Troy to Lacedaemon, where he was welcomed by Menelaus at 'Sparta'. At a feast, Alexandros plied Helen with presents. Suspecting nothing untoward, Menelaus sailed to Crete, leaving orders that all hospitality was to be accorded to Alexandros and his entourage. As soon as Menelaus had gone, the Trojans abducted Helen along with a mass of treasure belonging to Menelaus and returned to Troy. When Menelaus heard what had happened, he returned to Greece, conferred with his brother Agamemnon, and they planned a punitive expedition to Troy to get Helen back. Menelaus visited Nestor, king of Pylos (Messenia), and together they travelled all over Greece mustering the leaders.

There was a hosting of ships at Aulis and the combined Greek fleet sailed across the Aegean, but made landfall at the wrong place. The Greeks mistook Teuthrania for Ilios, and therefore attacked the wrong cities. After this abortive expedition there was a second muster at Aulis. After causing offence to the gods, Agamemnon was instructed to sacrifice his daughter to ensure a following wind for the fleet, but a stag was substituted at the last moment. The combined fleet set sail, landing briefly on the island of Tenedos before going on to Troy, where an embassy was sent straight to the city of Troy to ask the Trojans for Helen and the treasure to be given back. The Trojans refused. The Greeks attacked the walls of Troy, then went and sacked other cities in the area. They were keen to return home, but Achilles checked them. He sacked the cities of Thebe, Lyrnessos and Pedasos to the south-east of Troy, where in the customary way women were taken as prizes.

The narrative in the *Iliad* overlaps slightly with that of the *Kypria*, suggesting that they were intended for separate performance and lending support to the idea that the *Kypria* may originally have included more, and perhaps the whole of the Trojan War. The Achaeans (Greeks from all the kingdoms of central and southern Greece) planned to sack Troy and bring Helen back. The Achaean confederation was led by King Agamemnon, the brother of the wronged Menelaus, as commander-in-chief. There was an initial quarrel among the Greek leaders over two more abductions. King Agamemnon had taken Chryseis, the daughter of the priest Chryses; he then took Briseis away from Achilles when he was forced to give Chryseis up. Achilles appealed to the gods to inflict loss on the Achaeans, and Zeus was won over to his cause.

The *Iliad* was first written down in the eighth century BC and has been known as the *Iliad*, 'The Poem about Ilios', since at least as early as the fifth century BC, though it could as well be entitled 'The Wrath of Achilles' and some commentators have argued that it started off as a shorter poem with that title. The poem seems straightforward enough, yet it raises many questions. Is it a work of fiction based on poetic invention much later than the events described, or a genuine historical inheritance from the bronze age, or a mixture of the two? Was Homer a historian or a pseudo-historian? It is self-evident that it would be unwise to cite Homer as a historical source without corroboration.

Homer may have been reflecting the concerns and interests of the eighth century, either importing political and cultural concerns that were not part of the bronze age scenario, or simply placing emphasis on bronze age realities that had a particular resonance for people living five hundred years later. The dialect and geographical knowledge suggest that the 'final' form of the epic poems was arrived at on the west coast of Greek-colonized Ionia.[2] An Ionian-Greek poet might well tailor Epic Cycle subject matter to make an *Iliad* and *Odyssey* that would interest an audience of ex-patriot Greeks living in Anatolia. The *Iliad* tells a story of a successful Greek conquest in Anatolia and the *Odyssey* a story of an ultimately safe passage home to Greece, so the bard was adapting or selecting from the oral tradition to suit the interests of his audience.

The Cause of the War

The Epic Cycle gives us the rescue of Helen and the need to avenge her abduction as the twin reasons for the Trojan War. This rationale, along with all other aspects of the war, will have to stand up against the archaeological evidence. Many commentators have remarked that the *Iliad* calls up far too many ships and men to be true. It is one of the things that, for some, marks the piece out as a work of fiction. They have also said that a bronze age siege of Troy could not have lasted as long as ten years. A certain amount of scaling down has to be done to make the scenario credible. Even the motives for the attack can be called into question.

It is evident from Homer that women were regarded as legitimate spoils of war. Achilles took a trophy woman for himself from the Lelegian town of Lyrnessos. Agamemnon took a trophy woman too. Helen was similarly taken by a Trojan prince during a state visit to the court of Menelaus in Laconia; the capture of this one woman is presented to us by Homer as the mainspring for the Trojan War, as the single and only cause.[3]

Archaeology confirms that women were indeed taken during raids on the west coast of Anatolia and the adjacent islands. The Pylos tablets list rations for hundreds of slave women, many of whom are identified by adjectives indicating their place of origin – Knidos, Miletus, Lemnos, Zephyrus (Halikarnassos) and Chios. 'Aswija' on the Pylos tablets is thought to be the 'Assuwa' of the Hittite archives, the area in western Anatolia later known as Lydia. There was also a 'servant of the god' at Pylos who was 'To-ro-ja', a Trojan woman. She may have been brought back to Messenia after the sack of Troy, or her mother may have been brought back as a captive.

Sometimes there is more detail. The size of these ethnic groups is given: '21 women from Knidos with their 12 girls and 10 boys'. The tablets often use the word 'lawiaiai', meaning captives. It is the same word used in Homer to describe the women Achilles took as captives at Lyrnessos.[4]

There is a satisfying convergence here between the evidence from the tablets and the evidence of Homer. Homer names places in the eastern Aegean as the homes of women taken in Greek raids: Skyros, Lesbos and Tenedos.[5] These women must have been captured during Greek raids on those islands, or bought from entrepreneurs at a major Mycenaean colonial centre such as Miletus.[6]

Once landed back in Greece, the women were kept together in their original ethnic, cultural and social groups. Keeping all the women from one area together may have made it easier to communicate with them; perhaps it kept the slaves happier and therefore made them work better. It was evidently a regional practice, not just a Mycenaean practice. There are contemporary tablets at Ugarit, in what is now Lebanon, which mention 'the sons of the slave women of Kition'. Kition was in Cyprus.

The collection of women as textile workers and for other services – including sex, to judge from Homer – was a routine part of the Mycenaean way of life, so the raid on Troy may well have been carried out with the intention of picking up a hundred or more women. The *Iliad* tells us in no uncertain terms what happened to the Trojan men: most were killed out of hand. The Linear B tablets tell us by implication what happened to the Trojan women.

Enslavement and the slave trade were essential for the generation of wealth in Mycenaean society. The powerful grandees needed a huge labour force to sustain their extravagances, their rich war gear, their treasure, their fancy furniture, their royal ceremonies, their opulent tombs, and probably lavish hospitality too. The Aegean raids and the large-scale use of slave labour were probably essential to maintain the Mycenaean royal families in this style – in what were intrinsically rather poor kingdoms.

If 'fancy furniture' sounds fairly marginal, let us look at the sort of thing a Mycenaean aristocrat expected to sit on. Here is a description of a chair from a Pylian tablet: 'One chair of spring type, inlaid with kyanos [blue glass paste] and silver and gold on the back, which is inlaid with the figures of men in gold, and with a pair of gold finials, and with gold griffins and griffins of kyanos.' That is just one chair, one item of furniture among scores listed.[7]

The collection of slaves was one likely motive for the war, but there is another – the loss of Miletus. Hittite archives suggest that the Hittite Great King regained control of Miletus between 1260 and 1250. If the Mycenaeans lost Miletus, their most important colony on the Anatolian coast, they might well have decided to look further north in their search for slaves, raw materials – and a potential colony town or emporium to replace Miletus. The towns of the Troad presented themselves as obvious targets. If Hittite resistance was stiffening in south-western Anatolia, it was natural for the Mycenaeans to look to the north-west instead.[8] And of the towns in the Troad, the richest prize was Troy itself.

A third possible motive for war was glory, which mattered enormously to the Mycenaean aristocracy. The greatest accolade Homer can give a Mycenaean prince is the title 'sacker of cities'. Agamemnon was a sacker of cities. Nestor, the old king of Pylos, had been a sacker of cities when young. It was a Mycenaean warrior-king's greatest claim to glory. Leading an expedition against another city may have needed no other motive. A quarrel might be picked on a pretext, even envy, which must have been a major factor as far as the wealthy and sophisticated city of Troy was concerned. The main thing was the act of aggression, the attack itself.

The first destruction of Boeotian Thebes happened in around 1300 BC. This may have been the result of a large-scale attack by a confederation of Mycenaean states, in other words much like the concerted attack on Troy fifty years later, or it may have been a more local affair, an expression of the ongoing enmity between Thebes and its neighbour, the fortress-city of Orchomenos. The later Greek tradition of an Argive sack of Thebes a generation before the Trojan War fits the model of a confederate attack rather well.[9]

There was also a strong Greek tradition that the Mycenaean citadels were inhabited by men of blood, violent men constantly engaged in warfare. This was a militaristic, aggressive world where an attack on Troy would have been just one act of violence among many.

The Trojan War could alternatively have had a cold, commercial motive, an attempt to take control over an important trade route or, better still, to take control over an emporium and nodal centre at the junction of several important trade routes. The Trojans were evidently controlling the passage of ships through the Hellespont, especially those approaching from the south, who faced contrary winds. Maybe the Trojans were overcharging in harbour dues. Maybe they were behaving piratically, like the medieval robber barons in their castles along the Rhine Gorge. Maybe they were confiscating precious raw materials coming out of the Black Sea. The persistent northerly winds that still blow for much of the year in this area would have blown many a ship into the Bay of Troy, which functioned like a spider's web, catching cargo vessels as prey. Troy, crouching in the south-east corner of the bay, was the spider. Certainly the exceptionally high quality of the masonry for the citadel walls of Troy VI suggests that the Trojans of the 1250s were able to afford to set themselves up in grand style.

Chapter 7

The War according to Contemporary Sources

War – I know it well, and the butchery of men.
Well I know, to shift to the left, shift to the right
my tough tanned shield.

(*Iliad* 7. 275–7)

The Epic Cycle
Hittite sources tell us that epic poems and dramas involving gods were being composed in Anatolia in the late bronze age. There is no longer any need to assume that such works must have been created anachronistically, in the iron age, using a few oral traditions from the bronze age as raw materials. Whether the Mycenaeans wrote down any account of the Trojan War at the time will probably never be known; it is equally likely that their version of the narrative was handed on in the form of songs, stories and epic poems that were memorized and learnt by heart by successive generations of storytellers and bards. The narrative was eventually written down, though not all at once, from the mid-eighth century onwards, to make a sequence of poems known as the Epic Cycle. The most important surviving poem from this sequence is undoubtedly the *Iliad*.

The *Iliad*
The *Iliad* contains much of what we know about the Trojan War. The following summary outlines the main events narrated in the *Iliad*, but with the supernatural elements stripped away to clarify the progress of the military action.

Book 1. The Greeks encamped in huts by their ships on the shore near Troy, and they were there for nine years before the action of the story begins. Chryses came to the Achaean ships, begging for the return of his captured daughter. A 'plague' swept through the Achaean camp, killing many Greeks.

Book 2. The Greek warriors assembled, pouring out of the ships and huts onto the Plain of Troy, facing the Trojans. The Catalogue of Ships lists the contingents present. The Trojans gathered at Priam's door to confer. Priam's allies were assembled in the city, each commander in charge of his own men, because of the language difficulties. The gates of Troy were opened and the whole army poured out – chariotry and infantry. Outside the city, the Trojan army and its allies assembled on Thorn Hill, which carried a high mound known as the Tomb of Myrine, with open ground all round.

Book 3. The Trojan host advanced across the dusty plain, shouting, while the Greeks advanced towards them in silence. The two armies were about to clash when Paris stepped forward to offer single combat. Menelaus leapt down from his chariot to fight him. Paris took fright and hid among the Trojans. Hector rebuked Paris, his brother. Paris agreed to fight after all. Hector stepped into the no man's land, holding the Trojan line back. The Trojans sat down. The Greek archers fired arrows at Hector, until Agamemnon stopped them. Hector and Menelaus made speeches. Priam and Antenor rode out from Troy in a chariot to a point midway between Greeks and Trojans, offered sacrificial lambs, agreed that the single combat should determine Helen's future, and returned by chariot to Troy. Lots were cast to decide who would throw the first spear. Menelaus and Paris fought. Paris was beaten and disappeared.

Book 4. Menelaus was wounded, and his minor wound was tended. The Trojan army advanced in a babel of different commands, the Greeks put their armour back on, and Agamemnon toured his troops to encourage them. The Greeks advanced. The armies met in a great roaring clash. Many were killed on both sides, including one of Priam's sons, Democoon.

Book 5. The battle developed by a sequence of separate individual initiatives. The Greeks pushed back the Trojan line. Menelaus drove a spear into Scamandrius' back as he ran away. Many other Trojans were killed as they retreated across the plain. The Greek Diomedes butchered one Trojan after another. It looked as if Diomedes' successes would take the Greeks right into the city of Troy. A spear thrown by Pandarus penetrated Diomedes' shield. Pandarus thought for a moment he had killed Diomedes, but Diomedes shouted back, 'A miss! You never touched me.' Diomedes cast his spear at Pandarus, striking him full in the face and killing him. Aeneas jumped down from his chariot to defend Pandarus' corpse. Diomedes threw a rock at Aeneas, injuring his hip. Diomedes threw himself three times at Aeneas, intent on killing him and taking his splendid armour. Hector roused his men to turn and fight the Greeks.

A veil of darkness covered the battlefield, enabling Aeneas to leave the sanctuary where he had taken shelter. The Greeks were encouraged to fight by the Aiantes, Diomedes and Odysseus. Several individual duels were fought. Telamonian Ajax killed Amphius son of Selagus, but when he tried to strip him of his armour the Trojans fired a volley of javelins at him, many hitting his shield. Afraid of being surrounded and overpowered by the Trojans, Ajax retreated. Tlepolemus drove his long spear through Sarpedon's thigh. Sarpedon was carried from the battlefield by his followers, who for some reason didn't think to pull the spear from his wound and they found it difficult to move him. Hector arrived at Sarpedon's side; Sarpedon told him he would be content to die in the city of Troy and asked for his help; he was not going to see his home country again. Hector raced by without a word, driving the Greeks back so that Sarpedon could be carried away by his followers and laid under an oak tree. Sarpedon's squire pulled the spear from his thigh and he fainted, but recovered. Meanwhile the Greeks neither fled to their ships nor counter-attacked, but fell back steadily. Many Greeks fell as the Trojans advanced – Teuthras, Orestes, Trechus, Oenomaus, Helenus, Oresbius.

Book 6. The battle swayed to and fro across the plain, midway between the River Simois and the distributaries of the Scamander. Telamonian Ajax was the first to break a Trojan company, when he killed Acamas the Thracian. Other 'hits' included Agamemnon killing Elatus of Pedasos. Menelaus captured Adrestus alive. Adrestus' horses had bolted across the plain, crashing his chariot into a tamarisk branch, snapping the chariot shaft before galloping off on their own towards the city. Adrestus fell out of the chariot and soon had Menelaus standing over him with his spear in his hand. Adrestus offered to pay a ransom. Menelaus was ready to agree, when Agamemnon ran up to ask why he hadn't killed him. All the Trojans must die. Agamemnon killed Adrestus with his spear. It looked as if the Trojans would be driven back into their city. Hector urged his troops on. Glaukos and Diomedes approached each other in the open ground between the two armies, ready for single combat. They addressed one another at length, describing their ancestries. It turned out that their grandfathers were friends, so they too must be friends. Meanwhile Hector reached the oak tree at the Scaean Gate; he went in and made his way to Priam's palace, where he persuaded Paris to rejoin the battle.

Book 7. Hector and Paris passed through the gate and rejoined the battle. Paris killed Menesthius; Hector killed Eioneus. The Trojans gained on the Greeks. Hector challenged the Greeks to send out a champion that he could fight; his condition was that if he died, the Greeks could take his arms but must return his body to Troy for cremation. No one volunteered. Ashamed, Menelaus began to arm himself, but Agamemnon stopped him. Nestor made a speech, after which several Greeks volunteered. They cast lots. Ajax won, putting on his armour and striding towards Hector with his spear. They duelled with rocks. Hector proposed they call a truce as the light failed; they exchanged gifts. Ajax returned to the Greek encampment.

The Greek warriors had a meal. Out on the plain, the Scamander's banks were stained with Greek blood. They decided to call a truce, cart the bodies back to the encampment the following morning, burn them and raise a single burial mound. Then, using the mound as a base, they would quickly build a high wall to protect the ships and themselves. It was to have strong gates to let chariots in and out, and a little way outside there would be a deep ditch parallel to the wall as a further defence against the Trojans. At dawn, a Trojan messenger arrived at the ships with the news that Paris was ready to return all the property he had taken, together with some of his own, but he would not give up Helen. The Trojans also wanted a truce to dispose of their dead. Agamemnon agreed the truce, but Paris's offer was beneath discussion. The messenger returned to Troy.

Trojan and Greek work parties met at dawn to collect bodies. They burned them on pyres out on the plain, then returned to Troy and the camp. Before the following dawn, a Greek detachment went out to build a barrow over the pyre, then the wall, then the ditch and a palisade. Ships arrived at the Greek camp from Lemnos with cargoes of wine for the troops. The elaborate defences took all day to build.

Book 8. Dawn. The Greeks breakfasted in their camp, then armed themselves. The Trojans also armed; they were fewer in number than the Greek army. The gates of Troy were 'all thrown open' and the Trojan army poured out. The two armies converged and clashed. The earth ran with blood. The Greeks began to fall back. One of Nestor's chariot horses was hit by an arrow, throwing the other horses into confusion. Nestor was struggling to deal with this when Hector bore down on him. Diomedes called to Odysseus to help Nestor, but Odysseus did not hear him and rushed past on his way to the ships. Diomedes went to Nestor's aid himself, collecting the old man in his own chariot and leaving Nestor's squires to take charge of the horses. Diomedes hurled a spear at Hector, but killed Hector's charioteer instead.

Now the Trojans were in retreat, pushed back towards their city. There was a thunderclap; the lightning made Diomedes' horses shy. Diomedes was reluctant to turn back, but Nestor insisted on turning the chariot back. Hector shouted insults as Diomedes retreated. Hector incited the Trojans to follow them to the ships and set them on fire. Agamemnon climbed onto Odysseus' ship, in the centre of the line, so that his voice would carry to either end (the huts of Telamonian Ajax and Achilles); he urged the Greeks not to let the Trojans overwhelm them. There was fighting at the ditch. The Greeks pushed the Trojans away, then the Trojans pushed back to the ditch again.

Night fell, a great relief to the Greeks. Hector drew the Trojan army back to hold a conference beside the river, where the ground was clear of corpses. He told them to go and fetch food and firewood from the town, so that they could eat and have lots of fires. Guards must be mounted in the town to prevent the enemy stealing in. They would resume the attack on the ships at crack of dawn. The Trojans unyoked their chariot horses and sat up all night under the stars, eating and keeping the fires going, horses standing by the chariots munching barley and rye.

Book 9. Agamemnon called his captains together to tell them they had no hope of taking Troy. He proposed that they board ship and return home. Silence. Diomedes accused Agamemnon of cowardice; he, Diomedes, would fight on. The Greeks shouted their approval. The plan agreed was to deploy horse and infantry in front of the ships the next morning, but Agamemnon was still deeply despondent.

Book 10. Agamemnon looked across the plain and saw the many fires of the Trojans in front of Troy. Odysseus and Diomedes left the camp before dawn, moving silently across the plain. Hector sent a scout, Dolon, to reconnoitre by the ships, to find out if they were guarded and if the Greeks were discussing the possibility of flight. Dolon set off. Odysseus and Diomedes saw him, but pretended not to, letting him run past. They let him get ahead, then gave chase, caught him and forced him to tell them what Hector's intention was. He revealed that Hector was conferring with his advisers by the barrow of King Ilus, away from all the noise, and where the Trojan forces were disposed. Diomedes killed Dolon to silence him. Diomedes and Odysseus crept up on the sleeping Thracians and killed fourteen of them before returning back to the ships with the Thracians' horses. This exploit gave the Greeks new courage.

Book 11. The Greek and Trojan warriors prepared for battle. Then they collided in about equal numbers and fought all morning. The Mycenaeans under Agamemnon drove the Trojans back. By noon, the Trojans had fled past the barrow of Ilus, past the wild fig tree, and were halfway across the plain. The Greeks chased them until they reach the Scaean Gate and the oak. Then the Trojans stopped to let the slower ones catch up, because some were still out on the open plain, and being caught by Agamemnon. Hector encouraged his men to turn and fight the Greeks. This led to another skirmish. Agamemnon was wounded and taken at speed in his chariot back to the ships. Hector took heart from Agamemnon's departure. The Trojans surged forward and pushed the Greeks back towards the ships. Odysseus and Diomedes managed to hold the Trojans, but Paris shot an arrow and succeeded in wounding Diomedes. Odysseus shielded Diomedes while he pulled the arrow out. Trojans circled them, but Odysseus fought them off, sustaining a wound. The Greeks formed a line, crouching behind sloped shields; Ajax retreated to the safety of this friendly line and turned to face the Trojans. Achilles watched from his ship, with Patroklos. The two of them listened to a lengthy reminiscence by Nestor, leading up to the argument that the Trojans might be pushed right back to the city by two fresh fighters, Achilles and Patroklos.

Book 12. It began to look as if the trench and wall would give way before the Trojan attack. Later, when the siege was over, the gods destroyed all trace of the wall by turning against it all the united waters of the rivers running down from Ida to the sea. For nine days, they flowed together at one outlet in unceasing rain. Then the rivers returned to their channels.[1] The Trojans decided not to risk trying to take their chariots across the trench and wall; instead they dismounted and fought on foot. Asius alone risked his chariot, rode through the open gates and was killed by Idomeneus. Hector and other Trojans poured in through the gate.

Book 13. Hector reached the ships. The Trojan spearman Imbrius was killed by Teucer. Teucer tried to get Imbrius' armour off and was attacked by Hector. Hector tried to wrench the dead Amphimachus' helmet off, but Ajax attacked Hector. Hector withdrew. The two bodies were carried off by their respective sides. In anger, Imbrius' head was hacked off and hurled towards Hector; it landed at Hector's feet. Idomeneus and Meriones re-armed and re-entered the battle. Close hand-to-hand fighting followed with lots of stabbing. Idomeneus killed many Trojans. Aeneas marked him and Idomeneus was surrounded by Trojan warriors. The Trojan Harpalion attacked Menelaus and Menelaus killed him, infuriating Paris. Hector found Paris encouraging his troops and driving them forward on the left flank, and abused him. 'Where are Deiphobus, Helenus, Adamas, Asius, Othryoneus?[2] This is the end of Troy, and now you too must die.' Paris protested that he had never shrunk from fighting, pacified his brother and offered to go back into battle with him. There was a renewed attack by the Trojans. Ajax stepped forward and shouted to Hector that he would not take the Greek ships; the Greeks would take Ilium first. Hector led a charge against the Greeks, still intent on reaching the ships.

Book 14. Nestor in his hut decided to go and confer with Agamemnon. On his way he chanced on three royal lords who had been wounded – Diomedes, Odysseus, Agamemnon – and who were coming up from the ships. The ships had been drawn up in rows, as there was not enough room on the beach for them all side by side. The uppermost row was dragged right up onto the land, near the wall. Agamemnon was disappointed to find that Nestor was not fighting, and thought it likely that Hector would reach the ships and set them on fire. Agamemnon proposed dragging the ships out into the water and mooring them well out from the shore. Odysseus condemned this as brainless and cowardly. It would simply induce despair into the hearts of the Greeks. Agamemnon agreed, but asked for a better suggestion from them. Diomedes proposed that the leaders refrain from fighting, but visit all parts of the battlefield to urge the warriors on. They all agreed. Northerly winds sent breakers onto the beach. Ajax threw a rock at Hector. The Greeks swooped in, but the fallen Hector was immediately surrounded by his supporters. Penelaos killed and beheaded the Trojan Ilioneus, waving his head at the Trojans like a poppy-head on a spear. It frightened the Trojans. The Greeks at last drove the Trojans into flight.

Book 15. Fleeing Trojans went back across the palisade and trench, suffering severe losses at the hands of the Greeks. They did not stop till they reached their chariots. Hector lay on the ground, not fully conscious, with his comrades sitting round him. He recovered, recognized his friends, leapt up and rejoined the battle, which began to go more in the Trojans' favour. The Greeks gathered a small force of their best men (Ajax, Idomeneus, Teucer, Meriones, Meges) to face Hector and the Trojans, while the main force retreated to the ships.

There was another clash, with spears and arrows. The Greeks weakened, and the Trojans killed many – Arcesilaus, Stichius, Medon, Iasus and others. The Greeks were thrown back in disorder on the ditch trench and palisade. The defences were damaged, the wall knocked down. The Greeks reached the ships. Trojans poured across and there was close hand-to-hand fighting beside the ships. Some Greeks fought from the ships themselves. Teucer aimed an arrow at Hector, which would have stopped the battle, but missed. Ajax and Hector shouted to their men to encourage them. Trojans stormed the ships, but the Greeks stoutly resisted. As they fell back between the ships of the first row, they were protected by the upper works of the ships themselves. But the Trojans followed and the Greeks dispersed among the huts. Periphetes, a Mycenaean, tripped on the edge of his shield, and was speared to death by Hector. Ajax was storming up and down the decks of the ships swinging a 22 cubit-long pole. Hector laid hands on the stern of one of the ships and called for fire; his idea was to burn the ships. As Trojans arrived with torches, Ajax fended them off with his pole. He got beaten back to the 7 foot bridge amidships.

Book 16. Patroklos ran to Achilles to beg him to join the battle. He refused but agreed to let Patroklos wear his armour. Patroklos swept the Trojans from the ships, and put out the fire that had been started on one of them. Patroklos and Menelaus picked off some of the leading Trojans. Patroklos killed Sarpedon. Patroklos' arrival re-invigorated the Greeks. Hector turned his chariot and rode back towards Troy. Patroklos recklessly pursued the fight to the walls of Troy. Three times Patroklos scaled an angle of the wall, and three times he was hurled off. Hector pulled his horses up at the Scaean Gate, then drove at Patroklos. Patroklos picked up a stone and threw it at Hector's driver,

Cebriones. Hector jumped down and fought Patroklos for the body of Cebriones. Achilles' armour fell from Patroklos and Patroklos was left undefended, so he tried to escape by slipping back among the Myrmidons. Hector saw this, followed him and killed him with his spear, but not before Patroklos warned him that he would shortly die at Achilles' hands.

Book 17. Menelaus stood over Patroklos' body. Hector managed to strip it of the armour, leaving the body for the Greeks. His men carried Achilles' armour off into the town of Troy. Hector caught up with them, put on Achilles' armour himself and told his men to take his own armour into sacred Ilium.[3] Hector made a speech to the Trojans to encourage them, then they charged the Greeks, who still surrounded Patroklos' body. There was a raging battle, in which the Trojans tried to pull the corpse into Troy, and the Greeks tried to pull it to the ships. Fog descended. Then the sun came out, clearing the fog, and brought the whole field of battle into view. Gradually the Greeks succeeded in carrying the corpse back to their ships.

Book 18. Achilles, at the ships, saw the Greeks returning across the plain and guessed that Patroklos was dead. Achilles was visited by Thetis and Nymphs, who then disappeared into the heaving waters of the sea.[4] Achilles went out and stood by the ditch and gave his war-cry. The sun set. The Trojans drew back, unyoked their horses, and sat down to confer. They discussed whether they should stay where they were, ready for an early attack in the morning (which was Hector's advice) or retreat to the safety of Troy. They agreed with Hector.

Book 19. Dawn. Achilles grieved over the body of Patroklos. He was supplied with new armour and decided to join the battle, walked along the beach, and called out the Greek troops. Many of them were now suffering from their wounds. Achilles and Agamemnon formally put their dispute behind them. The Greeks armed, ready to attack.

Book 20. The Greeks assembled by the ships ready for battle. The Trojans drew up on Thorn Hill. A battle between the gods took place.[5] Some of the gods retreated with Poseidon to 'the lofty earthwork that the Trojans made as a refuge for Heracles from the great sea-beast when it came up from the beach to attack him on dry land.' Their divine opponents gathered on the brow of Callicolone. The plain meanwhile filled with human warriors. The earth shook beneath their feet as they rushed together. Aeneas and Achilles determined on single combat. Achilles taunted Aeneas with vain ambition: he wanted to fight Achilles because he wanted to supplant Priam as king of Troy. Aeneas made a dignified reply, detailing his pedigree. They threw spears at each other. Hector's brother Polydorus was killed by Achilles. Achilles was merciless, killing the young Tros.

Book 21. The Greeks moved forward to the ford of the Xanthus, where they split the Trojan force in two. Achilles drove one group across the fields towards the city of Troy; they spread out across the fields in wild disorder. They were confused by dense fog. The rest were chased into a bend in the river. They fell into the deep water. The banks on each side threw back their cries.[6] Achilles jumped in and killed the Trojans in the river.

Achilles took twelve young men out of the river to pay the price for Patroklos' death. Achilles cornered another son of Priam, Lycaon, who begged for his life. The river was choked with corpses, rose up and threatened to sweep Achilles away. An elm tree Achilles hung onto was uprooted by the flood water. Achilles waded through the flood water to safety. There was a heaven-sent fire on the parched plain, which burned up the bodies strewn there. Near the river were elms, willows, tamarisks, rushes, lotus and galingales; they were burnt by the fire, which also evaporated the floodwater. Priam, watching from the citadel, called out to open the city gates to let his routed forces in. The god Apollo disguised himself as Agenor and Achilles mistakenly pursued him across the fields away from the city, towards the Scamander, while the Trojans poured back into their city.

Book 22. Hector remained outside the walls. Achilles realized he had not been chasing Agenor after all and turned to head for the town. Priam groaned as he saw Achilles approaching and called to Hector, warning him not to engage in single combat with Achilles. Hector was uncertain what to do. When he saw Achilles running towards him, he fled before him round the walls of Troy, passing the lookout and the windswept fig tree, along the cart track, to the two springs that were the sources of the Scamander, one hot, the other cold. Beside the springs were the wide troughs where the Trojan women came in peacetime to do their washing. The two chased three times round the walls of Troy. More than once, Hector made a dash for the Dardanian Gate, hoping that as he dashed underneath the archers above would save him, but Achilles headed him off, keeping on the inside. Finally, Hector stopped running and fought Achilles. They threw spears at each other. Achilles ran at Hector with his lance, aiming at a gap in his armour (actually Achilles' own armour) at the gullet. Hector was mortally wounded and Achilles told him his body would be thrown to the dogs. Hector died. Achilles dragged Hector's body behind his chariot. Priam was distraught and had to be prevented from going out to stop Achilles.

Book 23. The Trojans lamented the death of Hector. The Greeks returned to their camp, dispersing to their respective ships. Achilles refused to wash until he had seen to the funeral of Patroklos, but first he lay down, in the open, on the beach and slept: he was exhausted. Agamemnon sent a sortie to collect wood on the slopes of Ida. A huge funeral pyre 100 feet long and 100 feet wide was built on the shore, on the spot where a mound was to be raised for both

Patroklos and Achilles jointly. Achilles sacrificed two of Patroklos' dogs and twelve Trojan prisoners. The fire did not kindle at first, then a north-west wind got up, raising the fire.[7] The flames were put out with wine, Patroklos' bones were taken out and sealed in fat inside a gold vase. Then Achilles asked Agamemnon to raise a small barrow over Patroklos' bones: it could be enlarged later. A stone circle was laid out round the pyre, to mark the outer revetment of the barrow. Then Achilles arranged funeral games. There was a chariot race. Nestor gave one of the charioteers advice, to look for a dead tree stump, an oak or pine, about six feet high, flanked by two white stones. The road narrowed there, and it might have marked an ancient burial place or a turning post; in any case it was the turning post Achilles had selected for this race. Nestor advised turning as tightly as possible. The race was from the beach to the mark and back. Other contests included a boxing match, a foot race, the discus, archery and javelin.

Book 24. The Achaeans dispersed to their ships for supper. Achilles went on grieving for days, and left the corpse of Hector unburied for twelve days. He

The Trojans drank from these vessels at the time of the Trojan War. The black tureen at the back is 20cm high and 30cm in diameter. The jugs in the centre are 17–25cm high. The largest of the cups, bottom left, is 11cm high (after Schliemann 1881).

was ready to hand over the body if Priam would offer him a ransom. The Trojans packed a mule-cart with treasure. Priam poured a libation and drove in his chariot, preceded by the mule-cart. They drove past the barrow of Ilus and stopped to let their horses drink at the river. Priam had a chance meeting with 'a young Achaean', who told him that Hector's body was still fresh. Priam was overjoyed and offered him money. The young Greek refused it, thinking that Achilles would sniff treachery. He offered to escort Priam into the Achaean camp. Achilles took the ransom and ordered Hector's body to be washed and anointed. Priam was at last able to eat, drink and sleep. Achilles ordered beds to be prepared in the portico. Achilles asked how many days Priam would allocate to Hector's funeral. Eleven days, Priam told him; the Trojans would be ready to fight again on the twelfth day. Achilles shook Priam by the hand.

Agamemnon and the rest of the Greeks did not know Priam was in the camp. Priam realized his danger, rose in the night and escaped back to Troy. As dawn broke, he reached the ford over the Scamander. Then he went on to the town. Cassandra was the first of the Trojans to see Priam returning, watching from the Pergamos.[8] Helen addressed the women of Troy, saying that it was nineteen years since she had left her home. At the next dawn, Hector's funeral pyre was lit. It was the same rite exactly as that for Patroklos, except that his bones were wrapped in a purple cloth and put in a golden chest; this was covered by a barrow.

The *Aithiopis* and the *Little Iliad*

That is where the narrative of the *Iliad* ends, with the story of the Trojan War not yet over. The next segment of the Epic Cycle, the lost *Aithiopis*, continued the story, opening with a digression which showed the sort of infighting that is likely to have gone on within a mixed force that included many rival chiefs. Although the *Aithiopis* has been lost, a summary made by Proklos survives, so we know what it contained.[9]

The Amazon Penthesileia, a Thracian, was among the Trojan allies. Achilles killed her and the Trojans arranged her funeral. The Greek trouble-maker Thersites reproached Achilles, saying that he loved Penthesileia, and was killed by Achilles. A quarrel arose among the Greeks over the murder of Thersites. After this, Achilles sailed to Lesbos, where he offered sacrifices to Apollo, Artemis and Leto, and was purified of the murder of Thersites by Odysseus.[10]

Achilles returned to Troy, routed the Trojans and rushed into the citadel of Troy, where he met his death at the hands of Paris. A battle followed for the body of Achilles. Ajax carried it back to the ships while Odysseus fought a rearguard action against the Trojans. After the funeral games of Achilles, Odysseus and Ajax quarrelled over Achilles' armour.

The narrative continued in the *Little Iliad*, another lost book, in which we learn how Odysseus won the armour of Achilles, and Ajax went mad and committed suicide.[11] Paris (Alexandros) was killed by Philoctetes. Paris's body was then mutilated by Menelaus. Troy was by this stage under full siege. The Greek Epeios built the wooden horse. Odysseus managed to get into Troy disguised as a beggar. Helen recognized him and together they planned the capture of Troy. Odysseus returned to the ships. Some Greek warriors hid inside the wooden horse. The rest set fire to their tents and sailed off to Tenedos. The Trojans believed the siege was over and that all the Greeks had gone. They broke down part of the city wall in order to pull the wooden horse into Troy.

In the first part of the Trojan Catalogue there is an authentic description of the geography of the Troad, or rather an account that is entirely consistent with the geography of the Troad. Walter Leaf makes the excellent point that the different components of the Epic Cycle were certainly written by different poets, possibly at different times, and yet the various accounts dovetail together very coherently; he argues that this is a strong indicator that the settings were real, not invented. It also indicates that, more likely than not, the events placed in those settings were real.[12]

The Hittite Texts

The poems of the Greek Epic Cycle give us the story of the war from the Greek side. But what of the Trojan view of events? It is extremely unfortunate that no Trojan texts at all have come to light. But Troy was on the western fringe of the Hittite empire and what happened there was of intense interest to the Hittite Great King, even though he resided 800km away to the east, at his capital, Hattusa – and many of his archives have survived.

The Hittite royal archive collection contains details about diplomatic crises, rivalries, negotiations with foreign powers, snubs and apologies. Found at Hattusa, roughly in the centre of Anatolia, many of the letters deal with treaties with the other great powers, and also with territorial and other political disputes. The tablets were so detailed and so many that there seemed to be a strong possibility that the Greek expedition and the fall of Troy would be there, somewhere, in this huge royal archive.

Since 1924 it has been generally accepted that the Ahhiyawans of the Hittite texts were the same people as Homer's Achaeans, and that Ahhiya (or Ahhiyawa) was the same as Achaea.[13]

The Indictment of Madduwattas, which dates from about 1450 BC, has a king called Attarissiyas, the 'man of Ahhiya', driving another king called Madduwattas from his western Anatolian kingdom so that Madduwattas had to seek asylum at the Hittite court. The Hittite king gave Madduwattas a small kingdom in the mountainous 'land of Zippasla', one of the twenty-two states in Assuwa, but here too he was attacked by the Mycenaean King Attarissiyas. The Hittite Great King, Tudhaliyas II, responded by sending an army. Tudhaliyas II was a dynamic Hittite high king who successfully controlled a huge empire stretching from the Aegean all the way to Aleppo.

In the pitched battle that followed, Tudhaliyas in person led his army against the Assuwan rebels. Attarissiyas deployed a hundred chariots and an unspecified number of foot soldiers, but he and the Assuwan rebels suffered a resounding defeat.

Tudhaliyas died, and the Hittite kings began to lose control of the kingdoms along the western Anatolian coast. In the reign of Tudhaliyas' successor, Arnuwandas (1440–1420), the Hittite kingdom started to disintegrate as cities of the central kingdoms were overrun by the Kaska peoples from the north. The Mycenaean Attarissiyas was able to exploit this opportunity, formed an alliance with Madduwattas and together they conquered the whole of the Arzawa Lands and launched a joint attack on Cyprus, both ventures that were every bit as ambitious in their way as the later Mycenaean confederate attack on Wilusa.[14] It is also significant that we are evidently seeing a 'king of Ahhiyawa' fighting with his own chariots alongside rebels on Anatolian soil – a century before the Homeric attack on Troy.[15]

One document (KUB XXIII 13) tells of events in the time of King Tudhaliyas IV, around the time of the Trojan War. It may even describe events that found their way into the Epic Cycle.

> Thus speaks tabarna [king] Tudhaliyas, the Great King. The Land of the Seha River transgressed again for a second time. They said: 'In the past, the great-grandfather of His Majesty [King Muwatallis?] did not conquer us by force of arms; and when the grandfather of His Majesty [King Mursilis III?] conquered the countries of Arzawa, he did not conquer us by force of arms. He would have conquered us, but we erased him for his transgression.' Thereafter Tarhunaradu [king of the Land of the Seha River] waged war and relied on the king of Ahhiyawa. And he took refuge on Eagle Peak. But I, the Great King, set out and ... raided Eagle Peak. And five hundred teams of horses and ... troops I brought here to Hatti, and Tarhunaradu together with his wives, children and goods I transported to [ ] ... and led him to Arinna, the City of the Sun-goddess. Ever since the days of Tabarna no Great King went to the country. I made a descendant of Muwawalwi ... in the Land of the Seha River king and enjoined him to deliver ... teams of horses ...[16]

Tarhunaradu was king of the Land of the Seha River in 1240, around the time of the Trojan War. The power of the Hittite Great King, when he was minded to use it, was enormous. He was able to send great armies huge distances and use them to quell insurrections and to depose or replace troublesome kings anywhere in his empire. He would, as we shall see, eventually intervene in this way at Troy, which was right on the edge of his sphere of influence.

For a long time scholars have seen evidence that the *Iliad* incorporates elements that date from the period after the Trojan War, from the supposedly non-literate dark age between 1100 BC and 750 BC. It would be quite likely for an oral tradition passed on through that period to acquire some anachronistic details along the way. But now we can see evidence in Homer of events that date from *before* the Trojan War of 1250 BC. There was, for instance, the expedition to the Gulf of Edremit, which may have happened months, years or even decades before the events described in the *Iliad*, and the account of the Edremit expedition may itself be a conflation of several separate raids. Some elements in Homer are much older than that. Ajax's tower shield and the use of silver-studded swords date from several centuries earlier. The sort of society described in the *Iliad*, the warrior-hero aristocracy, seems to me to belong to the Mycenae of the shaft graves of 300 years earlier. It is possible that some episodes embedded in the Epic Cycle originated in earlier epics describing the era before the Trojan War.

Certainly the expedition to Troy was not the only Mycenaean adventure in Anatolia. The letter about King Tarhunaradu shows that the king of Ahhiyawa, the Mycenaean Great King, fought as an ally of the king of the Seha River Land against the Hittite king, and that seems to have happened either just before or just after the Trojan War.

The first report of a connection between Ahhiyawa and the country (or later) city of Millawanda came in about 1330 BC, year three of the Annals of Mursilis II. Unfortunately both this reference and another shortly after are on broken tablets, and the location of Ahhiyawa is left unstated; one reference nevertheless does mention a ship, which supports the idea that Ahhiyawa was overseas. Mursilis fell ill and the divination priests opened an inquiry into the cause of the divine anger. A large tablet records the questions put to the oracle, and the answers. It mentions the god of Ahhiyawa and the god of Lazpas, whose statues were taken to Hattusa to succour the sick king, and inquires about the rituals appropriate to these foreign gods.[17] The divination tablet confirms friendly relations between the kingdoms of Hatti and Ahhiyawa; the loaning of cult idols is reminiscent of the modern practice of transnational loans of works of art for themed exhibitions, something that can only happen within a context of well-developed diplomatic relations – and strong mutual trust. I doubt whether the British Museum will be lending the Greeks the Elgin Marbles, because of the strong suspicion that they would not be returned.[18] Lazpas, Lesbos, was an island off the west coast of Anatolia where there were two Mycenaean settlements, so there is an implication that *both* of the portable gods came from across the water, from lands to the west of Anatolia.[19] At this stage, some seventy years before the Trojan War, Hittites and Ahhiyawans were on friendly terms. Some Greeks were even naming their boys Myrsilios after the Hittite king.

Another document is the so-called Tawagalawas Letter, addressed to the king of Ahhiyawa by an unnamed elderly king of Hatti, and dating to around 1250. The letter is hard to understand, because only fragments survive, but what is clear is that an Anatolian prince called Piyamaradus was causing disaffection in the Lukka country.[20] The Lukka Lands lay in south-west Anatolia and only the eastern part lay within the Hittite empire. Piyamaradus' base was the adjacent city of Millawanda, which was in the extreme west of the Lukka Lands, just outside Hittite control, in the coastal strip under the indirect control of the King of Ahhiyawa. The Hittite king wrote the letter to press the king of Ahhiyawa to hand over Piyamaradus and so restore peace in the Lukka Lands; it was an extradition request. The people of the Lukka Lands had already on their own account written appealing to the king of Ahhiyawa's brother, Tawagalawas, probably because he was currently living in Anatolia and therefore more likely to be able to help them. On another occasion, when the Lukka city of Attarimma was attacked, they called on the Hittite high king to help them. Everything points to the Lukka Lands being a buffer zone between Ahhiyawa and Hatti.

Piyamaradus was well enough established in the Lukka Lands to apply to the Hittite king for recognition as a vassal. The Hittite king was apparently willing to agree to this, and sent his son to fetch Piyamaradus, but Piyamaradus refused to accompany the prince to his father's court, probably sensing treachery, and insisted on recognition on the spot. After the Hittite king had suppressed the revolt in the Lukka Lands, he received a message from the king of Ahhiyawa telling him that he had instructed his agent (or regent) in Millawanda, a man named Atpas, to hand Piyamaradus over. The Hittite king arrived in Millawanda to discover that Atpas had allowed Piyamaradus to escape by sea, naturally the subject of a further complaint.[21]

The Tawagalawas Letter has by this stage confirmed not only that the king of Ahhiyawa was in control in Millawanda but that Millawanda was on the coast. The rest of the letter consists of reasons why the king of Ahhiyawa should accede to the Hittite king's request to hand over Piyamaradus. Among the suggestions is that the messenger bearing the letter should be kept as a hostage for Piyamaradus' safety. 'The messenger is a man of some importance; he is the groom who has ridden with me in my chariot from my youth up, and not only with me, but with your brother Tawagalawas.' This speaks of a close relationship between the dynasts.

There are even references to a Trojan War in the Tawagalawas Letter, two hints that Hittites and Ahhiyawans had already come to blows over Wilusa.

The tone of the letter is respectful and friendly. The Hittite king, Hattusilis III, even goes as far as apologizing to the king of Ahhiyawa for his 'soldierly' turn of phrase in case it is interpreted as aggressive.[22] He tactfully implies that his brother-king cannot be fully aware of the situation and will surely act appropriately as soon as he understands it. There is the clear implication that the king of Ahhiyawa is a *long way* from the scene of the events described. He is a remote figure, has probably been fed distorted and inaccurate information by his underlings and is not in direct personal control of what is happening at Millawanda.[23] The date of the letter, around 1250, is in legendary chronology close to the reign of Thyestes or Agamemnon, and also close to the likeliest date for the Trojan War.

The reference to the king of Ahhiyawa as the Hittite king's 'brother' has been widely discussed, as it shows that the Hittite king regards the Ahhiyawan king as his equal. The letter was not the only communication between the two kings on the Piyamaradus affair, and it is evident that a letter from the Ahhiyawan king must have contained some reproof for the content and tone of a still earlier letter. Hattusilis is conciliatory and defensive: 'If any of my lords had spoken to me, or even one of my brothers, I would have listened. But now my brother the Great King, my equal, has written to me, shall I not listen to the word of my equal?' Interpreting this is not easy, and it is possible to hear heavy sarcasm in it. Hattusilis was exasperated by continuing Ahhiyawan meddling in western Anatolia, and may well have felt that the king of Ahhiyawa was not only trespassing but overreaching himself – an upstart, a jumped-up Great King, not a real one.[24]

There can be little doubt that Millawanda (in some places 'Milawata', suggesting an early Greek form 'Milwatos') was the major Mycenaean colony of Miletus on the south-west coast of Anatolia.[25] One objection to Miletus as Millawanda is that Arzawa, a hostile country, would have separated Millawanda from the Hittites and prevented them from maintaining regular communication, though this is not necessarily so.[26] The most recent thinking puts the southern boundary of Arzawa somewhere close to the Meander valley. The Hittites may have had direct access to Miletus along the Meander valley, and they certainly had access by way of the Lukka Lands immediately to the south.[27]

The king of Ahhiyawa supported the powerful king of Arzawa in a war against Hatti in around 1320 BC, seventy years before the Trojan War. He also supported the king of the neighbouring Land of the Seha River in a similar war against 'the Great King of Hatti'. This repeated Greek interference in western Anatolia was on a larger scale than the slave raids suggested by the Pylos tablets, and is exactly the sort of background we would expect to an expedition against Wilusa in north-western Anatolia in the thirteenth century.

A fragmentary letter from the Hittite king to an unnamed sub-king, possibly the ruler of Millawanda, addresses him as 'my son'. Ahhiyawa is not mentioned, but there are references to the Piyamaradus affair, which would have been well known in Millawanda. There is also an implication in the style of address, friendly but proprietorial, that the outcome of the Tawagalawas Letter had been satisfactory from the Hittite king's point of view; he had regained control over Millawanda.

It is clear from all of this that, by the thirteenth century, Ahhiyawan interference in western Anatolia had become a continual problem to the Great Kings of Hatti. In the 1260s, just before the Trojan War, a deposed Hittite king requested help from the king of Ahhiyawa before going into exile in Syria. Shortly after this, Hattusilis was preoccupied with the sacking of his city of Carchemish by Assyrians in the east, but he was still aware of the ever-present threat of Mycenaean interference in the west. Ahhiyawa was seducing and destabilizing one western kingdom after another. War with Ahhiyawa was to be avoided; where possible, the Hittite kings preferred diplomacy.

It was the kings of Ahhiyawa of the thirteenth century who were accorded the status of 'Great Kings', by the Hittite Foreign Office in the reigns of Hattusilis III (1265–1239) and Tudhaliyas IV (1239–1209). These Ahhiyawan Great Kings correspond with the kings of the Atreid dynasty at Mycenae. It was the dynasty of the legendary Atreus, Thyestes and Agamemnon that was a particular worry to the Hittites.

Archaeology supports the idea of Mycenaean contact and trade with the coastal towns of western Anatolia, some of which were full-blown Mycenaean trading posts. Conversely, Hittite control penetrated a long way west, into the Lukka and Seha River Lands. The tablet references to Ahhiyawan activity at sea, the major Cyprus expedition in particular but also the long-distance trading with Syria, suggest a significant command of the seas and some major power base. The Greek traditions of successive sea empires emphasize that there was only room for *one* such sea empire in the Aegean at a time, and we know that it was the Mycenaeans who dominated the Aegean Sea from around 1400 BC onwards.

It is now generally accepted that Ahhiyawa was Mycenaean Greece. The Hittite picture of Mycenaean Greece was of a more or less unified confederation of the Greek mainland kingdoms under a High King. This is the picture Homer gives us as well, yet the circumstances described in the *Iliad* appear exceptional, a war coalition set up to deal with a particular emergency; it would not be surprising to find that in peacetime the twenty Mycenaean kingdoms went their separate ways. Yet the Hittite archives imply one man, a High King, an Agamemnon, at the helm throughout the centuries represented in the archive tablets. It is possible that the High King was the king of Thebes or Orchomenos, but both archaeology and Homer tell us that it was the king of Mycenae who held this office. The other significant implication from the Hittite archives is that the king of Ahhiyawa and his agents were busy along the western Anatolian coast, and that this disrupted the fraying western fringe of the Hittite empire. The king of Ahhiyawa himself was campaigning on the Anatolian mainland. This brings us very close to the Trojan War.

Forrer was sure he had identified Troy itself in the Hittite archives, in the name 'Taruisa', which could be the Hittite original of the Greek 'Troia'. 'Taruisa' might be pronounced Taruwisa, Tarwisa, Truisa or Troisa.

Unfortunately it only occurs once, in the records of Tudhaliyas I (1420–1400), the first Hittite king to visit this region, in a list of towns of the land of Assuwa. The towns seem to be listed in geographical order, starting in the south at the border with the Lukka Lands, and this puts Taruisa, the last in the list, in a northerly location – in the Troad.[28]

Just before Taruisa is the name Wilusa, and some seize on this as the Ilios of Homer. The name of the king of Wilusa in around 1280 BC, in the reign of the Hittite King Muwatallis II, was Alaksandus.[29] This is of course the same name as Alexandros, also in the *Iliad* called Paris, and he was a prince of Ilios or Troy.

The name 'Trojans' is used to describe the citizens of Troy or more loosely the people of the Troad as a whole. Homer uses another name, Dardanians, or Dardanoi, to describe some of the people of the Troad, and Egyptologists have pointed out that the contingent of 'Drdny', fighting as allies of King Muwatallis at the Battle of Kadesh in 1275 BC, were probably Dardanians.[30] In other words, as allies of the Hittite empire, Trojans fought for the Hittite king against Egypt. It is what one might have expected, and it means that the fathers of some of the Trojans who fought against Agamemnon in the Trojan War fought against Ramesses at the Battle of Kadesh twenty-five years earlier.

After the high point of the Hittite Empire, the peace treaty that was successfully concluded with Egypt in 1269 BC, a period of disintegration began, and the Mycenaeans played a significant part in it. The Tawagalawas Letter contains two hints that by 1250 the Hittites and Ahhiyawans had already fought over Troy, or at least over a town in Wilusa. The Hittite king says: 'Tell him [Piyamaradus] that in the matter of Wilusa over which we were at enmity, he has changed my mind and we have made friends ... A war is wrong for us.'[31] Later he refers again to 'the matter concerning the town of Wilusa over which we made war.' The phrase 'town of Wilusa' is tantalizingly ambiguous. It could mean any one of the towns in the kingdom of Wilusa, or the main town of the kingdom which would have been known by the same name; if the latter, then 'the town of Wilusa' must mean Troy itself, and the reference 'over which we made war' must be to the Trojan War.

Another letter, from around the same period, was from the king of the Land of the Seha River to a Hittite king mentioning that Piyamaradus had attacked Lesbos. Yet another document from the same period implies that the king of Ahhiyawa was himself present in western Anatolia, and refers to his withdrawal. These seem to be documentary references to the Trojan War itself.

The Egyptian Sources

There is a third strand of documentary evidence, from Egypt. As we have seen, the Hittite, Assyrian, Babylonian and Egyptian kings wrote to each other as brotherly equals, and there is a fleeting mention of the king of Ahhiyawa being an associate member of this exclusive jet-set of high kings. Support for an Aegean location for this potentate comes from the Egyptians, who kept their own independent records.

A statue base from the mortuary temple of Amenhotep III near Egyptian Thebes carries a list of names that have come from the Aegean. The list, which dates from about 1340 BC, opens with 'Keftiu' and 'Tanaja'. 'Keftiu' is known to mean 'Crete' or 'Cretans', and 'Tanaja' must mean 'Greece' or 'Greeks': the word is very close to 'Danaans', one of the names used in the *Iliad* for the Mycenaean Greeks. After distinguishing between Minoans and Mycenaeans, the inscription goes on to list the places where those envoys came from: the Cretans had come from Amnisos, Knossos, Lyktos, Sitia, Phaistos and Kydonia (Khania), while the Danaans had come from Mukana (Mycenae), 'Deghajas' (unidentified), Messene and Nauplion in the Peloponnese.[32]

An inscription from seventy years earlier, around 1450 BC, tells of tribute sent by 'Tanaja', the Greeks. This included a silver vase specifically of Cretan workmanship, which presumably either the Egyptians recognized for themselves from its style and quality or the Greeks, as great admirers of Minoan craftsmanship, were keen to point out. A similar list of tribute offerings from the reign of Amenophis III at Karnak mentions Greece in a list with Ugarit and Cyprus, reinforcing the idea of the Mycenaeans operating in the wider eastern Mediterranean sphere.

Overall, the Egyptian evidence shows that the Mycenaean realm was regarded in Egypt as significant enough to record. This is useful indirect evidence, as it adds weight to the idea that the rulers of Hatti would also have been interested in the Mycenaeans.

There is another way in which Egyptian sources tell us about the Trojan War. They contain detailed descriptions and even pictures of the Battle of Kadesh between Egyptian and Hittite armies, which included warriors from Wilusa. These descriptions and images supply useful information about military organization, strategy, command – and the general conduct of warfare in the thirteenth century.

The Trojan War: Towards a Twenty-first-Century Reconstruction

Any reconstruction of the Trojan War is necessarily speculative. Although the Hittite archives span a couple of centuries, there are still many gaps, and there are no Mycenaean archives for the period of the war. An outline reconstruction is nevertheless just possible.

The Hittite royal archives show that the thirteenth-century Hittite kings – Hattusilis III and Tudhaliyas IV in particular – had to push the resources of their empire to the limit to maintain their power. To the north they were threatened continually by the Kaska peoples; in Syria to the south-east they were locked in continuing rivalry with Egypt; to the east they were worried by the increasing power of Assyria; to the west, where a powerful group of states was led in disaffection by the Arzawans, there was unrest and instability. Embattled in their headquarters in Hattusa, the Hittite kings had to use all their skills in diplomacy to deal with some of these problems; their empire was very large and they simply could not deploy armies on three or four fronts at once.[33]

To this dangerously unstable situation we must add the increasing interest of the Mycenaeans in western Anatolia. For a long time, they had indulged in small-scale raids, taking slaves and probably other booty as well. They were raiding Anatolia in the fifteenth century, supporting the Assuwan coalition against the king of Hatti, and by the thirteenth century they had become more ambitious. The city of Miletus (Millawanda or Milawata) was well established as a Greek colony. The Hittite kings were understandably ambivalent about Miletus, but they were ready to concede that it and a certain amount of land round it were 'Achaean'. This concession may have hardened their attitude to the possibility of secession in the rest of western Anatolia, and they made it clear that they regarded Mira, Arzawa, the Seha River Land and Wilusa as vassal states of the Hittite empire. Any attempt at destabilization in those kingdoms would be met by force.

It is evident, again from the Hittite archives, that by 1250 the Mycenaeans' activities in western Anatolia amounted to deliberate and systematic destabilization. It is as if the Mycenaeans sensed that the Hittites were more interested in the east than the west and were losing their grip on the Aegean coastlands; there was a power vacuum that the Mycenaeans might exploit. The Mycenaean High King's brother aided Hattusilis' most dangerous enemy in the region. In around 1280 BC there had been a war between the Mycenaeans and the Hittites over a city in the kingdom of Wilusa, whose king was Alaksandus or Alaksandu; that city may have been Troy itself. It would not be long before the Wilusan royal family was moving into exile. The Mycenaeans' motives are unclear. They may have been keen to destabilize Assuwa as a step towards destabilizing Wilusa, which lay immediately to the north, and the motive for that may well have been a desire to gain control of the Hellespont. There is another possibility. There are mythic traditions of the Greeks that trace the bronze age dynasties at Argos, Tiryns and Mycenae back to Assuwa.[34] If there were blood ties between the royal families of Argolis and those of Assuwa, the Mycenaeans may have wanted to help their distant cousins to defend themselves against an invasion by king Tudhaliyas II – an invasion of their own ancestral homeland. If so, they failed.

After a war in around 1300 BC, a formal treaty known as the Alaksandu Treaty was drawn up between the Hittite king and the Trojan king:

> As follows His Majesty Muwatallis, Great King of the land of Hattusa, favourite of the Weather God of Lightning, son of Mursilis [II], the Great King, the Hero. Once upon a time, the tabarna, my

forebear, subdued the entire land of Arzawa and the entire land of
Wilusa. Later the land of Arzawa waged war [on us] for that reason;
however, I know, since the event lies far back in the past, no king of
the land of Hattusa from which the land of Wilusa has seceded. Yet
even if the land of Wilusa has seceded from the land of Hattusa,
close ties of friendship were maintained from a distance with the
kings of the land of Hattusa and envoys sent regularly to them ...

The thrust of the treaty is clear. The Arzawa lands to the south of Wilusa
were a continuing problem to the Hittite king, but Wilusa was not. Wilusa
might have seceded from the Hittite empire, though the Hittite king did not
really accept the secession, which as far as he was concerned had no
historical precedent; even so, the Hittite empire remained on friendly
diplomatic terms with Wilusa. It is also clear, from the many times he is
addressed in the text of the treaty as a whole, that the king of Wilusa in 1280
BC was Alaksandu.

There is also no doubt (from the archaeological remains in the region) that
Troy was always the largest and strongest of the Wilusan settlements and
therefore likely to have been the seat of successive Wilusan kings. Kukkuni and
his successor Alaksandu were kings of Wilusa and therefore almost certainly
kings of Troy too. The Alaksandu treaty gives strong evidence that there were
friendly relations between successive Trojan kings and the Hittite Great Kings
from 1420 until 1280 BC.[35] The title 'tabarna' was a very ancient one, and not
used after 1600 BC; this implies that the friendly relations extended right back
to that time.

The forces gathered by Agamemnon in Homer are colossal. Some have
suggested that the Catalogue of Ships was a poetic device, a means of
drawing in as many famous heroes as possible, and not a factual piece of
historical reporting.[36] The number of warriors seems grossly exaggerated. A
hundred thousand or more warriors, ferried in by 1,186 ships, would not have
been needed to take a relatively small citadel on a low, easily accessible coastal
hill. The Pylos tablets mention forces guarding the Greek coast counted in
hundreds, not thousands. On the other hand, the territories listed in the
Homeric Catalogue do coincide remarkably closely with the Mycenaean
heartland as we infer it from archaeological evidence, so it is possible that the
kingdoms listed really were part of the Achaean confederacy. The numbers
of warriors and ships each contributed were probably lower than Homer
mentions, and some did not contribute any at all; Homer says that land-
locked Arcadia contributed no ships, and there may have been other
kingdoms who gave diplomatic but not military support to the war on Troy.[37]

The muster point, Aulis, looks like an odd choice, when Agamemnon
might have been expected to summon the fleet to his own harbour, the Bay of
Argos. But Aulis really was a port in the late bronze age, and its position

towards the north-east meant that it was quite a short sailing distance from there to Troy.

The war over 'the city of Wilusa' was fought in the north-east of the Aegean, an area where the Mycenaeans had been taking slaves and where they had developed close trading links with one city in particular – Troy, possibly even then called something like Troia. What is still unclear is the reason for the Mycenaean attack. Many suggestions have been made.

The collection of women as slaves and concubines was common enough at this period. The motive given by Homer is not too far from this: the (re)capture of a woman abducted by a Trojan prince – but it seems unlikely that an expeditionary force would have been mobilized for just *one* woman. Another possible motive is economic strategy. As long ago as 1912 Walter Leaf proposed that Troy was extremely desirable to the Greeks because the city commanded the mouth of the Hellespont and had become a nodal point in trading operations. Tolls on foreign

The Greek impact on Anatolia: trade, raids, conquests and colonies.

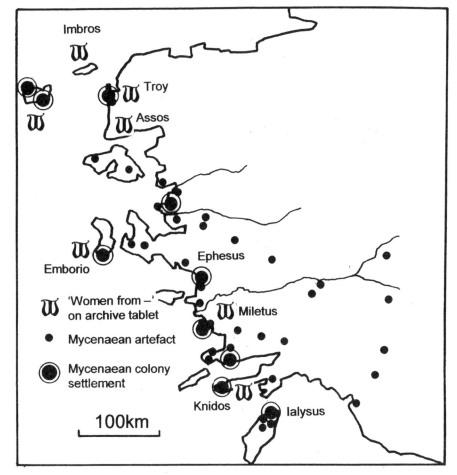

traders were imposed, the hypothesis continues, and the Greeks were goaded into putting Troy under siege, strangling it by cutting it off from its trade.[38] Nilsson believed that Leaf was applying too modern an approach to bronze age people.[39] Nevertheless, given that the Mycenaeans were conducting a significant volume of long-distance trade via the Black Sea route, the Hellespont would have been a key location; maybe the Mycenaeans wanted to secure Troy in order to be sure of the freedom of the sea route past it. Another possibility is that the Greeks wanted to gain control of the Scamander valley.[40] A simpler explanation is that, having developed a conventional trading relationship with Troy, the Mycenaeans came to realize just how wealthy the city was and saw it as a target for plunder. Strategy or robbery?

Certainly the Troy that fell to the Greeks in 1250 BC, Priam's Troy, would have been a prize worth taking. Sceptics have argued that Troy VI was too small to be the 'wide-spread Troy' described by Homer. The Troia Project of the 1990s has nevertheless resolved this problem by proving the long-suspected existence of a bronze age city on the slope to the south of the citadel. Manfred Korfmann, the project leader, shared Schliemann's view that more of Troy lay hidden. He and his team used a magnetometer survey to discover, a full century after Schliemann's death, the city streets of the Roman period and traces, beneath them, of the bronze age city.

The bronze age city of Troy turns out to have been thirteen times larger than previously thought, with a population of up to ten thousand, easily big enough to have been a major central place. Troy VI, with its city stretching away on the south side of the citadel walls, would have been every bit as imposing as Mycenae. The citadel itself rose on the top of steep cliffs from the shore of the bay as if defending the town from seaborne attack; approached from the sea, its reflection shimmering in the bay, it would have been as impressive to Europeans in the bronze age as Manhattan was to European migrants in the 1930s.

Another view, that of Carl Blegen, is that the Homeric Troy was Troy VIIa, a patched, earthquake-damaged city that the absence of imported pottery shows was in decline. This weakened city lasted for only a generation before being violently destroyed by fire – and looted. Blegen believed that *this* event was the Homeric sack of Troy, which he dated to about 1240 BC. Blegen's Homeric Troy was not a glamorous place. The threat of siege drove many of the citizens into the citadel for refuge, and small slum dwellings were crammed against the inside of the circuit walls. Scraps of human bones in the streets, a skull in a doorway, a man struck down in flight, were evidence of the moment when the Mycenaeans broke through the defences of Priam's Troy.[41]

At about the same time as the Trojan War, and perhaps even during the same campaign, the people of the Seha River Land rashly announced to the Hittite king that they no longer owed allegiance to him but to the Mycenaean king. The Mycenaean king seems to have arrived with an army, withdrawing when he had word of Hattusilis' approach, and leaving his Seha River allies to face Hattusilis unsupported. On the face of it, this was shameful and dishonourable. Hattusilis recorded his response: he ravaged the Land of the Seha River, deposed its king and installed in his place a loyal substitute. It was perhaps during this ignominious retreat from the Seha River Land that the Mycenaeans and their Anatolian allies sacked Thermi, the principal town on Lesbos.

Here we arrive at one of those refreshing moments when field archaeology, contemporary documents from the Hittite archives and the Epic Cycle all converge. Archaeological evidence of destruction at Thermi supports both the Hittite story of Lesbos being attacked by the infamous Piyamaradus, and the Epic Cycle story of the sack of Lesbos by the heroic Achilles. There is another possible reading of events, though. 'Withdrew' on the Hittite tablet could be interpreted as 'relied on'. The tablet is badly damaged and incomplete, and there is an alternative reading: that the Mycenaean king relied on the Seha River People to create a diversion, a smoke-screen behind which he might take Troy, if not unnoticed then at least unmolested by the great army of Hattusilis. Another possibility, which seems very probable to me, is that the Seha River People heard of the approach of the Mycenaean expeditionary force, thought it had come to liberate them, were mistaken in the Mycenaeans' intentions and made what turned out to be a fatally premature declaration of loyalty to the invaders.

It is hard to tell how important Wilusa was to the Hittite kings. One thing is clear from the surviving and very incomplete archive – and that is that the Hittite kings were polite, diplomatic and circumspect in their correspondence with the kings of western Anatolia. This may be in part a matter of custom and manners, in part a matter of trying to keep things quiet and orderly in the west so that what were seen as more serious threats from the east and south-east could be dealt with. But it was also possible for the power balance to shift unexpectedly as old alliances failed and new ones were formed. The kingdoms of the west could conceivably have united and marched on Hattusa. The identity of Parhuitta is still uncertain, but it is possible that he was the king of Wilusa. A fragment of a letter exists from the king of Hatti to Parhuitta, and the style of greeting is the one used from one Great King to another. In the nine short, incomplete lines of the letter, Wilusa is mentioned four times, which suggests that Parhuitta might have been its king. The Great King's greeting does not mean that the king of Troy was really a Great King, only that the Hittite king regarded him and his kingdom as politically significant at that moment, rather like an American president showing flattering cordiality towards a British prime minister. Parhuitta was being 'buttered up'.[42]

What is almost certainly true is that behind the tales told in the *Iliad* and the *Kypria* were many Mycenaean raids, very likely smaller in scale than the grand spectacle presented by Homer. The Trojan War of the Epic Cycle is a condensed account of events spanning as much as a couple of centuries, beginning about a hundred years before the supposed date of the Homeric siege.[43]

Chapter 8

Arms, Armour and Tactics

He stabbed his temple and cleft his helmet's cheek-piece.
None of the bronze plate could hold it – boring through
the metal and skull the bronze spear-point pounded.

(Iliad 20. 451–3)

Before we move on to reconstruct in detail the events of the Trojan War, we need to pause to look at the nuts and bolts of late bronze age warfare: the tactics that are likely to have been employed by the commanders and the weapons technology that was available to their warriors at the time. We have three sources of information available to us: the descriptions in the Epic Cycle, the artefacts surviving in the archaeological record, and contemporary images of weapons, armour and even sieges and battles. After 3,250 years, a surprisingly large amount of detailed information has survived.

Transport and Logistics

Transporting huge numbers of warriors and support staff, weapons, horses, chariots and siege engines across from Greece to Troy in the late bronze age might seem an almost impossible undertaking. Yet the Mycenaeans were very experienced in the logistics of this kind of operation; they had carried out attacks like this many times before. They were also experienced navigators. They had controlled the island-hopping trading routes across the Aegean for over a century by the time of the Trojan War. There were so many islands that ships were rarely out of sight of land for more than an hour, and the captains doubtless navigated by the sun and a sequence of sea-marks. They knew not only the way across but which of the islands would be useful sources of supplies for the campaign.

The ships had keels, but their hulls were broad and shallow, drawing very little water. This, combined with the square rig – a single square sail mounted on a central mast was the rule – meant that crews had no choice but to sail before the wind. The keel was sometimes extended to make either a ram or a landing gangway. At the stern, the keel was curved up to make a firm mounting for the large oar-rudder. Immediately in front of this was a square kiosk, rather like the wheelhouse on a small modern fishing vessel: this was the captain's cabin.

The shallow draught made it easy to navigate shallow water, to sail in very close to the shore, and to beach the ship easily in sandy bays. It was standard practice for crews to haul their ships ashore and chock them upright with blocks or props.

Ships varied in size, and different types of vessel were used for different purposes. Light, fast vessels would have been used for transporting the warriors; more stoutly built but slower vessels would have been used for transporting supplies, chariots and siege engines. The larger ships had cabins fore and aft. The forecastle had a banner mounted on it, while the stern-post was often decorated with a large carved animal's head.

All the ships were equipped with oars and seats for oarsmen. On days when there was a head-wind or no wind at all, the sail was furled and the crew would row. When approaching Troy from the south-west, Mycenaean captains must often have ordered the sails furled; they must often have had to give the unwelcome order for the oarsmen to row against a persistent north-east wind. The meltemi was the Trojans' best defence against the Greeks – but it was not enough to save them. The rowers were probably slaves. A raised walkway connecting the two cabins on the larger galleys enabled the ship's officers to move up and down the ship without interrupting the rowing.

The Mycenaeans might have brought some food with them, and they probably arrived in the Troad with enough for a week or two. They might expect to plunder the Trojans' food supply from the fields if they arrived at the right time of year, but if they came at the start of the campaigning season, in early summer, there would have been little to take. Success would in any case depend on a significant early military success giving them control of the Plain of Troy.

Once fighting started, the crops growing on the Plain of Troy would have gone untended, and the eventual harvest would have been slight. Hoping for food in the Troad would have carried enormous risks. It is clear that a campaign lasting at least several weeks, and possibly for several campaigning seasons, *must* have been resourced from outside.

The Mycenaeans had several offshore bases on islands off the Anatolian coast. We know from a variety of sources that they had bases on Lesbos, Tenedos and Lemnos. Food and wine were gathered at these safe havens and sent in to the Greek camp from time to time as needed. The Mycenaean trading network spread right across the Aegean, so it is reasonable to suppose that fruit, vegetables, cereals, nuts, olives and wine produced on islands elsewhere in the Aegean, and perhaps even the Greek mainland, were shipped to the offshore bases. As far as the *Iliad* is concerned, this huge catering and transport operation lies largely, though not wholly, hidden. The campaign against Troy would nevertheless have been impossible without it.

Homer: Weaponry and Command

The most distinctive and unusual item of military equipment mentioned in the *Iliad* is the Mycenaeans' boar's tusk helmet. Nothing like it had ever been seen by anyone living when the *Iliad* was written down in the eighth century; it was a genuine bronze age artefact, described in the *Iliad* just as it would have looked in the bronze age, yet no longer available for the poet to see for himself. The description of the helmet must therefore have been handed down by oral tradition from the bronze age. It was made principally between 1570 and 1430 BC, but was still in use two hundred years later.

Boars' tusks were not easily come by, and many were needed to make just one helmet; it was only the aristocrats who could afford the leisure to go boar-hunting often enough to collect the number of tusks needed to make a helmet. A boar's tusk helmet was a very expensive item and, once made, it became a family treasure. Homer confirms this; the boar's tusk helmet belonging to Meriones was stolen from Boeotia by Autolycus, given by Autolycus to Amphidamas of Kythera, and then by him to Molos, the father of Meriones. By the time Meriones gave it to Odysseus it was a priceless heirloom.[1] Only a few aristocratic warriors would have been able to afford these helmets; they were not exported, and must have been made to commission for specific princes, who were probably expected to supply the trophy tusks themselves. The helmet became a visual boast of the wearer's prowess as a huntsman.

The vogue for making boar's tusk helmets was over long before the Trojan War, yet remarkably there were some still in circulation then, two hundred years later.[2] By then they must have been priceless heirlooms, whose origins were lost in the mythic past – and these are exactly the terms in which Homer describes them.

The ordinary Mycenaean foot soldier would have had nothing so elaborate as the boar's tusk helmet, nor even the cone-shaped bronze helmet that other élite warriors wore. Most common soldiers at the time of the Trojan War probably wore simple leather helmets. These had a prominent ridge crest; they were made out of two pieces of leather sewn together to make the keel running over the top of the head. Some leather helmets may have had bronze disks or plates sewn onto them: that, I think, is what we are being shown on the Warrior Vase.

The cone- or bullet-shaped bronze helmets were sometimes decorated with horse-hair plumes sprouting from the crown. An ivory depiction of a boar's tusk helmet shows that it too had a socket for a plume. Schliemann found the remains of two bronze helmets at Troy. Although their lower parts had disintegrated, the corroded crests had survived well enough for him to be able to reconstruct them. They were made in two pieces, one permanently fixed to

A boar's tusk helmet, shown on an ivory plaque 8.5cm high (made in about 1225 BC, found at Mycenae).

the crown of the helmet, the other, holding the horse-hair plume, attached to it with a pin; the plume was detachable.[3]

In the *Iliad* we read of heroes duelling with spears, and though swords were definitely in use – every lancer would have had a short sword at his side for hand-to-hand fighting – the thrusting spear was still the weapon of choice. Some of these bronze-headed spears were very long and must have required a great deal of training and practice to handle effectively. Hector is described as wielding a spear 'eleven forearms long'.

Homer gives us relatively little about tactics or the nature of command. The generals conferred at various points during the war. We are told that early on the Trojan leaders gathered outside Priam's house to discuss strategy. We hear that when the Trojans were in disarray, having reached the Greek ships, the Trojan Polydamas persuaded a headstrong Hector to draw back:

Call the best of our captains here, this safe ground.
Then we can all fall in and plan our tactics well.

Hector saw the sense in this, told Polydamas to muster the captains:

I'm on my way over there to meet this new assault –
I'll soon be back, once I've given them clear commands.[4]

Even so, what followed seems little more co-ordinated than what went before, as Hector ranged among the ships looking for his captains, and stopped to rage at his brother Paris. Paris's riposte in effect restates the prevailing spirit of command. He emphasized that all the Trojans were 'right behind' Hector and that he would not find them 'short on courage'. There is no strategy here at all, just an injection of adrenaline. This runs parallel to accounts of Ramesses' behaviour at the Battle of Kadesh. Instead of giving specific, rational orders, he inspired valour by example and shouting inspirational encouragement: 'Take heart, my soldiers! You see my victory! Amon is my protector and his hand is with me.'

There is nevertheless a hint that though the commanders-in-chief shouted only inspirational generalities the generals gave more specific directions. At one point Agamemnon toured his generals, giving them and their troops a pep talk, first the two Ajaxes, then Nestor, and so on. After Agamemnon had passed, Nestor gave more specific commands to his combat units, each under captains (Pelagon, Alastor, Chromius, Haemon and Bias), who were responsible for carrying out Nestor's tactical orders.[5]

The Trojan attack on the ships caused Agamemnon to lose his nerve; several leaders were wounded and the defensive wall was breached. It was Nestor who gathered the Greek generals together to discuss tactics. Agamemnon advocated retreat. Odysseus questioned the quality of leadership, telling Agamemnon bluntly, '*You* are the disaster. Would to god you commanded another army.'[6]

We also hear through the Trojan scout Dolon that Hector, the Trojan commander-in-chief, discussed plans for the next day's battle during evening meetings. The Greeks held similar meetings; in some of them, Agamemnon, the Greek commander-in-chief, put forward ideas that the other Greek leaders disapproved of, and he was ready to back down. These 'evening councils' are very credible.

Homer nevertheless supplies little information about tactics during the battles. We hear of the two armies colliding and clashing; we hear of the Greeks sometimes advancing to the walls of Troy, and being beaten back to their camp at others. A great deal is left to brute force, courage and chance. There is little information about command, apart from the occasional shout of encouragement. The warrior élites are portrayed as taking all the initiative in hand-to-hand fighting, but there is no description of generals or other officers giving orders for the rest of the warriors to move forward or back, or adopt a specific formation. The general soldiery is described as moving forward or back, but moving as if in a tide rather than on instructions or commands from officers. If this is the way the battles were fought, with no commands given once battle was joined, the commanders were using their armies as blunt instruments, and, if so, it could explain why it took the Greeks a long time to achieve their goal. It seems that it was only in lulls in the fighting that the commanders could confer and decided on changes of tactic.

There is just one occasion, when things were going very badly for the Greeks, when a decision was made – evidently a revolutionary one – that the commanders should tour the battlefield and encourage and inspirit the warriors rather than losing themselves in hand-to-hand fighting.[7] This is a look forward to a later style of command; eventually generals would watch battles from vantage points to get an overview and send officers onto the battlefield with instructions.

What Homer describes – the exploits of a handful of heroes – would be more appropriate to a small-scale raid in which perhaps a hundred men could act entirely individually. But the huge numbers involved, the 130,000 Mycenaean warriors implied in the *Iliad*, means that the commanders would have been far more usefully employed guiding and directing their troops. If, in fact, once battle commenced, there was an incoherent mêlée of hand-to-hand fighting, the style of fighting would have been similar to the one the Romans encountered when they invaded Britain; indeed it may be that the use of chariots and shouted insults during the Boudiccan revolt was a backward look to this earlier, bronze age way of fighting. I suspect that the warrior-heroes did in fact lead, encourage and direct those of their countrymen who were within earshot, so that there would have been patches of co-ordinated action, oases of purposeful (or foolhardy) action within the general mêlée.

What is missing from the Epic Cycle is any credit for the efforts, exploits and achievements of the huge numbers of ordinary soldiers involved. The official Egyptian accounts of the Battle of Kadesh praised the heroic exploits of Ramesses, who overcame enormous odds single-handed. It was Ramesses who commissioned the history and was in a position to inflate his own personal contribution to the battle, frequently at the expense of that of his own armies. After Troy, it was, of course, the Mycenaean officers who commissioned the poets and bards, and this socio-political fact is enough to explain the very high profile the princely heroes acquired in the Epic Cycle record of the war. The bards were merely boasting on their patrons' behalf, and inevitably inflating the parts they played in individual actions and the outcome of the battle.

Greek Weaponry from Archaeology

The ordinary Mycenaean foot soldier wore a simple belted tunic with short sleeves, narrow waist and full but short skirt; a loincloth was worn under the skirt. In artwork warriors are sometimes shown barefoot, but they are also shown wearing sandals; the simple lattice of black lines in fresco images tells us that the Trojan War really was a sword-and-sandals epic. I suspect the sandals were for high summer wear only, and that laced boots were worn at other times.

Mycenaean warriors wore greaves on their shins. What they were made of probably depended on rank, with ordinary soldiers wearing greaves made of leather. The fact that they are often painted white on the frescoes suggests that aristocrats had greaves made of polished metal that shone in the sun. They extended up to cover the kneecaps like cricket pads and were tied on, with leather laces wrapped round three or four times just below the knee and again just above the ankle. The loose ends of the laces were allowed to hang free. A curving line shown on several fresco images suggests that the leather greaves might have been made as flat sheets of soft leather with curving outer edges. Each leather greave would have been wrapped round the leg so that the curving edge was on the outside, where it could not snag the greave on the other leg and trip the wearer. Some finely made bronze greaves have been found, for instance at Enkomi. Warriors were invariably shown wearing greaves. Grooms wore only tunics, whereas warriors wore greaves and helmets as well.

Greaves were worn by warriors to protect their shins from disabling slashes by enemy swords, but also to stop them from being chafed and bruised by the lower edges of their huge shields. Greaves would also have been indispensable when hunting on foot in scrubland.[8]

Some warriors, presumably the higher status warriors on both sides, wore kilts with chequered braid and a fringe round the hem.[9] A painted papyrus from El Amarna in Egypt shows an Egyptian view of what seem to be Mycenaean warriors, wearing helmets apparently made of boars' tusks. Some warriors are bare-chested, others wear short, rib-length capes of mottled brown and black oxhide which hang down front and back to the same level. The function of this cape is unclear: perhaps to reduce sunburn, or to indicate rank, or to reduce

A bronze greave 26cm long found at Kallithea. This one was made in 1160 BC (after Papadopoulos 1979).

chafing if shouldering loads. The El Amarna warriors wear white loincloths and short kilts.[10]

The main metal in use was bronze, which provided the cutting edges for sword and dagger blades, spear points and arrowheads. It was also used for chariot wheel fittings, helmets and suits of armour.

Spears were the main weapon that many warriors had. This is shown in the frescoes. Duels of the sort described by Homer were probably fought using a thrusting-spear or lance. Once a throwing-spear is thrown it has gone, and that implies that warriors who threw spears must have kept a second one, a thrusting-spear, for self-defence. They could not expect to retrieve thrown spears, or take one from an enemy, or pick one up from a fallen enemy, except by chance, though all of these methods of re-arming are mentioned by Homer and common sense says that they must have occurred all the time in battles.

Some lances had composite shafts, made in sections; this made it possible to manufacture very long spears. Homer describes Ajax defending his beached ship with a spear that was an astonishing 22 cubits long, double the length of an ordinary lance.[11] This may have been brought on the expedition for use in sea-fighting, though it is not clear how effective such an unwieldy weapon would have been. Even so, some massive spearheads have been found, 60cm long, so very big spears were certainly made. I have a hunch that the big spear Ajax was using on the ships was actually intended for use mounted inside a 'wooden horse' or siege engine, and specifically for dislodging the mudbrick parapets on the fortification walls of Troy.

Spears, slings, bows and arrows were the main weapons at this stage. Many arrowheads were still made of Egyptian flint or Melian obsidian, which could be sharpened to finer points than metal. A special kind of whetstone for smoothing the shafts of arrows, the 'arrow shaft polisher', was imported from northern Europe. Bronze arrowheads were just coming into use at this time. The bowstrings may have been made out of horse or ox sinew. A Mycenaean archer depicted on a Minoan steatite vase is shown shooting up in the air. This suggests that he was firing a shot up at the defenders on the rampart of a fortification wall. When a fortified town was attacked, the archers and spearmen were the main force against the town, unless the garrison could be tempted out to fight hand-to-hand outside the walls, or unless they could be starved out by siege. Sieges were regularly undertaken, though they could be lengthy businesses now that many fortresses had their own internal water supplies; both Mycenae and Troy had these.

The technology for making reliable and effective swords was still in an experimental stage. The fine-looking swords and daggers found in the Mycenaean shaft graves show the skilled use of complicated moulds for the relief decoration of blades and midribs, and in the covering of hilts with *repoussé* goldwork.[12] So elaborate and beautiful are they that it seems likely that many of these were for ceremonial use; they look far too good to have been used in battle. The large number of swords found nevertheless confirms the aristocrats' preoccupation with fighting; at least ninety swords were buried with the three princes in Shaft Grave V. The long rapier, which was the commonest type of sword in the shaft graves, was a borrowing from Minoan Crete. These unwieldy weapons, a metre long, were good for thrusting like spears and stabbing, but they were prone to break if given a sharp blow on the blade edge; then they were likely to snap, especially at the tang, the thin spike which fitted into the hilt, and most of the rapiers found are broken in this way.

The foot soldiers or lancers also carried a short sword that seems to have been a Mycenaean invention, with a broader blade and a tang enlarged into a proper, strong hilt; this was an altogether more serviceable weapon than the old rapier. This cut-and-thrust sword had a short, heavy blade. The early Mycenaean swords at the time of the shaft graves had but a single edge, but the first proper cut-and-thrust double-edged swords with a serviceable point appeared just at the time of the Trojan War. The blade had either no midrib or a very wide, flat rib that did not impede a slashing stroke. The blade was parallel-sided until its final taper to the point. Some blades widened slightly from the hilt to a point about two-thirds of the way along before tapering. The blades were 75–81cm long. Hilts were usually finished with a pommel, held in place by a tine in the bronze end of the handle. Many Mycenaean swords had round pommels made of white alabaster.

The new weapon, the Mycenaean short sword, made sustained hand-to-hand fighting possible for the first time. Maybe this historic change in the nature of warfare was one of the features that made the attack on Troy such a memorable landmark.[13]

Homer's heroes took considerable risks to take their opponents' armour from them.[14] It was not just a matter of killing the enemy, but of taking his weapons as trophies. It is very understandable, in the context of relatively scarce raw materials and the high technology involved in making the artefacts, that Homeric heroes would undergo great dangers to acquire a fine set of armour and weapons. After the battle was over, the battle trophies were often dedicated at an appropriate temple as thank-offerings to the gods. Pausanias mentions seeing in the front chamber at the Argive Heraion, a short distance from Mycenae, the shield that Menelaus had taken from Euphorbus at Troy and had himself dedicated at the temple.[15] Surviving examples of the aristocrats' weapons are often highly decorated – objects of great beauty as well as indicators of high status – and they must have been seen as such in antiquity; this too must have made them greatly prized.

For over a hundred years before the Trojan War, Mycenaean warriors had protected themselves with tall rectangular tower shields or figure-of-eight shields. Both of these giant shields were in use at the same time, as we can see in the picture worked on the blade of the Lion Dagger. The tower shields which were depicted on rings and other images were covered with dappled

A Mycenaean warrior on an ivory plaque found on Delos. Dating from 1250 BC, it shows a warrior proudly bearing a spear and a figure-of-eight shield. He is wearing a boar's tusk helmet.

cowhide, just like the figure-of-eight shields, and they had semicircular extensions at the top to protect the warriors' heads.[16] Both types of shield were large, and must have been made out of hide rather than bronze, or they would have been too heavy to carry. The dappled texture shown in fresco images of the figure-of-eight shields proves that they were covered with cowhide. The hair was left attached to the hide, partly to save unnecessary work in removing it, but also because the bristles deflected and absorbed a certain amount of energy when a weapon struck them. The figure-of-eight shields as shown in frescoes had visible lines of stitching round the edge – three lines at Knossos, two lines at Tiryns. The stitching represents the strips of rawhide that were used to stitch the hide round the wooden frame.

The figure-of-eight shield evolved into what looks like a very unsatisfactory design, called the dipylon shield. This was shaped like a capital H on its side and made by stretching a hide on a vertical stave, with horizontal struts at the top and bottom. In time, the hide shrank, creating the narrow waist.[17]

Homer describes tower shields, but in a way that cannot be historically accurate; Ajax carries 'a shield like a tower, made of bronze and seven layers of leather'.[18] This would be too heavy to carry, and Homer was probably combining an oral tradition of the cowhide tower shields of the Mycenaean period with the smaller eighth-century round shields, which were indeed made of bronze covered with layers of leather – and would have been familiar to an eighth-century bard and his audience from first-hand observation. Agamemnon is described as being armed with two spears and a round shield, which sounds like eighth-century, iron age, gear, though round shields were in use at the time of the Trojan War. Ajax's shield is also described as having a boss, which his tower shield (as big as a wall) would not have had. Both the figure-of-eight and the tower shields must have been very unwieldy. Hector's shield, slung over his back, bumps against his neck and ankles as he runs. Periphetes, a warrior from Mycenae, trips on the rim of his shield, which must therefore have been large, but could have been of either figure-of-eight or tower design.[19] Elsewhere, Homer has warriors bearing round shields; Aeneas has one.[20] Round shields did in fact appear in the Mycenaean period, in the fourteenth century.[21]

A piece of pottery from the Geometric period just after the Trojan War shows three warriors each carrying a different type of shield, round, rectangular and dipylon, and this confirms what we might have expected – that several different types of shield were in use at the same time.[22] Possibly tribal or family traditions dictated which shield type a warrior might use; possibly it was the particular type of fighting the warrior was involved in. A big figure-of-eight or tower shield would have been impossibly unwieldy in a chariot, except on ceremonial occasions, but it would have given better protection to an infantryman attacking a wall or defending a siege engine.

The Warrior Vase shows yet another type of shield. This was round but with a curved 'bite' taken out of one side only, unlike the dipylon shield, which had bites taken out of two opposing sides. It is not certain what purpose this unusual shape served, but it was in service at the time of the Trojan War.[23] The

Mycenaean warriors: two images from contemporary artwork. The boyish figure on the left was painted 27cm high in the porch to the Banquet Hall at Pylos. On the right is one of the marching figures from the Warrior Vase. Both Greek and Trojan warriors sometimes wore horns on their helmets.

shape may have been dictated by the need to hold the shield in front, covering as much of the chest and abdomen as possible, but allowing a space on one side for a forward-thrusting sword or spear.

The shield was a vital piece of equipment: mislaying it meant death. It is likely that as a precaution warriors often did what Euphorbus did, and inscribed their names inside them.

Some of the weapons were elaborately decorated. A distinctive decorative technique used on daggers was *niello*. The Lion Dagger is the best-known example of this; its broad bronze blade is inlaid with gold and silver cut-outs, forming an elaborate and lively scene of a lion hunt in full swing. The technique for making *niello* decoration came from the east, and it may be that the Mycenaeans and perhaps the Trojans too imported Syrian craftsmen to make these fine weapons for them.[24]

Homer's description of Hector as 'covered with bronze all over' used to be seen as an anachronistic description of hoplite armour from a later period, but the discovery of a complete bronze suit of armour at Dendra has changed all that.[25] Hector could indeed have been clad in a metal suit. The Dendra armour was elaborately made, with fifteen curved and carefully jointed pieces of bronze. It was very impressive, and doubtless an object of great status, but it must also have been heavy, cumbersome and hot. No warrior could have run in it, and even walking any distance in summer would have been exhausting; it is likely that he would have been ferried onto the battlefield on a chariot for quite a short period of hand-to-hand fighting.

It seems likely to me that the Dendra armour was for a royal figurehead to wear for token appearances on the battlefield. The *Iliad* is full of the daring deeds of kings and princes, but much of that is spin; the truth, I strongly suspect, is that some kings preferred to stand back and watch from a vantage point, like Charles I at Naseby. One can imagine a figure like old Nestor, static and imposing in his chariot with his armour flashing in the sun, supervising his Pylian warriors in this way and acting as a kind of living battle standard; in a similar way the Hittite Great King Muwatallis was described by the Egyptians as *observing* the Battle of Kadesh, not participating in it. Maybe the Dendra suit of armour was an experiment, an attempt to replace the big tower and figure-of-eight shields, which must have been totally unmanageable in a chariot.[26] It is worth bearing in mind that the Dendra armour dates from well before the Trojan War, and may by then have been seen as very old-fashioned, even obsolete. That does not mean that some kings did not wear it; aristocrats have habitually worn anachronistic dress in order to authenticate themselves by embedding their images in the ancestral past.

The clay tablets mention the *to-ra-ka*, which is the same word the later Greeks used, thorex, for an armoured tunic or corslet. In some cultures at the time of the Trojan War warriors had metal scaled tunics, in effect bronze shirts. They were in use in the Middle East and may have been in use as far west as

Greece. A few bronze scales from a corslet have been found at Troy. These scales measure roughly 8cm by 3cm, and are rectangular in shape with the lower end rounded into a semicircle. They have several holes for stitching along the top and one edge, made so that they could be sewn securely onto a fabric or leather tunic; the scales would have overlapped like the tiles on a roof to cover the stitching and allow the warrior considerable flexibility of movement as well as protection from swords, spears and arrows.

Under the plate armour or the thorex, the warrior wore a cloth tunic, a chiton, as an undergarment. Where this hung down below the level of the thorex or plate armour, it was reinforced with small bronze discs sewn onto it. References on the Mycenaean tablets to 'tunic fittings' may refer either to these light bronze discs or to the heavier bronze scales. Because of the flexibility of movement it allowed, this type of body armour was a huge advance on the Dendra type.

Archers may have worn altogether far less, partly to give them even more freedom of movement, partly because they were of lowly social status. Minoan artwork shows what seem to be Mycenaean archers wearing only shorts, belted round the waist and extending to mid-thigh. They were sometimes loose, like modern shorts, and sometimes tight-fitting, more like swimming trunks. The trouser legs were hemmed with a broad strip of braid. Decorative braid strips were often used in Mycenaean clothing, for both men and women, for hemming, to stop the cloth fraying. The archers and slingers shown on the Siege Rhyton from Mycenae are naked, though it may be that it was the artist rather than the warriors who omitted the shorts.[27]

Both Mycenaeans and Trojans had horses. Their bones have been found in tombs; they appear in sculpted low relief on the stones marking the shaft graves; their images are seen on gold rings, wall paintings and carvings. Horses are known only in association with Mycenaean aristocrats and mainly when harnessed to chariots, though it is likely that both Mycenaean and Trojan armies had a few mounted messengers. Horses were indispensable for chariot teams, and were probably reared for this specific purpose. Horses meant status, and their appearance was enhanced accordingly. Their manes were tufted into a row of plumes by Mycenaean grooms, by pulling bunches of hair through rings at intervals down the horse's neck, beginning at the top of the head. This is shown on many images and was very much a Mycenaean custom; it was not done in Egypt or the Near East and I do not know whether the Trojan charioteers adopted this custom. The tails were left long, undocked and they are shown very full, as if they were regarded as a fine feature of a horse. Some paintings imply a tail sheath, which may have been added for neatness or for decoration.

Horse harness is shown in the frescoes. Homer tells us that both the Greeks and the Trojans were noted for horse-rearing; it was evidently a very important activity in the Mycenaean world, as the armies of the many kings required

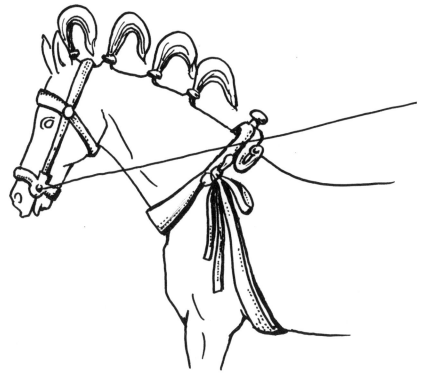

A Mycenaean chariot horse in harness.

chariot teams. The colour of the horses seems to have been significant. Black, white and piebald horses are shown in murals, but white horses were preferred, presumably so that the warrior-princes would be even more visible when driving their chariots and cut even more of a dash.[28]

Horses may have been used for riding. There are vase paintings and terracotta figurines from 1300–1250 BC that show men on horseback, and they may have been used by noblemen to carry them quickly to and from the field of battle. There is no image of cavalry as such (mounted troops fighting on horseback) until the ninth century BC, and this was in the Middle East, where there had been a long-developing tradition of using horses with chariots beforehand, so it is unlikely that the Greeks and Trojans, who acquired horses later, fought each other on horseback on the Plain of Troy.[29] Horses were used to pull chariots in battle long before they were ridden as fighting platforms.

Horses were certainly used for pulling chariots; they are shown doing this on gravestones, vase paintings and listed on Linear B tablets. Because they were vital for powering the new lightweight war-chariots, horses acquired a tremendous importance to all the chariot powers. In Homer we hear of chariot horses called names like Golden, Whitefoot and Silver Flash, names that are simple and descriptive, just like the names given to cattle on the Linear B tablets; Ramesses characteristically gave his chariot team the high-flown name Victory in Thebes.

Roads that might have been designed for chariot-driving have been identified at Mycenae. It has been assumed that these carefully graded roads with their minimal gradients, their tortuous avoidance of ravines and ridges, must have been for military chariots, but there is no overriding reason to assume this. The roads would have been equally useful for transporting agricultural produce and other resources, and we can imagine them used more by the carts of farmers, potters and blacksmiths than the chariots of the warrior aristocrats.

The earliest chariots the Mycenaeans used were box chariots, literally rectangular boxes on two four-spoked wheels. They were not a Greek invention by any means, but a borrowing from the Near East, where they had been in use since about 1800 BC, but the early chariots were four-wheeled and rather heavy. The light war-chariot that was to prove such an effective fighting machine came into use throughout the Near East and Anatolia around 1580 BC.[30] The Mycenaeans were using them from about 1550 BC onwards.

A second type was the quadrant chariot. The sides of this type were curved down towards the back, presumably to ensure that the warriors would be able to mount and dismount without getting snagged on projecting corners. By the time of the Trojan War the sides of the chariot had been modified yet again. Obviously the chariot was open at the back to enable rapid mounting and dismounting. The square sides were back, but with semicircular wings added behind them. The wings were probably mudguards, to keep off some of the dust, stones, mud and water spinning up from the chariot wheels.

In plan, the chariot box was D-shaped, a metre wide and between 0.5m and 1m deep. The one-metre width made it possible for two men to stand side by side, which they regularly did, while the extra depth made it possible for a third man to stand behind. A fragmentary model from Tiryns seems to show a three-

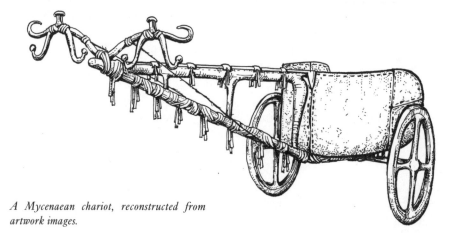

A Mycenaean chariot, reconstructed from artwork images.

Homer.

The Menelaion, the place where the Trojan War began. This hill-top site near Sparta, with its spectacular view across to the Taygetus Mountains, is where Menelaus and Helen lived. Paris abducted Helen from this beautiful place.

The South Gate of Troy I, dating from a thousand years before the Trojan War, was buried under the centre of the citadel of Troy VI. *(Nic Fields)*

Schliemann's great trench. In his enthusiasm to reach the oldest layers – here the remains of Troy I houses – Schliemann destroyed much of the Troy VI citadel. *(Nic Fields)*

Mycenae: the ruins of Agamemnon's citadel.

The citadel wall at Mycenae stands on top of an outcrop of bedrock that has been artificially smoothed. Was this done in imitation of the battered walls of Troy?

The Bay of Argos. The Argive fleet, commanded by Diomedes or Agamemnon, sailed from the most sheltered part of the bay, Nauplion harbour, to the right. The harbour was guarded by a Mycenaean citadel on the promontory in the centre of the picture.

Troy VI: the East Bastion *(left)* defending the East Gate *(centre background)*.   *(Nic Fields)*

Troy VI: the South Bastion *(left)* defending the South Gate *(right)*.   *(Nic Fields)*

Beşika Bay, looking south. The site of the Greek camp is in the bottom left-hand corner and the ships were drawn up centre left. Tenedos in the distance. *(Nic Fields)*

The Triple Spring *(foreground)*. The walls of Troy passed from the right centre to the hilltop on the left. The citadel stood on the flat-topped hill on the skyline.

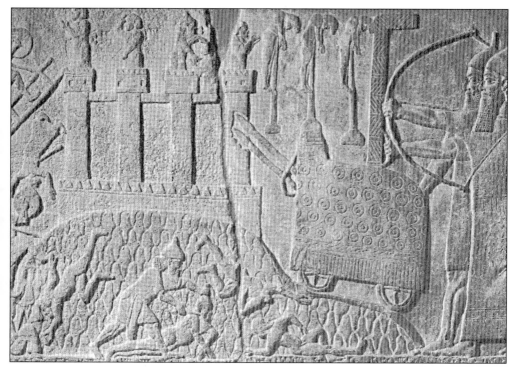

Assyrian relief showing a siege engine being used to break down the walls of a city.

The restored royal tomb at Pylos, which stands just outside the so-called 'Palace of Nestor'. King Nestor himself may have been buried here. The beehive tombs in the west of Greece were free-standing like this one, whereas those at Mycenae were built more securely into hillsides.

A seventh-century BC representation of the Trojan Horse, as portrayed on an amphora from Mykonos.

The Warrior Vase, showing Mycenaean warriors of about 1200 BC.

(Athens National Archaeological Museum)

Carl Blegen, one of the excavators of Troy.
This bronze bust stands outside
the museum at Hora, close to the Palace of
Nestor at Pylos, which Blegen
also excavated.

Heinrich Schliemann.

man chariot team. As we shall see from other evidence, the three men had distinct functions, to attack, to defend and to drive.

The structure of the chariot was very simple, consisting of a box mounted on an axle with a wheel on each side. The box had to be as light as possible, so probably the frame was made of bent wood, lashed together with rawhide. The floor was probably a lattice of rawhide thongs covered with leather, which would have made a resilient, springy platform that was comfortable to stand on; the chariot had no other form of suspension. The front and sides were wooden-framed, with cross-frames for strength, but covered on the outside in leather, cowhide, linen or basketwork. Above all, the material had to be very light. The Mycenaean chariots were all painted blood red. A tablet at Pylos describes a chariot as 'inlaid with ivory, painted crimson, equipped with bridles with leather cheek straps and horn bits'.[31]

The Mycenaean chariots were very similar to those in use in Egypt at the same time, except that the Egyptian chariot boxes did not have wings and their wheels had six spokes instead of the Mycenaean four. Otherwise, the technology was very similar.

The chariot was pulled by a pair of horses, trotting one on each side of a stout pole attached to the centre of the axle. The horses were harnessed under an elaborate wooden yoke, also painted red by the Mycenaeans. Two leather thongs passed from the yoke saddles back to the chariot box, to make sure that the yoke stayed at right angles to the pole and ensure that the horses ran straight. Some of the pull would have been transmitted through these yoke braces, giving the whole chariot more resilience. Surviving images of chariots show no padding beneath the yoke, but some sort of padding must have been used, especially since horses' withers (shoulders) are not at all prominent. Some of the strain of the pull was taken by the leather neckstrap round the horse's chest and the leather girth, which passed immediately behind the front legs.

The horse was controlled, just like a modern horse, by way of a metal bit, which consisted of a mouthpiece and two cheekpieces. Each cheekpiece was joined by a leather rein to the chariot driver. The reins passed through a curved loop attached to the yoke, terminating in an upward-pointing knob or terret. The charioteer therefore controlled his pair of horses by dexterously pulling on the four reins.

The bit was held in place by a headstall made of a lattice of leather straps, including a crownpiece, going over the horse's head behind the ears, a noseband, passing over the horse's nose, a browband, passing over the forehead, and a throatlash.

The leather harness was decorated with bronze discs, attached in rows, and polished to catch the sunlight. The appearance of the horse meant a great deal and was an integral part of the warrior's image projection. As we have already seen, the mane was carefully dressed. The tail may have been enhanced by a shining metal tailguard. The leather harness with its metal appliqué ornaments was doubtless waxed and polished by the grooms till it shone. Some horses were given an additional crest of fine plumes, mounted on a cap attached to the leather headstall. Whether these plumes were the privilege of a specific élite group, a mark of rank, or just down to the personal taste of the chariot team leader we can only guess. It may be that some warriors wanted to draw attention to themselves, and the decoration of their chariot team was a good way to do it.

Charioteers made their horses run faster using both whips and short wooden goads or prods. Murals in the throne room at Mycenae showed horses being led by grooms to be harnessed and hitched up to waiting chariots, warriors standing in chariots, others jumping off chariots ready to fight, hand-to-hand fighting on foot, and two warriors lying dead on the ground.

There were several ways in which chariots might be used in warfare. They were used in the Near East from 1500 BC as firing platforms for archers, though this was never shown in Mycenaean art and was therefore presumably never done. The Mycenaeans preferred wielding spears to bows and arrows or even swords, and they are more likely to have used their chariots as platforms for spear thrusting and throwing. Chariot charges were probably rare in Greece and over large areas of Anatolia too, simply because of the nature of the terrain, though, significantly, the Plain of Troy was ideally suited to this manoeuvre. The Hittite warriors mounted in chariots seem to have used a single long spear. The Hittites and their allies, who would have included the Trojans, are shown in this way in Egyptian depictions of the Battle of Kadesh.

Chariots could be used en masse to charge the enemy and prepare the way for an infantry attack. They could be used at speed to outflank and even attack the enemy from behind.

They were probably sometimes used as taxis, to deliver élite warriors into battle and out again. The aristocratic élite warrior could cut a dash with a finely caparisoned chariot and team of horses, as he was hurtled into the thick of the battle by his driver. Once there, he may have dismounted for hand-to-hand fighting, as shown in the Mycenaean mural images, and indeed as described in Homer, or returned to a place of safety behind the lines.[32]

Great cities like Mycenae, Knossos and Troy would have had large fighting forces and something of the order of two hundred chariots each. Building and maintaining a fleet of chariots would have sustained an industry in itself. There are tablets listing chariots and referring to the workshops where they were repaired, even giving the names of the men in charge at these important service centres. The lightweight chariot drawn by a team of two horses was a spectacular new weapon in the late bronze age armoury. It is difficult today to imagine the impact it had on warfare – perhaps something akin to the combined impact of the aeroplane and the tank in the First and Second World Wars. Thirteenth-century kingdoms that had chariots belonged to an élite group of superpowers. They were the equivalent of the nuclear powers of the second half of the twentieth century AD.

Both the Mycenaeans and their Anatolian enemies had siege engines. The Mycenaeans and Trojans had built ever more imposing fortifications to withstand sieges and head-on attacks; it follows that they must have developed equally ingenious methods for attacking those defences. The story of the Wooden Horse contains a garbled description of an engine for attacking city walls. The story as passed down in legend is not in the *Iliad*, as many non-readers have assumed, but belonged to another segment of the Epic Cycle, the *Little Iliad*.[33] It was mentioned in passing in the *Odyssey*, then elaborated by Aeschylus in the *Agamemnon*, and by Euripides in *The Trojan Women* and *Hecuba*.[34] Later the story was developed further in Virgil's *Aeneid* and many other works. In the re-tellings, the Wooden Horse was said to contain varying numbers of Greek warriors, from nine in the *Aeneid* up to an absurdly impossible 3,000 in the *Little Iliad*.

The Wooden Horse of tradition was and still is a vivid and compelling image, but it is fundamentally a fable of treachery and gullibility, a fable of the human condition. It is not a literal account of an incident in the Trojan War. Many even in antiquity saw that, and recognized that something rather

A Mycenaean siege engine.

different lay behind it. Pliny the Elder proposed that the Wooden Horse was really a siege engine.[35] Pausanias went even further: 'Anyone who does not think the Trojans were utterly stupid will have realized that the Horse was really an engineer's device for breaking down the walls.'[36] Even though a solid-looking 'facsimile' has stood at Troy since 1974, the Wooden Horse of popular imagination does not quite represent the historic reality of the siege engines.

Perhaps surprisingly, we know what the Wooden Horse looked like. Assyrian bas-reliefs show siege engines dating to 870 BC. The Assyrians regularly used them to break down the defensive walls of cities. The engine was a large timber-framed box up to about 8m long, 2m wide and 2m or more high which held the crew. It was apparently covered with hides and mounted on four wheels. The horse could be pushed up to the base of the enemy's fortification wall, often up a ramp made of logs or earth, presumably so that it could reach the mudbrick upper wall.

Some siege engines, depicted in carvings made in 740–700 BC, had towers at the front to enable the crew to reach higher up the walls. This would have made them look distinctly like animals, though rather more like elephants than horses, elephants complete with tusks. The crew of perhaps four or six men operated two long spear-shaped drills or prods, which stuck diagonally upwards out of the front. This is clearly shown in a bas-relief at Nimrud. Marcus Vitruvius Pollio, who lived around 50 BC, described the instrument used in a contemporary siege engine as a beam 25m long with an iron point. The Mycenaean siege engine 'spear' would have been similar, a stout spear shaft of unusual length and thickness, fitted with a hefty bronze tip – in fact exactly the sort of thing Ajax is described as picking up and using as an improvized weapon against the Trojans when they attacked the Greek ships.[37]

Siege engines do not appear in bas-reliefs earlier than the reign of Ashurnasirpal II (883–859 BC), but there is evidence from Mari and Hattusa that very similar siege engines were in use as early as the eighteenth century BC. They certainly existed in between, in Anatolia, in 1250 BC and were in use at the time of the attack on Troy. The Egyptians used them too. In other words, all the great chariot powers also possessed siege engine technology.[38] We know from their literature that the Hittites used towers, battering rams and ramps when they laid siege to their enemies.[39]

The prods were used to jab at the base of the mudbrick superstructure, first exposing and loosening the joints between the bricks, then prising some of the bricks out. The siege engine was not a battering ram; it was simply a means of picking and prying at the vulnerable mudbrick wall until it crumbled. Very soon a hole was opened in the wall and the parapet and walkway above it collapsed. Warriors waiting behind the siege engine or sheltering behind big tower shields or wicker pavises then rushed forward with scaling ladders to get through the breach in the defence. Also behind the siege engine was a support team, responsible for moving the engine into position, defending it from attack, and standing by with buckets of water in case the Trojans tried to set fire to it with flaming arrows.

The Mycenaeans doubtless took the siege engines with them in their ships, either fully assembled or more likely in a dismantled form. Transport in kit form is suggested by the Ajax incident mentioned above.[40] Transporting siege engine kits implies a high level of planning, organization and preparation for the expedition.

Trojan Weaponry from Archaeology

We have far less evidence of the way the Trojans were armed, but it is reasonable to assume that, with a few notable exceptions, they were equipped in a similar way to the Mycenaeans. As far as is known, the Trojans did not possess any boar's tusk helmets. The Egyptian images of Hittite warriors at Kadesh, which we know included a contingent of Dardanians from Wilusa, show some interesting differences in dress, but the weapons would have been broadly similar to those in the Mycenaean armoury.

Some Trojans wore bullet- or cone-shaped bronze helmets, like the Mycenaeans, while most common soldiers probably wore simpler and cheaper helmets made of leather. The two bronze helmets Schliemann found at Troy, and mentioned above, could have belonged to either Trojan defenders or Mycenaean attackers; there is no certain way of knowing which.[41] The evidence they give of detachable horse-hair plumes could therefore equally apply to Mycenaean or Trojan warriors. The Egyptian carvings show Hittite warriors with thick luxuriant hair falling to their shoulders and down their backs. The hair seems to have been held in place, to some extent, by a thin circlet, possibly made of plaited leather, pulled down over the crown to keep the face clear. Much of this hair hung down below the neck-piece attached to the rim of the helmet at the back. The helmet was also fitted with broad cheekpieces to protect the warrior's cheeks and ears from injury.[42]

Sometimes the plume and the rather weighty crest that held it in place must have made the helmet top-heavy; to prevent the whole thing from toppling off, a chinstrap would have been necessary. In fact Homer mentions that Paris's helmet had a chinstrap, which may be taken as evidence that his helmet was overloaded with plumes.[43] Entertaining though this image of the vain and dandified Trojan prince may be, there is another possible explanation for his chinstrap. The bronze helmet had hinged cheek-pieces – some of these have been found, for example at Ialysos, and they appear again and again in artwork – and to stop them flapping about they would need to be laced lightly together under the chin.

Paris's helmet seems to have been his weak link. He could be throttled with his chinstrap and his 'nodding horsehair plume' was something that his adversary could seize and use to drag him down.[44] In fact what is described in Homer is an understatement. Hittite art shows that Hittite princes in the late bronze age wore helmets with long streamers hanging to waist level, and sometimes both streamers and plumes sprouting from separate sockets.[45] The streamer in particular would be an extremely impractical extra that must in many situations have been dangerous; it could be caught in a chariot wheel or seized by an enemy. It was too absurd a detail to invent – another detail in Homer that appears to be a genuine recollection of the Trojan War, though only half understood 500 years later.

Paris? A Hittite warrior wearing an elaborate helmet embellished with plume, streamer and horn. From a drawing incised on a clay vessel from Hattusa.

Hittite warriors wore tight kilts, probably with a loincloth underneath, just like the Mycenaeans. Egyptian carvings show them as prisoners wearing long robes with short sleeves; the ankle-length robe may have been an overgarment worn on the march, a greatcoat normally taken off when fighting was imminent and left with the baggage train.[46]

The Trojan infantryman wore a thorex, or an armoured tunic or corslet, like his Mycenaean counterpart. As mentioned above, the Trojan warriors had adopted metal-scaled tunics, in effect bronze shirts, from the Middle East, and a few of these bronze scales from a corslet have been found at Troy. It must have been an extremely effective coat of mail, as many foot soldiers appear in artwork without shields. A drawing on a clay vessel shows a thorex with bronze discs attached to it – presumably one of many variants that would have been seen in the Hittite lands. Under the thorex, the warrior wore a cloth tunic, a chiton, as an undergarment, and this is shown on some Hittite carvings.[47]

Warriors lining the ramparts of Troy and defending the city from the wall-walks would have been armed with throwing-spears, slings and bows and arrows. The slingshot found among the debris of Troy VI could have belonged to warriors of either side. The stones appear to be water-rolled beach pebbles, and were presumably carefully collected in peacetime, from certain chosen locations; it is not immediately obvious where the Trojans (or Mycenaeans) gathered their stone bullets. Various images show Hittites using spears and bows. The Trojans used a spearhead with a tubular socket for fitting onto the wooden spearshaft: several examples of these have been found in Troy VI, though Schliemann commented that he found exactly similar spears at

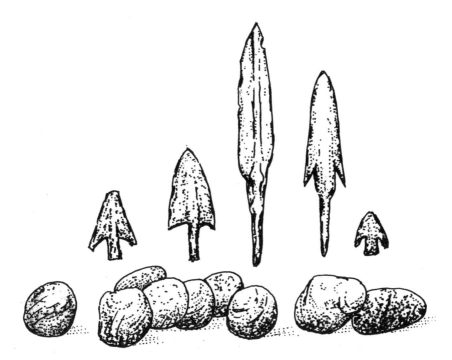

Weapons used in the attack on Troy. The arrowheads and spearpoints (above) and slingshot (below) were found in the debris of Troy VI.

Mycenae, implying that the spears found at Troy might after all have been thrown *at* the Trojans rather than *by* them.[48]

The Trojans also had swords, but with short and slightly curved blades; several were found in the debris of Troy VI.[49] They were really daggers or short stabbing swords, and they were worn in scabbards with a tight and distinctly oriental-looking curve at the end. Some curious and very distinctive curved daggers with tightly curled tips were found in the debris of Troy III, so the curving dagger seems to have been a distinctive part of the Trojan armoury.[50] The destruction debris of Priam's Troy nevertheless also yielded a small straight knifeblade with parallel sides about 13cm long; gold-plated, it must have belonged to a member of the royal family.[51]

The hilt of the Trojan short sword usually terminated in a white alabaster pommel held in place by the bronze end of the sword handle. As we saw earlier, the Trojan sword pommels are identical to their Mycenaean counterparts and may well have been imported. There was also a very different weapon, the slashing-sword. This had a broad curving blade, like a sickle but with the cutting edge on the outside; again it had an eastern look to it, rather like the later Turkish scimitar.[52]

Several whetstones have been found at Troy. These distinctive pencil-shaped stones were used for sharpening sword blades.[53] Warriors probably spent a little time each evening retouching their sword blades by the light of their camp fires, while they told stories and sang songs. It almost goes without saying that popular songs of the sort that soldiers sang have disappeared without trace – the scribes would not have thought them worth writing down – but a fragment of one of them was recorded. It ran as follows:

> Nesas' tunic, Nesas' tunic
> dress me up in, dress me up.
> Bring me down my mother's clothes, to
> dress me up in, dress me up ...[54]

The Hittite armoury included a battle-axe. This had an elaborately designed bronze head with a strongly curved blade and a series of vicious-looking spikes projecting backwards from the slender and slightly sinuous haft.[55]

The repertoire of different Mycenaean shield shapes was reflected in variations in Anatolia too. The Trojans had more than one type of shield. One was rectangular. Another was apparently related to the last Mycenaean type described, the round shield with a bite taken out of one side. The Trojan version of this had bites taken out of both sides, making it look a little like a double-axe, the powerful religious symbol of the Minoans.[56] Possibly it was made symmetrical for efficiency and safety, so that the shield did not have a significant left or right side or top or bottom. Possibly the 'left hand' bite was created to ensure that the right hand of the foot soldier to the left was not impeded; in the phalanx formation that was already in use, that would have been a consideration. A Hittite warrior in an Egyptian image of the Battle of Kadesh is shown holding up one of these distinctive shields to protect another member of his chariot team who is about to throw a spear.[57]

Homer said that Troy was noted for horse-rearing, and as a chariot power it must have raised horses to draw its chariots. The Trojans had chariots that were of the same general type as the Mycenaean chariots, though they may have painted them a colour other than red. The Alaksandu Treaty dating from 1280 BC assumes that the king of Wilusa owned battle chariots as well as teams of trained horses and skilled charioteers with which to deploy them. The reference shows that the Hittite Great King acknowledged that Wilusa was a significant military power; not all the kingdoms in Anatolia had this profile.[58] The Hittites were second to none in their prowess in chariot-driving; they knew better than anyone else how to wield this brand-new weapon. Homer might well call them 'these *headlong* Trojans'.[59]

The Hittites' chariots were very similar in design to the Mycenaean chariots, except that their wheels had six spokes, like the Egyptian chariot wheels, instead of the Mycenaean four. As mentioned above, there is a Mycenaean model that seems to show a chariot team consisting of three men. The Egyptian portrayals of the Battle of Kadesh show Hittite chariots also with crews of three men who had distinct functions: one attacking, one defending, one driving. Presumably when they dismounted, the three men continued to function as a co-ordinated team. They must have learnt both to think and to function very closely together, as their survival as a chariot team would have depended on split-second timing, on long experience of working together and anticipating one another's thoughts and actions.

Chapter 9
The Landing

And once offshore of Achaea's vast encampment
they eased her in and hauled the black ship high,
far up on the sand, and shored her up with timbers.
(Iliad 1. 577–9)

The *Iliad* tells us that the Greek warriors disembarked on the beach in front of Troy. There is no beach immediately in front of Troy today, but modern geographers infer that there was once a Bay of Troy extending far inland, with its south-eastern corner close to the walls of Troy. Applying even the most rudimentary knowledge of river processes tells us that silting by the Rivers Scamander and Simois must have gradually filled the bay in.

Walter Leaf tried to reconstruct the shape of the ancient coastline by analysing accounts in Strabo and Pliny. Unfortunately, he did not take seriously enough Strabo's perceptive remarks on the process and rate of silting, which he, Strabo, recognized must have filled in the bay; Strabo even made a startlingly accurate estimate of the bay shore's position at the time of the Trojan War.[1] Modern assessments of rates of accretion based on sections and bore-logs are a far more reliable and scientific basis for reconstruction. Even so, Strabo got much closer to the bronze age landscape than Leaf.

One recent study by a distinguished team of researchers concluded that the Greek fleet sailed into the Bay of Troy and set up camp near its south-west corner, due west of Troy. The main reason for selecting this location is the existence of a deep defensive ditch, the Kesik Cut, across the narrow ridge to the west, which is taken to be the ditch described in the *Iliad*. But the ditch in question is more likely to be associated with the later fort which stands immediately to the north of it. It is also, in my view, extremely unlikely that the Mycenaeans would have taken the trouble to dig a ditch 6m deep; 2m would have been more than adequate to prevent chariots crossing.

It is also very unlikely that the Mycenaeans would have sailed their fleet into the Bay of Troy, where they could so easily have found themselves bottled up

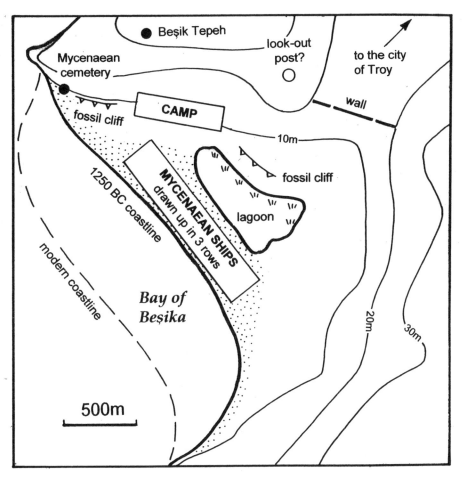

The Greek camp at Beşika Bay.

and trapped by the north and north-easterly winds, the meltemi, which blew and still blow incessantly through spring, summer and autumn. Instead, it is more likely that the Mycenaeans beached their ships in the Bay of Beşika on the open coast of the Aegean 8km to the south-west of Troy. In the *Iliad* the beached ships are referred to several times as being on the Hellespont. While the Bay of Beşika is not strictly on the Hellespont, it is on a coastline fronting open sea adjacent to the Hellespont.

Boreholes in the sediments flooring the Bay of Beşika and the adjacent plain show that the late bronze age bay was slightly larger and slightly more sheltered from north winds than the present one. It was 3km across from north to south, and 700m deep from west to east. There was a curving sandy beach, rare on this coastline, which would have been suitable for dragging ships ashore. Behind that was a high storm beach and sand dune complex 1.5km long. Behind that there was a slope down into a saltmarsh and lagoon about 800m long and extending 450m inland.[2] The storm beach and the sheltered slope down towards the lagoon would also have been suitable berths for ships, and the location certainly lends itself to the accommodation of three rows of beached ships.

The Bay of Beşika is fairly small, its beach just 3km long, and it may have been the shortness of the beach that made it necessary to draw the ships up in rows as Homer describes. There was a broad sand barrier between the bay and the lagoon, which gave plenty of backshore space to do this. Though not mentioned in Homer, the lagoon with its fringing saltmarsh would have provided the ships with a certain amount of protection on the landward side from a direct attack by the Trojans.

The Greeks raised a 'wall', presumably to the east of the lagoon, to protect their ships and their camp from such an attack. The likeliest location for this barrier is the narrow neck of lowland connecting Beşika Bay with the Plain of Troy. At its narrowest point, this connecting valley is but 500m wide; this would have been the likeliest route for a Trojan chariot attack and therefore also the likeliest place for a Mycenaean defensive work.

The lower part of the wall was, according to the *Iliad*, built of stone, though it may be that it was a core of earth dug up from the fronting ditch, revetted with a stone facing. The wall had a wooden superstructure with a ledge and a parapet along the top. There were two barred and gated gaps in the wall, to let the chariots through, and these were inside a single gap in the outer ditch. The gate to the south was for returning chariots, so by implication there was a one-way system.[3]

At the northern end of the bay, under the lee of a hill, was a Mycenaean settlement of some kind. The excavators sensed that it was an unusual settlement; the remains were scanty, suggesting a collection of lightly built temporary structures; the location in terms of both site and situation seems to have been overwhelmingly strategic. As far as the excavators were concerned, a connection with the Homeric attack on Troy was inescapable. The settlement may have been established well before the arrival of the invasion fleet, the base of a support group for Mycenaean traders wanting to use the Bay of Beşika as a refuge before or after passing through the Hellespont at the time when the Mycenaean trading empire was at its peak. Another possibility is that it was a community of Mycenaean adventurers trying to force their way into Wilusa.[4] Alternatively, it may be a vestige of the Greek camp described in the *Iliad*. The settlement the archaeologists found was not substantially built, and it may only have been occupied during the summer sailing season in the period before and after, as well as during, the Trojan War. In the winter months there would have been very little coastwise traffic to justify being there; nor would there have been any chance of rescue by Greek naval reinforcements if the Trojans or any other Anatolian power attacked. It is likely that the settlement was evacuated for the winter and reoccupied afresh each spring. With a Mycenaean settlement planted here, fighting may have broken out fairly often as exasperated Trojans made their resentment felt.[5]

The *Iliad* supplies some confirmation of the seasonal nature of bronze age warfare. In two places there are hints that the attack was launched in the spring. The Greek army is described as advancing from the camp for the first time onto a Scamander floodplain just breaking into flower. A few lines later a spring date is indirectly implied in an apt metaphor; the armies mass like flies swarming over the shepherds' stalls 'in the first spring days'.[6] A spring attack is entirely consistent with what is known of contemporary practice; the Hittites certainly conducted their military campaigns only in spring and summer.[7]

The Mycenaean cemetery was at the top of the beach at the extreme northern end of the bay, almost at the headland and close to the conical mound of Beşik Tepeh, one of two mounds pointed out in the ancient world as the Tomb of Achilles and still a conspicuous landmark today.[8] Manfred Korfmann's team uncovered this extensive cemetery in 1984. It was very close to the late bronze age shore, and a flight of steps led from the shore the 4m up to the graveyard. In it were about fifty-six graves, some communal, all dug out of the loose beach sand, and all facing south-east. There were several different sorts of burial: graves surrounded by a light covering of sand, stone box-tombs made of regular slabs, and formal grave-houses. Most of the burials were in large or medium-sized jars (pithoi) covered with stone slabs. Some of the remains were cremated, some not. At least fifty of the burials included imported goods.[9]

The pottery found there shows that the cemetery dates from the very end of Troy VI – VIh – or the beginning of Troy VIIa, in other words precisely from the time of the Trojan War. At the centre of the grave complex there was a substantial grave house, 4m by 3m, with a burial jar in its inner chamber, containing three cremations. The porch of the grave house was found to contain a black Mycenaean sealstone with a stylized human face on it. This is the first Mycenaean sealstone to have been found in Anatolia. There were also fragments of gold jewellery.[10] This was evidently the grave of a rich, high status Mycenaean family.

To the east of the cemetery a fossil cliff, a cliff no longer reached by the waves, ran along the head of the beach for about 200m. To the east of that was quite a large area of gently sloping ground with a southerly aspect, warm and sheltered from the north wind by hills at the back, invisible from the walls of Troy, and overlooking the sand barrier where the ships were drawn up. It was at the western end of this site that the archaeological remains of the Mycenaean settlement were located and in my view it is the likeliest site for the Greek encampment described in the *Iliad*. It runs for about 700m in all along the northern end of the sand barrier and lagoon and is up to 400m broad. This is a large area providing ample space for the Mycenaean encampment.

The camp was screened from the eyes of Trojan lookouts posted on the walls of Troy by a low ridge to the north and north-east. A short walk to the east, though, would have brought a Mycenaean sentry to the crest of the ridge. From there he would have had a panoramic view of the Plain of Troy and any troop movements on it; from there the city of Troy itself would have been plainly visible to the north-east, 8km away on the far side of the plain. The defensive wall of the Greek camp was immediately below to the south-east. This seems a likely place for a Mycenaean look-out post. In fact, the Beşika location as a whole is so tailor-made for a base for an invading Greek army, so perfect in every way for the purpose, that it surprises me that scholars have looked for alternative locations elsewhere. I doubt whether the Greeks themselves would have looked any further than Beşika Bay.

Chapter 10

The Attack on Troy: a Minimal Reconstruction

What god drove them to fight with such a fury?

(*Iliad* 1. 9)

Now, in the light of the foregoing discussion, we can attempt a narrative reconstruction of the events of the attack on Troy. Complications arise because there is more than one way to reconstruct the Trojan War. There is a minimal way, which infers from all the strands of evidence that, yes, there was a Mycenaean raid on Troy, but it was a small affair and just one raid among many on the coastal towns of western Anatolia. It would allow for some earlier attacks or sorties on other coastal towns further south, followed by a fairly brief and perhaps small-scale attack on Troy. The numbers of warriors involved would be small and the historical importance of the raid would be slight.

There is also a maximal way, which takes the series of raids on other sites to the south as part of a grand regional strategy on the part of the Mycenaeans that culminated in an attack on the richest and most powerful city in Wilusa, its capital, with a view to capturing and taking it over as a Mycenaean colony, and so transforming the Northern Aegean. The large-scale invasion by the king of Mycenae and all of his allies was met by an armed host consisting of the Trojans and all of their allies. This maximal view would take the Catalogue of Ships and the Catalogue of Trojans at something close to their face value, though we still do not need to take the numbers of men involved literally. The Battle of Kadesh involved a Hittite army of over 40,000 men, and this was the largest military force ever raised by a Hittite Great King.[1] Common sense dictates that the maximum size of the army the Trojans would have been able to raise to defend Troy must have been less than half that. The Mycenaean attack on Troy was a major event in Wilusa, but in Anatolian terms it must have seemed a very local matter and for local emergencies of that kind the armies of the homelands and the contiguous kingdoms would be adequate.[2] But even when reduced to perhaps one-quarter the figures spoken of in Homer, the number of warriors is still very large and the historical significance of the war would be correspondingly great.

It would also be possible to advance 'halfway-house' reconstructions that are neither maximal nor minimal but lie somewhere between these two extremes.

The *Iliad* and the other poems in the Epic Cycle show gods and goddesses deeply involved in the action; it is what both the Greeks and the Trojans of the late bronze age actually believed. The later Pylians had Hades fighting on their side, and Pausanias comments that this was entirely consistent with Homer's Argives being assisted by Poseidon.[3] This view of divine intervention was widespread, and confirmed by the contemporary carvings at the Kazilikaya sanctuary in Anatolia, where a whole regiment of gods is shown marching into battle, each divine warrior wearing the tall pointed hat of the weather god. These warrior gods were carved in the decades leading up to the Trojan War. Hattusilis III, Great King at the time of the Trojan War, mentions in his 'autobiography' that as a child he was dedicated to the goddess Ishtar; during the course of his adult life Ishtar had repeatedly intervened to help him to overcome his enemies. Hattusilis wrote of the goddess's participation in his military career in the most graphic terms; it was she who had shut one of his enemies up in a city 'like a pig in a sty'.[4]

Some of the gods and goddesses of the classical period had already emerged by the time Pylos fell in 1200 BC. The tablets speak of Zeus, Hera, Athena, Artemis, Paiawon (Apollo), Enualios (Ares), Poseidon and Hermes. We cannot tell whether these deities had the characteristics and responsibilities attributed to them later. Three aspects of the Minoan Great Goddess stand out – Mistress of Animals, Goddess of Vegetation and Household Goddess – and they correspond to three great goddesses of the classical period, Artemis, Demeter and Athena. The Mycenaean gods and goddesses carried responsibilities for various aspects of the natural world, and those were vividly recalled in Homer, where we hear of Poseidon the Earth-shaker and Zeus the Cloud-compeller, Zeus of the Lightning Flash.[5] The Anatolians too had their all-powerful weather gods.

The warriors on both sides certainly believed that the gods were implicated in their war. At times during the fighting they would have been encouraged at the thought that this or that god or goddess was on their side. At other times they would have despaired at the knowledge that their deities had deserted them. That was part of their way of thinking, but for the purposes of both of the narratives I shall leave the divine voices and apparitions out; they form part of that important inner world, the world of self-talk and auto-suggestion, that is inaccessible to the historian.

What follows is one version of what actually happened. The names of the generals may not have been as Homer listed them, but for convenience and orientation I have kept to them, rather than referring colourlessly to nameless officers as 'the Mycenaean generals' or 'the Trojan commander-in-chief'.

As we have already seen, Homer put great emphasis on the role played by the heroic leaders of the expedition to Troy, but we have to remember that bards were employed to entertain the aristocracy and therefore reflect their vainglory. We can safely assume that the *Iliad* flatters and exaggerates the part played by the war-leaders on both sides. The Great Kings of Hatti were great boasters, as were the Egyptian pharaohs. In the reliefs at the Temple of Luxor showing the Battle of Kadesh, Ramesses is shown huge – a colossus several times larger than the other warriors – and leading a single-handed charge against the enemy. Absurd and conceited boasting by kings was the norm for the period. If we seek to reconstruct what might actually have happened in the attack on Troy, we need to de-emphasize the part played by the heroes and think rather in masses of chariotry and infantry, sometimes following and sometimes perhaps not following their war-leaders' orders.

Many scholars have been worried by the colossal scale of the war envisaged by Homer – the thousand ships, the tens of thousands of men, the ten-year siege – and assumed that it was exaggerated for poetic effect. Can we see a smaller-scale scenario that would have fitted the known evidence from the bronze age?

A generation before the attack on Troy in 1250 BC, there was an earlier Mycenaean attack on Troy. It was then that the Mycenaeans led by the legendary Heracles stormed Laomedon's city of Troy with the crews of only six vessels,[6] or eighteen ships if we listen to later authors,[7] but in either case a relatively small force. The later raid on Troy could have been a similarly small-scale affair, involving just ten or twenty ships.[8]

It is also clear that laying siege to a coastal city was a fairly common event in the bronze age, not just along the coast of western Anatolia but throughout the Eastern Mediterranean world. Ugarit was the great city and port at the eastern end of the Mediterranean Sea. It is known from archaeology that it was destroyed by fire at the close of the bronze age, in 1185 BC. It was so badly damaged that it was not reoccupied afterwards. Within the destruction layer are arrowheads that show that some warlike force of unknown origin attacked and destroyed Ugarit. Was this an attack on the same scale as the Homeric attack on Troy? Remarkably, some tablets found among the debris unexpectedly tell us exactly what we need to know. One of them is a draft of a letter to the king of Alasiya (Cyprus) from the last king of Ugarit, whose name was Hammurabi.

> Behold, the ships of the enemy are already here, and they have set fire to my towns and done very great damage in the country. Does my father not know that all my infantry and chariots are in the Hittite country, and that all my ships are in the land of Lukka, and have not yet returned? So, the country has been abandoned to its own devices. My father, consider this; there are seven ships of the enemy that have come and inflicted very great damage upon us.

Shortly after the letter was written, great Ugarit and the nearby towns that depended on it were brought down by these seven ship-loads of warriors. Only seven ships.

Sixty or seventy years before the fall of Ugarit, the Mycenaeans were carrying out similar raids on the coastal towns of western Anatolia. They had control over Miletus, Ephesus and other towns in the south-west, which gave them a bridge-head from which they could destabilize not only towns but kingdoms to the north. These kingdoms were a long way from Hattusa and, although the Great King of the Hittite Empire sought to control them, there were continual disturbances.

As we saw earlier, the Tawagalawas Letter was a complaint from the Hittite Great King to the Great King of Ahhiyawa, about his complicity in the 'Piyamaradus' raids in south-west Anatolia. It is not known who Piyamaradus was. Given the peculiar relationship between him and Ahhiyawa it is not impossible that he was a Mycenaean ex-pat – a sort of Cecil Rhodes figure. If we think of Agamemnon as the king of Ahhiyawa in 1250 BC and Achilles as his war-leader, we are very close to inferring that 'Piyamaradus' was in fact Achilles.

King Hattusilis himself led the Hittite army in person all the way to Miletus to settle the disturbance that the Piyamaradus raids were causing. By the time Hattusilis reached Miletus, Piyamaradus had gone. By then he was in Greece, evidently a favoured protégé of the Ahhiyawan High King. With the Mycenaean king's approval, support and encouragement, Piyamaradus/Achilles instigated a whole series of raids along the Anatolian coast.

Sailing north towards Troy, no doubt calling in at various Mycenaean colonies and trading posts along the way, such as Ephesus and Emborio (on Chios), Piyamaradus, with his handful of ships, reached the island of Lesbos. Lesbos had a prosperous trading port, Thermi, on its eastern coast. It was culturally rich, belonging to the same culture as Troy VI. It was sacked and burnt at about the same time as Troy VI, and its destruction can be seen as one of the final coastal raids in the sequence that culminated in the sack of Troy. We know from archaeological evidence that both towns fell close to the year 1250 BC. Intriguingly, we have documentary evidence of both as well. The Hittite account is contained in the Manapa-Tarhunda Letter, which tells us that Lesbos was destroyed by Piyamaradus. The Greek account is contained, if obliquely and briefly, in the *Iliad*, where we learn that it was Achilles who sacked 'strong-founded Lesbos'.[9] So perhaps Piyamaradus and Achilles were one and the same.

The attacks on towns along the coast of the Gulf of Edremit immediately north of Thermi can be seen as part of the same sequence. Possibly these were relatively impulsive, sudden and rapid raids. The attack on Troy was quite simply the last in a sequence that had taken Piyamaradus/Achilles all the way along the western Anatolian coastline, ravaging, burning and stealing. There was plunder to be taken, and women were the greatest prize of all.

The Great King of Ahhiyawa sanctioned and sponsored these raids from mixed motives. First and foremost, they were a business proposition. They yielded many different kinds of wealth, manpower and womanpower in particular, but also livestock, including highly valued horses. Control over the various ports and trading posts round the Aegean also meant that levies could be extorted from the seaborne traders who criss-crossed the sea.

Piyamaradus/Achilles set up camp on the sheltered north side of the Bay of Beşika one spring. From there, he led his warriors across the Plain of Troy, wading across the River Scamander, and attacked the city of Troy. A well-ordered attack on such an accessible site could have resulted in the city falling within a matter of weeks or even days. Once inside the city with the help of siege engines, the Greek warriors killed as many men as remained, made for the citadel, took whatever valuables they could find, and returned to their ships with their booty. Before leaving, they knocked down the mudbrick ramparts of the citadel and possibly the town walls too. The spoils taken back to the twenty ships drawn up on the sandy beach in Beşika Bay would have included women, and some of those women would almost inevitably have been women the Trojans had acquired on very similar raids on Greek towns. From time to time, with repeated raids and repeated abductions, women must have found themselves by chance rescued and returned home. This, perhaps, is the mainspring of the story of Helen, a high-born Mycenaean lady abducted from a Mycenaean palace, taken to Troy and then taken back to her home.

The attack on Troy, launched overland from the Bay of Beşika, became the most famous in song and legend simply because it was the last. Troy was the northernmost of the sacked cities, the final one in the sequence. It may also have been where Piyamaradus met his death. That would have given the final adventure an extra poignancy as the 'war' fell back in time to become history or legend. The loss of Troy – initially to the Trojans, but also ultimately to the Greeks as well – was to resonate through antiquity for centuries, like the doleful gonging reverberation of a huge, deep-toned bell, a bell for the dead. In every sense, the loss of Troy was to become legendary. As the Revd James Bramston wrote in 1729:

What's not destroy'd by Time's devouring hand?
Where's Troy, and where's the Maypole in the Strand?[10]

Chapter 11

The Attack on Troy: a Maximal Reconstruction

So tribe on tribe, pouring out of the ships and shelters,
marched across the Scamander plain, and the earth shook,
tremendous thunder from under tramping men and horses ...
... men by the thousands, numberless
as the leaves and spears that flower forth in spring.
(*Iliad* 2. 549–54)

In the last chapter we looked at a minimal reconstruction of the attack on Troy: a small-scale raid on an Anatolian coastal town that, because of certain special circumstances, later acquired legendary status. Now we come to the more exciting possibility that the grand scale of the Epic Cycle version of the Trojan War was closer to the historical reality.

The Muster
The Mycenaean war-leaders assembled their contingent fleets at Aulis, a port with a spacious roadstead in the sheltered Euboea channel. There was no wind for the voyage to Troy. A sacrifice was required to win favour with the gods and, given the gravity of the enterprise, Agamemnon was required by Calchas the priest to sacrifice his own daughter, Iphigeneia, to appease the goddess Artemis, who had quelled the wind. Iphigeneia was fetched from home and sacrificed at the Sanctuary of Artemis at Aulis.[1]

Human sacrifice is mentioned in the Epic Cycle as an integral part of the world of the bronze age heroes. Priam's daughter Polyxena was sacrificed on Achilles' tomb; by this act of appeasement the Greeks hoped to gain a fair wind for the voyage home.[2] Menelaus resorted to a similar rite in similar circumstances, sacrificing two children when he was detained in Egypt for a long time by storms.[3] Some Linear B tablets imply human sacrifice. One from Pylos, belonging to the final days of Pylos, is incomplete, but begins with a date and a place, and the name PYLOS written six times. The text refers to offerings for the gods, including 'sacrificial victims'.

Released from Artemis' curse, the huge confederate Mycenaean fleet set sail across the Aegean, stopping at the island of Tenedos, just 7km short of the coast of Wilusa. On Tenedos, the Mycenaeans set up a base camp from which the attacks on the mainland of Wilusa could be mounted.[4]

The Trojans evidently saw what was happening and prepared a reception. When the Mycenaeans tried to land at Beşika Bay, the Trojans, under Hector's leadership, were initially able to stop them. The *Kypria* adds the detail that Hector succeeded in killing the Greek Protesilaus, who became the first of the Greek champions to fall in the war.[5] A task force of Mycenaean infantry under Achilles rushed the Trojans and pushed them back from the coast. This enabled the Mycenaeans to land, disembark and drag their ships up onto the beach. The beach was quite short, and to fit the scores of ships into the space they were drawn up in three rows. Once ashore, the Mycenaeans set up camp and prepared for their attack on Troy.

The huge numbers of ships and warriors assembled in Homer may have become exaggerated in the continual retelling of the saga. Even so, there is fairly reliable contemporary evidence that very large armies were mustered in the late bronze age. In 1275 BC the Egyptian pharaoh Ramesses reported that the Hittite Great King Muwatallis mustered 3,700 chariots and 37,000 infantry for the Battle of Kadesh, though he was probably exaggerating somewhat.[6] Kadesh was a major clash of empires and the confrontation at Troy was not seen as being of that order of importance, but the force enumerated in the catalogues may have been exaggerated only tenfold. Later, in 853 BC, the Hittite kings of Hamath and Damascus were able to call up contingents of twelve subject chiefs to fight against the Assyrians at Qarqar. Between them they mustered 2,000 cavalry, 4,000 chariots and 63,000 infantry. Clearly, the scale of these early battles *could* be very large.[7]

The unwieldy and unlikely-sounding confederations of allies in the Greek and Trojan catalogues may also have been exaggerated in scale. But, again, the official Egyptian report of the Battle of Kadesh shows that Great Kings were indeed in the habit of calling up contingents from their subordinate kingdoms; the command structure had evidently been in place for a generation before the attack on Troy – and would prevail for hundreds of years afterwards.

The Attack on South Wilusa

Having already established the strength of the Trojans' resistance, the Mycenaeans decided to delay a direct onslaught on the well-defended capital of Wilusa. Their strategy was to weaken the defence of Troy, which depended heavily on the collusion of allies, by attacking several towns in southern Wilusa, along the north shore of the Gulf of Edremit, before attacking the city of Troy itself. Walter Leaf believed the references to these preliminary attacks come from another poem (not the *Kypria*) and now lost, which he called the *Poem of the Great Foray*. This expedition was really much more than a foray; it was a serious military operation with strategic importance and an integral part of the campaign against Troy.[8]

The expedition to the Gulf of Edremit, the entrance to which lay 50km to the south of the Bay of Beşika, took place in the middle of summer, as we are told of cattle already driven up onto the high pastures on the treeless upper slopes of Ida. Leaf assumed that Achilles took a large force of at least fifty ships, and between 3,000 and 6,000 men (assuming that the poet based his 'facts' on the Greek Catalogue or a common source). He probably took a subsidiary fleet of cargo ships with him in which to stow the anticipated plunder.

A plundering expedition starts work at the furthest point in order to minimize the transport of booty, which would include women and animals. If embarking from the Bay of Beşika encampment, Achilles' fleet would have taken perhaps one or two days, depending on the wind, to sail and row the 125km to the head of the Gulf. The fleet probably sailed up the middle of the Gulf, so as not to alarm the towns on the northern shore, and probably without stopping, to maximize surprise. The slower cargo ships were sent ahead, so that all the ships would arrive at the head of the Gulf at about the same time.

The Cilician town of Thebe, the modern Edremit, now stands an hour's march from the sea at the head of the Gulf, though then it was probably somewhat closer. Thebe on its spur of high ground was well defended with walls and high gates, and may have felt itself safe against ordinary pirates.[9] But the Mycenaeans were determined, experienced, well-equipped, and they attacked and sacked the town. The Thebans were not entirely alone in their resistance to the Mycenaeans. Reinforcements came to their aid from Masa (Mysia), the large country to the north-east of Cilicia. Among the Mysians was the hero Telephos, who was reputed to be a son of Heracles. The duel between Telephos and Achilles was afterwards depicted in sculpture on the pediment of the Temple of Athena at Tegea in Arcadia.[10] Telephos fell, wounded by Achilles.

Once their champion had fallen, the men of Thebe were systematically massacred, including King Eetion, the father of Princess Andromache. King Eetion, Hector's father-in-law, was killed by Pelides, who took as a prize the ball of iron which the king had used to shot-put.[11] Andromache's brothers, Eetion's sons, were up in the hills of the Mount Ida range with their cattle and so were safe, for the moment.

The women of Thebe were sent off to the ships along with the rest of the plunder. Eetion's widow and Chryseis were among the woman captured.[12] The Mycenaeans showed respect to their royal victims. They raised a funeral pyre for Eetion and he was burnt on it with his armour, which less scrupulous attackers would have stolen from the corpse.[13] The Mycenaean commanders took the best spoils for themselves. Achilles took the horse called Pedasos, which he considered worthy to run in harness with his own horses.[14] Achilles also took a lyre with a silver bridge, to which he sang songs about the deeds of heroes, and the iron shot belonging to Eetion which he later offered as a prize.[15]

Next, the flocks and herds up on the hills had to be gathered in, partly to cut off supplies from the enemy (the Trojan 'confederation'), partly to feed the Greek host. There was a long and easy path running north-west from the site of the modern village of Zeitunlu, diagonally up the mountain side, and it still forms the natural route between the plains of Edremit and Bairamich. Achilles and his men followed this path up to the high pastures, where they found that herdsmen had gathered not only from Thebe to the south-east but from Dardania to the north; there were herds of Dardanian as well as Theban cattle grazing the high summer pastures. Aeneas, the leader of the Dardanians, was there, thinking himself safe up on Mount Ida because he never dreamed that the Mycenaeans would attempt this sweeping flanking manoeuvre. He had as a result taken no warriors with him onto Mount Ida.[16] Eetion's seven sons were there too. They tried to defend their father's flocks, but the Mycenaeans killed all seven of them.[17]

Achilles and his men moved quickly round to the north to stop any escape towards Dardania and rounded up both herds and surviving herdsmen. He drove them at breakneck speed through the pine woods on the hill slopes and the olive groves nearer the shore, down, down towards the ships. The men at the ships concentrated on rounding up the cattle. The herdsmen meanwhile managed to escape to the west, along the coast, to the town of Lyrnessos.

Achilles and his men had not killed at random, though. Among the herders were two sons of Priam, king of Troy – Antiphos and Isos. These he captured and took down to the ships and freed for a ransom; this is how Agamemnon later, in battle on the Plain of Troy, was able to identify the two brothers as they stood together in one chariot. Then he would kill them both.

The Mycenaean fleet sailed westwards along the coast, attacking Lyrnessos with the same result as at Thebe. The king of Lyrnessos, Mynes, was killed. Among the many women taken there was Briseis, whose husband was killed. She was taken on board one of the ships. Some escaped, and Aeneas was one of these, managing to struggle back home to Dardania by following paths across the Ida range. Aeneas was one of the lucky ones, or perhaps he just had a strong survival instinct; he escaped from the Mycenaeans over and over again.

The Mycenaeans' return voyage to the west took them past the coastal town of Pedasos. Sheltered from the north winds, its harbour was an attractive haven for those travelling from the south northwards towards Troy. The Mycenaean invasion had put a stop to commercial traffic for the time being, but the Mycenaeans still saw it as a potential prop to Troy as it could offer support to auxiliary troops arriving from the south. The citadel of Pedasos stood on a steep, craggy hilltop and may have been hard to capture. The king of Pedasos was old King Altes, one of Priam's fathers-in-law and the father of Lykaon.[18] It is not known what happened to him, but it is not recorded that he was killed, so perhaps he was allowed to live. Afterwards, some of the surviving Lelegians (the people of the Troad's south coast) went back to the ruins of their town.

The siege of Pedasos (the town of Assos in later antiquity) became more famous than the sieges of Thebe or Lyrnessos. This may have to do with the strategic importance of Pedasos. The high ridge separating the Leleges from the kingdoms to the north dropped to a height of only about 100m just beside Pedasos. Pedasos therefore commanded the route over the col and northwards to the land of the Pelasgians, then on to Dardania and Troy, a route still followed by a present-day main road.[19] Arzawan allies might sail north as far as Pedasos, disembark there and then march overland to Troy, without having to brave the difficult northerly headwinds in the exposed water between Lesbos and the Hellespont. Lying at the entrance to the Gulf of Edremit, opposite the north coast of Lesbos, Pedasos also commanded the west–east sea route into the Gulf. It was a key strategic town and it is easy to see why the Mycenaeans wanted to slight it before going in to attack Troy.

On the same expedition, Achilles attacked 'the citadel of Lesbos'.[20] It was common for principal towns to share the names of their kingdoms, a practice that must have created even more problems in antiquity than it does today. The name 'Lazpaz' could be used to mean both the island of Lesbos and the main town on the island, so phrases such as 'founding Lesbos' or 'taking Lesbos' are ambiguous. Agamemnon later said he would give away seven of the women of Lesbos who were part of his booty from this raid. The place name is mentioned incidentally, implying that the whole island was not taken, just the principal town on Lesbos, though there is no tradition of one of the settlements there having been called Lesbos. Walter Leaf thought it might have been the modern town of Molivo (ancient Methymna), which has a harbour and is well situated to trade with the north.[21] It is on a stretch of the north coast that is visible from Pedasos, and the sight of it may have tempted the Mycenaeans across on impulse, although the expedition as a whole seems to have been carefully organized and planned. A late poem by Parthenios (in *Erotici Graeci*) describes the Mycenaean raid on Lesbos, very possibly borrowing part of the story of the raid on Pedasos; this is a later source, but he gives as an authority for the story an old poem on the founding of Lesbos. Parthenios locates the raid at Methymna.

Archaeology has nevertheless come up with an alternative site at Thermi, on the east coast of Lesbos. This is known to have been a town in the late bronze age and must be considered a likelier alternative for an attack than Methymna. Thermi went through several building phases from the early bronze age onwards, creating a deposit 6m thick. It is possible to extract the town plan from the earlier phases. Initially, there were long, narrow houses arranged radially alongside radial streets, in much the same way as the Trojan citadel in Troy VI; this layout seems to have been a speciality of Western Anatolia. Later the evolving town was protected by a fortification wall up to 2m thick, reinforced with towers. Unfortunately the plan of the last phase, the one that corresponds to the period of the Trojan War, has not survived intact. But the Thermi known to the Mycenaeans and Trojans was, oddly, a town of oval houses – which made it quite unlike Mycenae or Troy. The excavator of the site, Winifred Lamb, thought late bronze age Thermi, complete with its Mycenaean pottery, ended in a catastrophic fire and total destruction. This may correspond to the attack on Lesbos during the Great Foray of Achilles. According to the *Iliad*, the king of Lesbos was called Makar. Diodorus Siculus traced Makar's ancestry back to an Achaean called Macareus, so Makar was a descendant of Mycenaean migrants.[22]

According to Hittite documents, Lesbos and the Caicos valley were ruled by an Anatolian dynasty around the time of the Trojan War. The Greeks seem nevertheless to have perceived Lesbos as in some sense Mycenaean. Maybe, instead of the Aeolic migration being a clear-cut event happening well after the time of the Trojan War as has often been supposed, it was a long drawn out process of infiltration, with Greeks arriving before, during and after the war.[23] The complex interaction between Mycenaeans and Anatolians would fit that explanation. There are hints at something of the kind in Pausanias, who mentions that Gras, the great-grandson of Orestes, set off with a fleet of Mycenaeans to settle both Mysia and Ionia; Penthilos, the *son* of Orestes, had already settled Lesbos, so the colonization of north-west Anatolia was envisaged as stretching across at least three generations.[24]

Tenedos lay on the way home to Beşika Bay for the Greeks. Even so, the raid on Tenedos in which Achilles killed its chief, Tennes, during the sack of Tenedos, is likely to have been a separate venture. Hekamede was one of the women captured there when Achilles raided the island, and she was given to Nestor.[25] Given that the Mycenaean fleet sailed from Greece by way of Tenedos, the raid on Tenedos is much more likely to have happened during that outward journey, at the time when the island was commandeered as a base. It is also likely that at the same time a similar base was set up on Lemnos, further out in the Aegean, as a preliminary to setting up camp at Beşika Bay. Later, we hear of additional supplies being landed for the Greeks at Beşika Bay from Lemnos, implying a considerable level of pre-planning.

From Lesbos, Achilles probably sailed straight home to Beşika Bay. As soon as the ships were beached, the division of the spoils began, and the unseemly squabbling over the captive women. This was the moment when Agamemnon chose Chryseis as his share, and apparently the pick of the Lesbian cargo as well, not realizing the momentousness of his choice. Achilles took Briseis and then Agamemnon took her away from him.[26] The mother of Andromache was ransomed at a high price, possibly through a neutral slave-dealer in Lemnos. Isos and Antiphos were ransomed too.[27]

Alternatively, there may have been a storm after the attack on Lesbos, preventing Achilles from returning home immediately. According to the account in the *Kypria*, a storm blew up, scattering the fleet before it could reach Troy, and Achilles was driven by adverse winds to the island of Skyros – 130km away, an incredibly long way off-course.[28]

This self-contained narrative was probably, as Leaf argues, the substance of a great lost poem in the Epic Cycle. That makes it interesting in its own right. But, more than that, it provides an insight into the strategy that lay behind the attack on Troy. It shows how the attacks and the selection of towns to be raided added up to a thoroughgoing regional campaign to gain control of western Wilusa. The Mycenaeans recognized that the Trojans had kinsmen and allies throughout the Troad and beyond, and that it was important to neutralize some of those most likely to be active in offering military help. By ravaging southern Wilusa, they were weakening the military strength of any help from the Kilikes (Cilicians), Leleges (Lelegians) and Dardanians, and also removing an important naval base for any warriors arriving by sea from allies in the Seha River Land or Arzawa-Mira to the south. We know from the Hittite archives that armies were moved long distances to resolve disputes over land or sovereignty.

The isolated references to the sacking of a town for the gathering of women slaves make these expeditions look like nothing more than opportunism. A raid on a vulnerable coastal town might yield an amount of plunder, a number of slave-girls, that would raise a certain sum of money. It was a business venture. But what this reconstruction of the campaign against southern Wilusa represents is much more than a mere series of random raids on a number of coastal cities. It was a systematic slighting of the region of Wilusa that might have supported auxiliary troops arriving from the south.

The Trojans' Allies

When the Trojans were attacked by the Mycenaeans, it was to be expected that neighbouring tribes and townships would rally to the Trojans' aid. The detailed Catalogue of Trojans in the *Iliad* recounting their disposition round Wilusa and across the Hellespont shows that the Mycenaeans were conscious of this. The preliminary raids on Thebe, Lyrnessos and Pedasos on the Anatolian mainland and Thermi on Lesbos show that they could apply this knowledge effectively too. The Catalogue goes on to list allies in the surrounding territories, outside Wilusa, though this list is vaguer, suggesting that the Mycenaeans (or maybe the later Greeks) were less certain about the affiliations and locations.

The first part of the Catalogue is in effect a tour of Wilusa, crossing it diagonally and then going round the circumference. The second part is entirely different, and made of radial paths leading away from Wilusa. One radial path consists of Thracians, Kikones, Paionians 'from far-away Amydon on the River Axios'. A second is Paphlagonians and Halizones 'from far-away Alybe'. A third is Mysians and Phrygians 'from far-away Askania'. A fourth is Maionians,

Carians and Lykians, 'from far-away Lykia on the River Xanthus'. These four radii are probably four ancient trade routes that converged on Troy as a common trading post.

Thrace was very likely beyond the Mycenaean sphere of influence and therefore possibly aligned with Troy in the war. Coincidentally, Wilusa-orientated Thrace occupied the same area as modern-day European Turkey. The Kikones lived along the north Aegean coast between there and the island of Thasos. The Paionians lived even further to the west; Leaf believes they lived in the area of modern Salonika. This grouping therefore made a northern Aegean axis.

The Paphlagonians and Halizones lived along the southern shore of the Black Sea, forming a similar trading axis leading away to the east.[29] The Mysians lived to the south-east and east of Wilusa, on the southern shore of the Gulf of Edremit and in a great arc from there to the north-east. The Mysian war-leaders were Chromis and Ennomos. Mysia was adjacent to Phrygia, which lay further off to the north-east. The Phrygians were led by Phorkys and Askanios. Masa was a very large kingdom and it may be that what Homer calls 'Phrygia', essentially a later place name, was in reality eastern Masa.

The Maionians lived to the south of the Mysians and were led by Mesthles and Antiphos. The Carians, led by Nastes, lived further south, but still on the Aegean coast of Anatolia. The Lykians, led by Sarpedon and Glaukos, lived in the far south-west of Anatolia.

It has often been said that the Trojan Catalogue may truly represent the political geography of the region a century or so after the time of the Trojan War, but not exactly contemporary with it. That may be the case, and it is certainly true that the kingdom of Phrygia seems not to have existed in 1250 BC; 'Phrygia' as such does not appear in any of the Hittite documents. On the other hand, a kingdom called Masa certainly existed at the time of the war, in the area that became Phrygia, and its name is fairly close to the Mysia of the Catalogue. Mysia also spread across the territory that the Hittite archives refer to as the Seha River Land, which lay immediately south-east of Wilusa. The kingdom of the Maionians was known as Mira to the Hittites, which again is close. The Lykians lived in the Lukka land. There may be one or two anachronisms, but most of the names and the locations are close enough for us to take the Catalogue of Trojan allies seriously.

But did all these far-flung kingdoms really come to the aid of Troy when it was attacked by the Mycenaean fleet? One reason for believing that such a confederation was formed is that there is contemporary evidence that such confederations were set up to meet military emergencies. At the Battle of Kadesh, the Hittite Great King called up contingents from all over Anatolia, while the Egyptian pharaoh called up contingents of Nubians, Sherden, Libyans and Canaanites to swell his army. The Homeric catalogues are therefore consistent with the normal call-up practice of the late bronze age.

It is distinctly possible that the Trojan Catalogue is authentic, not least because the kingdoms listed are the ones that were sufficiently far from Hattusa to have been just within the Hittite sphere of influence, or just beyond it, and trying to lead a semi-independent existence apart from the Hittite Empire. The lands of the north Aegean coast were far enough from both the Hittite and Mycenaean Great Kings to try to resist control by either. It begins to look as if the Catalogue of Trojan allies represents a loose confederation of independent states, non-aligned states who wanted to remain non-aligned and were ready to fight to do so. Some of the allied forces may have been mercenaries: Troy was rich enough to pay for military assistance.[30]

Not all of the allies were mercenaries, though. The Lykians, from the far south, the Lukka Lands, had much to lose if Troy went under as a result of the Mycenaean attack. They were merchants and probably made their money by acting as middlemen between the lands to the south-east and the emporium at Troy. If they lost their control over the coastal trade to the north, they stood to lose everything. According to the *Iliad*, the Mycenaeans were by this time in possession of Rhodes, which is supported by archaeology, and this would have meant that the mercantile activities of the Lykians were already severely cramped. With the Mycenaeans ensconced on Rhodes, commanding the narrow channel between Rhodes and the Anatolian mainland, the Lykians would already have felt under pressure. Tradition has it that, after the fall of Troy, Rhodes controlled the eastern Aegean trade routes.[31] The Lykians desperately needed their friends in the north, the Trojans, to act as a bulwark against the Mycenaean supremacy. The Lykians were allies of the Trojans in a very special sense. It must be significant, in this context, that in the Trojan War the Lykians were led into battle by their kings. The warriors of other kingdoms were led by distinguished noble warriors, but in most cases not by their kings. The Mycenaean host was most actively led by Achilles, rather than Agamemnon. The Trojan host was led into battle by Hector, not Priam. But the Lykians were led by Sarpedon and Glaukos – two kings, the respective heads of the two branches of the Lykian royal family. In the Homeric description of the battles on the Plain of Troy, Sarpedon is shown as second in importance only to Hector, which implies that the Trojans recognized the Lykians as very special allies. Sarpedon is also shown, immediately before his final fight with Patroklos, in combat with Tlepolemos, the war-leader of the Rhodians; in the circumstances, this duel had a special edge.[32]

Troy's allies were able to come to her aid unhindered and apparently unnoticed, like the relief troops from Askania.[33] Abydos and Sestos were able to keep open communication with Thrace. Rhesus was able to enter Troy from that direction with his warriors and chariots.[34] The ransomed and liberated Lykaon was returned from Imbros to his family by the same route.[35] The siege was not a completely effective one. Supplies, troops and hostages were able to break through the Greek cordon. Troy was not starved out by famine. Instead it was bled to death by being deprived of its living. As the weeks and months passed, its economic resources dwindled. It may have been possible for Trojan warriors and their allies to come and go relatively easily, but the normal passing traffic of trading vessels had ceased because of the war, Troy would have been starved of its income, and much of its accumulated wealth was being spent maintaining forces of mercenaries.[36] Hector himself said, 'Are you not sick of being caged inside those walls? Time was when the world would talk of Priam's Troy as the city rich in gold and rich in bronze – but now our houses are stripped of all their sumptuous treasures, treasures sold off and shipped to Phrygia, lovely Maionia.'[37]

War with the Trojans Begins

The opening section of the story covered by the *Iliad* gives us the Greeks encamped in huts by their ships on the shore near Troy, when Chryses came to beg for the return of his daughter, who had been captured by the Mycenaeans during their attacks on towns in the Gulf of Edremit. The ships were, as we have seen, dragged up in three rows on the sandy barrier that lined the Bay of Beşika, the aptly named 'Cradle Bay'. The camp was set up on the south-facing hill slope at the northern end of the beach barrier. There were springs in the hills to the south, but it seems that either the water was contaminated in some way, perhaps deliberately by Trojan scouts, or the food supply was not fresh.[38] Whatever the cause of the outbreak, the Mycenaeans were overtaken by a serious illness – 'the arrows of Apollo' – that swept through the Achaean camp for nine days, and many Mycenaean warriors died – and this was before the fighting started.[39] It was not an auspicious start.

To make the camp secure from another surprise attack by the Trojans, the Mycenaeans decided to build a defensive barrier. The likeliest route for a Trojan attack was the narrow valley that connected the Bay of Beşika with the Plain of Troy; chariots could be driven through it at high speed. The valley was sealed off by digging a ditch and using the upcast from it to make an embankment on the Mycenaean side. The *Iliad* describes the wall as being made of stone, with an elaborate timber rampart and walkway along the top. On the whole, this seems unlikely, and a more ad hoc defence is probable. There would, even so, have been some gaps left in both ditch and bank to allow the Mycenaean troops and chariots through, and these may well have been fitted with gates. The *Iliad* tells us that the defences took all day to build but, in one day, it would not have been possible to build a defence as elaborate as the one Homer describes. The reality was probably a simple earthen bank made from the upcast from a ditch, possibly with a wooden palisade along the bank top. The ditch was lined with sharpened stakes.

The Greek warriors assembled, pouring out of their huts onto the beach. The Mycenaean warriors were rallied by commanders wielding sceptres. A fine gold sceptre was found in a royal burial dating to around 1100 BC at Kourion in Cyprus, though it was even then an antique piece made at least a century earlier, in other words close to the time of the Trojan War. Of Late Mycenaean workmanship, it consists of a plain gold rod, surmounted by a granulated astragal. On top of that is a globe with two hawks perching on it. The globe and the hawks are covered by cells of white, green and purple enamel. No doubt Mycenaean kings regularly commissioned wonderful regalia like this from their craftsmen.

Agamemnon held his sceptre so that the warriors mustering on the beach in front of him could see it.[40] The sceptre had been made by a god, Hephaestus, for another god, Zeus himself; it had been passed in turn to Hermes, Pelops the great charioteer, Atreus shepherd of the people, and Thyestes rich in flocks. Thyestes bequeathed it to Agamemnon, to be held in token of his empire. Throughout time, kings have ceremonially validated their rule by owning and flaunting inherited crown jewels like this sceptre, and Homer tells us explicitly that the Mycenaeans subscribed to this ancient concept of god-given regalia.

Assembled in front of their commanding officers and given their marching orders, the Mycenaeans advanced eastwards, past the lagoon and the saltmarsh, then north-east through the valley connecting Beşika Bay with the Plain of Troy. They passed through the wall and its fronting ditch, and almost immediately after that a panoramic view across the Plain of Troy towards Troy itself opened up. The great Mycenaean host marched onto the plain of the River Scamander, facing the Trojan army.

This first view of Troy showed the walled city on its low, steep-sided hill commanding a broad bay below it and stretching away to the left (north) towards the open gate into the Hellespont guarded by Cape Sigeum to the left (west) and Cape Rhoeteum to the right (east). The Bay of Troy was shallow, spread like a huge mirror, but fraying out indeterminately at the edges into fringes of reedy lagoons, saltmarshes and sand dunes. Directly between the Greek army and the city of Troy was a great sweep of alluvial plain with the meandering River Scamander passing across with its riparian reed beds and scattered small oak trees. Away to the right (south) was the winding path the Scamander had followed from Dardania, where the Trojans had stalwart allies; alerted to the threat by news of the setting up of the Greek camp and the systematic sacking of towns from Thebe to Pedasos, the Dardanian warriors had already arrived from that direction, emerging suddenly from the gorge, then assembling on the low valley side immediately south of Troy, alongside the other allies. Troy would be a prize too great for the Greeks to resist.

In amongst the Scamander's reed beds were all kinds of wild things the Trojans habitually hunted for food. Soon the Ṭrojans would be cut off from that food supply. On the open plain were fields of barley. The Greeks would cut them off from those too.

There was pasturage on the plain for many horses, the horses the Trojans traded and used to draw their war chariots. The Trojans exported foals and full-grown horses to the chariot kingdoms of the Near East; it was one of the ways they had grown rich.[41] They knew this plain well, with its strong points, quagmires and places where the Scamander could be forded. This was a potential killing ground, and the Mycenaeans must have felt disadvantaged and daunted, in spite of their superior numbers. The walled city was impressive on its low tell.

What the Mycenaeans did not see was that there was pasturage *behind* the city for substantial flocks of sheep and goats, interspersed with small arable plots. There were also, indiscernible in the distance, vineyards, olive groves and stands of cypress trees. The Trojans would be able to make unseen sorties from the Dardanian Gate, the back door of their city, to gather food and firewood. The Trojans would be able to withstand a longer siege than the Mycenaeans realized.

The Trojan generals gathered 'at Priam's door' to confer. The likeliest location for this meeting is the public space immediately outside the South Gate of the citadel. The armies of Priam's allies were assembled beside the town of Troy, arrayed along the low ridge to the south, each allied army under the immediate command of its own war-leader, partly because of the language difficulties, partly because of long-established group loyalties. The main gate of Troy was the Scaean Gate, which was probably the gate in the south wall or the one in the south-west wall. It was this that gave access to the Plain of Troy, to the *west*, as the name 'Scaean' implies.

The Mycenaeans stood some way off on the western part of the plain, west of the Scamander. From the Mycenaean standpoint, the Trojan army and its allies could be seen assembled on the low hill called Thorn Hill or Thicket Ridge. At this moment the two armies were 4km apart at their closest, 6km at their furthest. The Trojans and their allies were ranged along the eastern side of the Scamander valley, along the southern flank of Thicket Ridge. In the days when it was assumed that the Greeks had dragged their ships ashore on the modern coast between Cape Sigeum and Cape Rhoeteum, it was not immediately obvious where this isolated ridge 'in front of Troy' might have been. If the Greeks had approached Troy from the north or north-west, they would have encountered no ridge or hill at all in front of Troy on that side. Now that we can see that the Greeks approached Troy from the south-west, a very obvious candidate for Thicket Hill emerges. It is the well-defined west–east ridge projecting into the plain immediately south of the Scaean Gate, on the far side of the Chiblak valley. Viewed from the Mycenaean position to the west, this west–east ridge would indeed have looked like an isolated hill. In the *Iliad* we are told, 'A sharp ridge rises out in front of Troy, all on its own and far across the plain, with running-room all round it, all sides clear. Men call it Thicket Ridge, the immortals call it the leaping Amazon Myrine's mounded tomb, and the Trojans and allies ranged their troops for battle.'[42] A few hundred metres back from the tip of this finger of high ground there is indeed a 'mounded tomb', now called Pasha Tepeh, but also identified as the Tumulus of Myrine or Batieia, the daughter of Teucer. There are several of these large tumuli round the Plain of Troy, and it has been assumed for 2,000 years that some of them at least represent the tombs of the heroes who fell in the attack on Troy. (See Appendix 2.)

Barrows were certainly raised in the bronze age, and it may well be that Pasha Tepeh, the Tomb of Myrine or Batieia, was already a conspicuous landmark at the time of the attack on Troy. In the dust of battle on the plain, it would have been useful to have a landmark to aim for or return to as an agreed muster point, a landmark such as a large tumulus, especially if it had a whitewashed building such as a shrine or tower built on top. The Trojans and their closest allies, the Dardanians, mustered close to the barrow. The Carians, Paionians, Leleges, Cauceones and Pelasgoi mustered along the ridge to the west of them. The Lykians, Mysians, Phrygians and Maionians mustered along the west-facing slope to the south-east of them, 'towards Thymbra'. Thymbra was a small Trojan walled town on the eastern side of the Scamander valley, and one of the few (purely) Trojan settlements other than Troy itself that is known to have existed. The Thracians arrived late, probably sailing their ships

The Trojan muster, reconstructed from the Iliad.

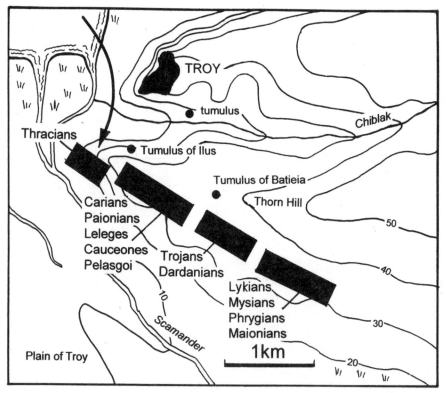

fast before the wind right into the Bay of Troy. They landed in the shallows of the bay as close as they could to the walls of the city and took up their position at the westernmost end of this impressive host ranged along the side of the Scamander valley.

It was standard practice to muster on high ground if possible and it is easy to see why the Trojan commanders gathered their troops on Thorn Hill. The sharply rising ground gave them a fine view of the entire Plain of Troy, enabling them to see exactly where the enemy units were from the plumes of dust they raised. It also enabled them to see over the trees and shrubs growing along the banks of the Scamander: elm, willow, tamarisk, lotus, bulrush could all provide cover for the enemy. Thorn Hill was directly opposite the valley leading to the Greek camp, and afforded plenty of space for the host of warriors and their tents. It was also easy to descend the short slope onto the plain. The Scamander flowed across the plain in front of the site, giving the Thorn Hill encampment a significant defence. It would not have been possible for the Greeks to charge across the river and make a surprise attack on the allies' camp. The river was negotiable, but only slowly and with care. The Thorn Hill site was also very close to the south gate of Troy, the Scaean Gate, if they were in desperate need of a refuge, or if Hector and the other Trojan leaders needed to consult King Priam, who was watching everything from his vantage point in the citadel.

The camp or camps of the Trojans and their allies spread perhaps 3km along the valley side from close to the South-West Gate of Troy halfway to Thymbra. Each contingent had its cluster of tents, its waggons laden with provisions, its host of supporters: cooks, grooms, surgeons, vets, armourers, joiners and wheelwrights.

The First Battle

The two huge armies were drawn up, ready to engage in battle. The Mycenaean host had emerged from the valley leading to the Bay of Beşika. The Trojan host was poised on Thorn Hill. We can imagine them pausing, while their respective commanders assessed the situation, guessed what the enemy might do, made last-minute tactical decisions and issued instructions to their subordinates. Once the battle was begun, opportunities for clear and reasoned communication were going to be few and far between.

The warriors assembled in formal groups, chariots all together in one or more blocks, the infantrymen or lancers all together shoulder to shoulder in a phalanx, the archers and slingers similarly grouped together. One obvious reason for this was social custom and training: charioteers were an élite force that would have considered themselves far superior to slingers. Archers and lancers would have been trained in different skills and be commanded by different officers. The different groups were differently equipped and encumbered and moved at different speeds, so for efficiency they moved separately. It is likely that the lightly armed archers and slingers, who had no shields, assembled behind the more heavily armed lancers. The lancers formed a human shield in front of the archers and slingers, who at the same time were able, on command, to fire into the oncoming enemy lancers (or even oncoming chariots) over the heads of their lancers. It was a symbiotic relationship that was no doubt maintained for as long as possible during battle. The chariots were possibly divided into three divisions, one on each flank, ready to accompany the infantry as the whole army advanced and to defend its flanks, and another directly in front of the infantry.[43] If need be, the chariot units could race forward ahead of the infantry and attack the enemy from the flank – or even from behind. The new light chariots were highly manoeuvrable and could if deployed with skill and daring completely encircle the enemy and produce a quick victory. If the battle went less successfully and there was a long drawn out retreat, enemy foot soldiers could be chased and routed as they tried to leave the field.

But regardless of the specific manoeuvres attempted, and no doubt there were many different possibilities, as far as possible the units remained together for mutual support and safety throughout the battle. Much depended on discipline and unified action. Units could disintegrate in a matter of seconds into an unruly horde deaf to all command. One effective manoeuvre was to send a chariot unit right through an enemy infantry unit, breaking it in two and snapping the chain of command; with confusion came defeat. This was a favourite Hittite trick, and we can be sure the Trojans attempted it. The second worst thing that could happen to you in battle was to become separated from your unit. At Kadesh, Ramesses himself was in this predicament, his chariot completely surrounded by Hittite warriors. Afterwards, he was recorded as lamenting, 'No prince is beside me and no chariot driver, no officer of the infantry and none of the charioteers. My foot soldiers and my charioteers have abandoned me to the enemy.' Ramesses asked his god why he had forsaken him.

Large hostings like those at Troy were regularly divided into more manageable smaller divisions. The huge assemblage of warriors summoned by Ramesses to Kadesh, perhaps 20,000 men, was grouped into four huge field armies, each dedicated to a god. The Mycenaean and Trojan field armies were probably also put under the protection of named deities; the *Iliad* makes much of individual heroes being under the protection of specific gods or goddesses, and it is likely that whole units and divisions were dedicated in the same way.

The decision was made to commence battle. The Trojan host moved slowly forwards, all at the same walking speed, down the hill to the bank of the River Scamander. A small corps crossed the river to secure the west bank and offer protection as the rest of the army followed. The Scamander was forded slowly, with care; we know from Kadesh that whole chariot units were able to cross rivers. The army then advanced westwards, shouting, willing the Greek host to engage. The Thracians at the north-western end of the host were drawn up on the end of the Thorn Hill ridge, only 300m from the Scamander, and were therefore able to get into position quickly; the Phrygians and Maionians at the Thymbrian end of the line-up were a full kilometre from the river. It would, even so, have taken perhaps only an hour to transfer the Trojan host to a position on the plain on the west bank of the Scamander, a position where the Greeks could be engaged in battle. From there it was a short march of only 2km to the middle of the plain where a clash of arms might be anticipated.

The Hittite commanders were masters of strategy, and the Trojans would have known that their greatest strength lay in their light, mobile and very fast chariotry and their knowledge of the local terrain. They needed to engage the enemy on a smooth open plain, and here on the plain of Troy they had exactly what they wanted.[44] The Trojans' first move appeared to put them at a disadvantage, because they now no longer had the river in front of them as a defence; worse, they had the river immediately behind them, and being driven backwards into it could be disastrous. They had also lost their height advantage. The Greeks must have thought the Trojans very foolish. The Greeks obligingly advanced eastwards across the plain, in silence but raising a great cloud of dust. The two armies were only a few hundred metres apart when Paris went ahead of the Trojan line in his chariot to offer single combat. It was a regular procedure in both bronze age and iron age warfare for champions to engage in single combat, either to settle the outcome in a duel or as a preliminary to general battle.

In the iron age, shouted boasts and abuse were routine in the preamble to fighting, and Homer's account suggests that this was customary in late bronze age warfare too. There is also some corroborative evidence from the Hittite archives. The Hittite Great King Mursilis II (1333–1308) sent this challenge to the king of Arzawa: 'You called me a child and made light of me. Up then! Let us fight, and let the Storm-god, my lord, decide our case!'[45]

Paris stepped down from his chariot, ready to fight the Greek champion, whoever it might be. Paris was the abductor of Helen. He was the alleged cause of the war. It was naturally the wronged Menelaus who leapt down from his chariot to fight him. Paris had second thoughts when he saw the enraged Menelaus and hid among the Trojans. Hector rebuked Paris, who agreed to fight after all. Hector stepped into the no man's land, holding the Trojan line back. The Trojans sat down. The Greek archers fired arrows at Hector, until Agamemnon stopped them. Hector and Menelaus made speeches.

Priam and Antenor rode out from Troy in a chariot to a point midway between Greeks and Trojans, offered sacrificial lambs and agreed that the single combat should determine Helen's future, then returned by chariot to Troy. The warriors of both armies took off their helmets. Lots were cast to decide who would throw the first spear. Menelaus and Paris fought. Paris was beaten but vanished from the battlefield.

Menelaus sustained a minor wound in this short duel, and went back behind the Greek lines to have his wound tended. The warriors put their helmets back on, ready to do battle and Agamemnon toured his troops to encourage them. The Greeks advanced. The Trojan army advanced in a babel of commands in different languages. The armies met in a great roaring clash in the middle of the Plain of Troy. Many warriors died on both sides in this first great collision of the two armies.

The Mycenaeans pushed back the Trojan line, jabbing with their swords and spears. Many Trojans were killed as they retreated across the plain. It looked as if the Mycenaeans would succeed in penetrating with a single sweep right into the city of Troy.

The Mycenaean warriors were urged on by their commanders, including Diomedes and Odysseus. Many individual hand-to-hand fights followed, and we must imagine these as happening within a general mêlée, rather than as formal set pieces like the Paris–Menelaus duel. The Mycenaean thrust ran out of steam, and the Mycenaeans were pushed gradually and steadily back, many of them falling as the Trojans advanced.

So far, the battle had moved like a tide, taking the Mycenaeans north-eastwards across the plain towards the walls of Troy, then back again. And so it continued, ebbing and flowing across the plain.

It started to look once more as if the Trojans would be driven right back into their city. Hector urged his troops on. In a rather farcical episode, Glaukos and Diomedes approached each other in the open ground between the two armies, ready to do single combat. They addressed one another, describing their ancestries at length. It turned out that their grandfathers were friends, so they

The first battle on the Plain of Troy. Subsequent battles followed a broadly similar pattern. Each night the Trojans usually withdrew to Thorn Hill and the Greeks to Beşika Bay.

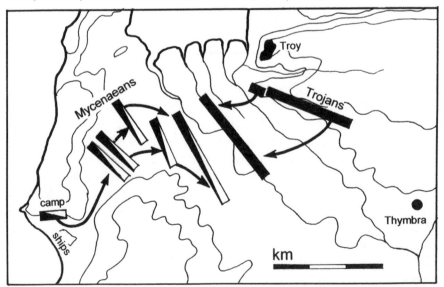

decided that they could not fight. Meanwhile Hector reached the oak tree that grew just outside the Scaean Gate; he went into the city and made his way to Priam's palace in the citadel. Paris was skulking in the citadel, and Hector urged him to rejoin the battle.

Hector and Paris returned through the Scaean Gate and rejoined the battle. Paris killed Menesthius. Hector killed Eioneus. The Trojans gained on the Mycenaeans. In a break in the fighting towards evening, the warriors took off some of their armour. The Trojan war-leader, Hector, challenged the Mycenaeans to send out a champion that he could fight. To begin with none of the Mycenaeans volunteered; Hector was too formidable an opponent, a warrior with a legendary reputation. Nestor made a speech, after which several Greeks volunteered. The volunteers cast lots. Ajax won. He put on his armour again and strode towards Hector with his spear. The two heroes duelled with rocks. Then the evening light failed and Hector proposed that they call a truce; they exchanged gifts to mark the truce.

The armies settled down to eat and rest after a hard day's fighting. The Mycenaeans decided to call a truce, cart the bodies of their dead warriors back to the encampment the following morning, burn them and raise a single burial mound.[46]

At dawn the next day, a Trojan messenger arrived at the Greek camp with a compromise solution. Messengers were in regular use, some possibly on foot, others certainly mounted; they were used to transmit orders from one part of a battlefield to another, to offer terms to the enemy, to call truces. There were also scouts or spies who were sent out to gather intelligence about the enemy. Spying was a routine part of warfare, as was the spreading of disinformation. Some scouts allowed themselves to be caught and then gave a false account of their troops' position. This was clearly a dangerous occupation, and beatings and other forms of torture were employed to try to get the truth out of enemy agents.

This Trojan messenger came with a peace offer. Paris had decided he was ready to return all the property he had taken, together with some of his own. But he would not give up Helen. The Trojans also wanted a truce so that they could dispose of their dead. Agamemnon agreed the truce, but Paris's offer was beneath discussion. The messenger returned to Troy. Trojan and Greek work parties met early that morning to collect bodies from the field of battle. They burned them on pyres out on the plain, then returned to Troy and the camp.

Homer has been criticized for describing cremation as the standard method for disposing of the dead, but warrior aristocrats killed on campaign far from home at Troy could not have been buried in the customary Mycenaean way in family chamber tombs or *tholos* tombs back in Greece; nor would there have been time to build such tombs in the Troad. As a matter of expediency it would have been necessary to dispose of their bodies in some other way.

It is estimated that it took as long as a year to build a *tholos* tomb like the magnificent Treasury of Atreus at Mycenae. It was time-consuming and therefore expensive. The *tholos* was the standard type of tomb for a Mycenaean king in 1250 BC, and consisted of a beehive vault built of oversailing courses of drystone masonry. A horizontal entrance passage went into the mound on one side, leading to an impressive stone doorway. The tombs at Mycenae were built in cuttings in the sides of hills, so that the solid rock walls of the hill surrounding the tomb on three sides would effectively hold in the lower half of the vault. The *dromos* corridors were lined with huge ashlar blocks and were impressive pieces of architecture in their own right. The monumentality of the doorway, with its huge lintel, huge jambs and massive threshold, was not there just to impress, but to act as the lynch-pin, the three-dimensional keystone of the structure.

The last *tholos* tomb to be built at Mycenae was the so-called Tomb of Clytemnestra, built in about 1250 BC, and this very conspicuous tomb right beside the approach to the Lion Gate was covered in a coat of white plaster; it was probably the tomb of Agamemnon himself, murdered on his return home from Troy. The Mycenaean rulers wanted their graves to be highly visible: they were a major public statement about the rulers' status, a flaunting of social superiority.[47]

But none of this was practicable on campaign. Cremation and a more modest burial were all that was possible, and this is what we see in the cremations and jar burials in the Mycenaean cemetery at the northern end of Beşika Bay. In using cremation, the Mycenaeans were using an expedient rather than a customary method for disposing of the dead. It is highly significant that an elaborate cremation ritual with a strong similarity to the ritual described in Homer for both Patroklos the Greek and Hector the Trojan made its first appearance in Anatolia in around 1250 BC. It is also significant that these cremations are most abundant in north-west Anatolia – round Troy.[48] Perhaps the new practice was devised by the Mycenaeans.

Before the following dawn, a Greek detachment went out to build a barrow over the pyre. More ships arrived in Beşika Bay, drawing up on the sandy beach in front of the Greek camp. They had sailed 65km from the Mycenaean base on Lemnos with reinforcements and supplies – cargoes of wine for the troops.

At the dawn of a new day, the Mycenaeans breakfasted in their camp, then armed themselves. The Trojans did the same, putting on their armour ready to do battle again.

The Second Battle

The Trojan army once again marched down from Thorn Hill, cautiously crossed the Scamander under the protection of an advance guard, and assembled in formation on the river's west bank, ready to meet the Mycenaeans. The Mycenaeans advanced, as before, from their camp at Beşika Bay, confronting the Trojan army on the open Plain of Troy. The two armies squared up to each other. The Mycenaean lancers or foot soldiers stood very close together, side by side, so that their shields overlapped to make a continuous protective wall against the spears and arrows of the Trojans. It was the solid phalanx formation that would be used again and again in later centuries. Philip of Macedon, Alexander's father, would used it in conscious imitation of this Mycenaean practice.[49] The two armies converged and clashed in the middle of the plain as in the first battle. At first the Mycenaeans began to fall back, then they pushed the Trojans back towards their city, then they began to fall back again towards Beşika Bay.

The Trojans pursued the Mycenaeans to their ships, in the hope of setting the ships on fire. Agamemnon climbed onto Odysseus' ship, which was in the centre of the line, so that his voice would carry to either end, and bellowed at his troops, urging them not to let the Trojans overwhelm them. There was renewed fighting at the ditch, with the Mycenaeans first pushing the Trojans away, then falling back again.

Nightfall came as a great relief to the Mycenaeans. The Trojan army drew back from the Greek camp onto the Plain of Troy to confer beside the river, where the ground was clear of corpses. Hector ordered his men to go and fetch food and firewood, so that they could eat and make watch fires. He ordered guards to be mounted in the city to prevent the enemy stealing in; they would resume the attack on the ships at crack of dawn. The Trojans unyoked their chariot horses and sat up all night under the stars, eating and keeping the campfires going, their horses standing by the chariots munching barley and rye.

By this point Agamemnon had reached a momentous decision. The resistance of the Trojans had been fiercer than he had expected; the Mycenaeans were defeated. He called his captains together to tell them they had no hope of taking Troy. He proposed they board their ships and return home. There was a stunned silence from his generals, who persuaded him to stay and fight. The plan agreed was to deploy both chariotry and infantry in front of the ships the next morning, but Agamemnon was still despondent.

Lookouts on the ridge to the east of the Greek camp could see the many fires of the Trojans and their allies in front of Troy. Mycenaean scouts set off across the plain to see what they could find out, and succeeded in intercepting and capturing a Trojan scout who had been sent to find out if the Mycenaeans were preparing to take flight. The Mycenaeans forced the Trojan scout to tell them what the Trojan leaders were doing. He revealed that the Trojan leaders were conferring at a quiet spot away from the main Trojan host. The Mycenaeans then killed the Trojan scout, before creeping up on some sleeping Thracians (the late-arriving allies of the Trojans from across the Hellespont) and killing several of them before returning to the ships with the Thracians' horses. It was a shameful, ignoble act, but it gave the Mycenaeans some heart.

The Third Battle

The Mycenaeans and Trojans prepared for battle once more. They collided and fought all morning. The Mycenaeans drove the Trojans back. By noon, the

Trojans had moved halfway back across the plain. The Mycenaeans chased them on until they reached the oak outside the Scaean Gate. Then the Trojan vanguard stopped to let the slower warriors catch up, because some were still out on the open plain, and being caught up by Agamemnon.

Another skirmish followed as the trailing Trojans turned to fight the pursuing Mycenaeans. Agamemnon was wounded and taken at speed in his chariot back to Beşika Bay. The Trojans took heart from Agamemnon's departure from the battlefield and surged back onto the plain, pushing the Mycenaeans back towards their ships.

Achilles watched all this from his ship, with Patroklos. The two of them listened to Nestor, who argued that the Trojans might be pushed right back to the city if Achilles and Patroklos would only join the battle.

Now it looked as if the ditch and wall would give way before the Trojan attack. The Trojans decided not to risk trying to take their chariots through the defences, but dismounted and fought on foot. Only one Trojan rode through the gates (which were left open) on his chariot, and he was killed. The Trojan infantry poured in through the gate.

The Trojans reached the ships. Close hand-to-hand fighting followed with swords and spears. The effectiveness of the infantry was greatly enhanced by the introduction of the short sword. The spear or lance was still the main weapon of the infantryman, but if a spear was thrown and not retrieved or replaced, or if the shaft was broken, it was crucial to have another weapon in reserve. The first contact with the enemy would invariably have been with the tip of the long lance, while the warriors themselves were still some distance apart. Once that initial encounter was over and the warriors were much closer together, the lance became ineffective and it was dropped in favour of the sword. But the warrior never let go of the shield in his left hand.

After an onslaught by the Trojans, Ajax shouted to Hector that he would not take the Mycenaean ships; the Mycenaeans would take Ilium first. Hector led a charge against the Mycenaeans, still determined to reach the ships.

Nestor left his hut in the Greek camp at the northern end of the line of ships. He wanted to confer with Agamemnon. On his way he chanced on the Mycenaean lords who had been wounded – Diomedes, Odysseus, Agamemnon – and who were coming up to the huts from the ships. Agamemnon was still pessimistic; he thought the Trojans would reach the ships and set them on fire. Agamemnon considered launching the ships and mooring them well out in the bay. Odysseus condemned this proposal; it would demoralize the Mycenaean warriors. Agamemnon agreed that it was unsatisfactory, but wanted a better suggestion from them. Diomedes proposed that, instead of fighting, the leaders should visit all parts of the battlefield to urge the warriors on. They all agreed to this strategy.

The Mycenaeans at last succeeded in driving the Trojans into flight. Fleeing Trojans went back across the palisade and trench, suffering severe losses at the hands of the Mycenaeans, not stopping till they reached their chariots. Hector lay on the ground, not fully conscious, with his comrades sitting round him. He recovered, recognized his friends, leapt up and rejoined the battle, which began to go more in the Trojans' favour. The Mycenaeans gathered a small force of their best men to face Hector and the Trojans, while the main Mycenaean force retreated to the ships.

The Mycenaeans weakened, and many were killed. They were thrown back in disorder on the ditch and palisade. The defences were damaged, the wall knocked down.[50] The Mycenaeans reached the ships, but the Trojan infantry poured across the broken-down defences. Like many phases of these battles, this was a scene of total disarray, of totally uncoordinated action. Hand-to-hand fighting beside the ships followed. Some Mycenaeans fought from the ships themselves. War-leaders on both sides shouted to their men to encourage them.

The Trojans tried to storm the ships, but the Mycenaeans stoutly resisted. As the Mycenaeans fell back between the ships of the first row, they were protected from falling spears and arrows by the upper works of the ships themselves. But the Trojans followed and the Mycenaeans dispersed among the huts, which lay at the northern end of the beach barrier. Mycenaean warriors on the ships stormed up and down the decks swinging the giant prods brought as fittings for their siege engines, which it now looked as though they would never have an opportunity to use. The Trojans brought torches, with the intention of setting fire to the ships. They were fended off by the warriors wielding the gigantic spears.

The Mycenaeans rallied and pushed the Trojan host back from the ships, where the fires were extinguished, all the way to the walls of Troy. Mycenaean warriors, Patroklos among them, made valiant attempts to scale the sloping stone walls of the city, but they were pushed off by the Trojan defenders on the parapet above. Achilles' armour fell from Patroklos and Patroklos was left undefended while fighting Hector. He tried to escape by slipping back among the Myrmidons, but Hector saw this move, and followed him, killing him with his spear.

A fierce skirmish raged over Patroklos' body, with the Trojans trying to pull the corpse into Troy, and the Mycenaeans trying to pull it to the ships. Fog descended. Then the sun cleared the fog, bringing the whole field of battle into view. Eventually the Mycenaeans succeeded in carrying the corpse of Patroklos back to the ships.

The sun set. The Trojans drew back, unyoked their horses, and sat down to discuss tactics. They decided to stay where they were, ready to attack in the morning. At dawn, the Mycenaeans were still smarting from their losses. The Mycenaean war-leaders agreed formally to put their personal disputes behind them. The Mycenaean warriors armed, ready for a renewed attack.

The Fourth Battle

The Mycenaean troops drew up by their ships ready for the fourth battle, while the Trojan army reassembled on Thorn Hill. The Plain of Troy once again filled with warriors as the armies converged.

The Mycenaean warriors crossed the plain, moving forward to the ford on the Scamander, where they split the Trojan force in two. It is not clear how this happened, but it may be that a standard technique was used. Often when an army advanced, the foot soldiers were preceded by the chariots as a screening force. It may be that the Mycenaean chariot force moved forwards rapidly and succeeded in breaking the Trojan army in two. One group of Trojans went towards the city of Troy, spreading out across the fields in wild disorder; they were confused, losing their sense of direction in a dense fog that covered the plain. The rest were chased into a bend in the river. Trapped, they were forced back and many were killed as they floundered in the deep-flowing water. Achilles took twelve young Trojan warriors out of the river to pay the price for Patroklos' death. The river was choked with corpses. Its current threatened to sweep Achilles away; an elm tree that Achilles was hanging on to was uprooted by the strong flow of water. But Achilles extricated himself.

Watching from the walls of the citadel of Troy, Priam groaned as he saw Achilles approaching and called to Hector, warning his son not to engage in single combat with Achilles. Hector was uncertain what to do. When he saw Achilles running towards him, he fled.[51] Achilles killed Hector and dragged his body behind his chariot.

The Funeral and Burial of Patroklos

The Mycenaeans returned to their ships. Agamemnon sent a sortie to collect wood, probably in the hills immediately to the south-east of the camp. The funeral pyre for the princely casualties was built near the shore, on the spot where a commemorative mound was to be raised for them. There were sacrifices of horses, dogs and Trojan prisoners. The flames were quenched with wine and the bones were taken out and sealed in jars.

Burial in a jar was common at this time, and there are exactly contemporary jar burials in exactly the location described. The Mycenaean cemetery at Beşik Tepeh, beside Beşika Bay, 8km south-west of Troy, may be the burial ground for the Mycenaean nobles who died during the attack on Troy. The dead included men, women and children, suggesting that some warriors took their families with them. One grave is that of a warrior, who was buried with his sword wrapped round his ash urn, and who also had a very large krater set up over his grave as a marker – very like the practice of Athenian nobles in the ninth century, who set up masterpieces of Geometric pottery over their graves.

A small barrow was raised over the heroes' bones: it could be enlarged later. A stone circle was laid out round the pyre, to mark the outer revetment of the barrow. Then funeral games followed, including a chariot race, a boxing match, a foot-race, discus and javelin throwing and archery; then the Mycenaean warriors dispersed for supper.

The Mycenaeans were ready to hand over Hector's body if Priam would pay for it. Priam drove to the Mycenaean camp in his chariot, preceded by a cartload of treasure. The Mycenaeans accepted the ransom, and handed over Hector's body to be washed and anointed. Priam realized his own acute danger, and escaped back to Troy under cover of darkness, crossing the ford over the Scamander at dawn.

At the next dawn, Hector's funeral pyre was lit. Hector was given the same rite as Patroklos, except that after the cremation his bones were wrapped in cloth and put in a chest; this was then covered by a barrow.

The Fifth Battle and the Siege of Troy
The Mycenaeans launched a new attack, routed the Trojans, broke into the town and rushed into the citadel of Troy. This assault was led by Achilles, who

A besieged town defends itself. A scene on the silver Siege Rhyton (Mycenae, about 1550–1500 BC).

was killed in the citadel by Paris. A fierce struggle ensued for the body of Achilles. Ajax carried it back to the ships while Odysseus fought a rearguard action against the Trojans. After the funeral games of Achilles, Odysseus and Ajax quarrelled over Achilles' armour.

Odysseus won Achilles' armour. Ajax went mad and committed suicide. In a formal duel, Paris was killed by Philoctetes. Paris's body was then mutilated by Menelaus. Dardanian and Lelegian reinforcements arrived from the south to help the Trojans.

The Mycenaeans had succeeded in confining the Trojans in their city and Troy was truly under siege. Infiltrators had penetrated the city. The Mycenaeans down at the Bay of Beşika meanwhile assembled the siege engines and wheeled them across the plain towards the walls of Troy. The siege engines were wheeled up ramps of logs and earth so that the long spears could reach and demolish the mudbrick ramparts. The engineers jabbed repeatedly at the mudbrick superstructure to bring it down, leaving the defenders exposed to attack by spear and arrow, and make the raising of siege ladders possible. The support groups defending the siege engines and their crews saw to it that the Trojans did not set fire to the engines, occasionally dousing them with water, and offering covering fire with slings and arrows.

It was at this point in the campaign that the slingers and archers really came into their own, picking off the defenders on the ramparts to enable the siege engineers to do their work. Slingers are shown in action on the Siege Rhyton from Mycenae, and the *Iliad* tells us that stone-throwing was a routine feature of the fighting on the Plain of Troy.[52] The Mycenaean infantry, waiting beside the engines and sheltering behind large shields, were quick to run up the scaling ladders, over the breached wall and into the city.

Once the wall was breached, Troy was doomed.

Chapter 12

The Fall of Troy and its Aftermath

Breach these gates and thin long walls and devour Priam
and Priam's sons and the Trojan armies' van.

(Iliad 4. 40–1)

The Sack of Troy

At the critical moment, when Troy was *in extremis*, an extraordinary thing
happened. As the Mycenaeans overran the city of Troy, Aeneas dissociated
himself from the Trojans' fate and went home to Mount Ida. This could have
been portrayed as epic cowardice, a betrayal as terrible as Judas Iscariot's – yet
the reputation of Aeneas has somehow survived unscathed. The Epic Cycle
explains his intriguingly anti-heroic behaviour as a response to omens. The
reality may be that when he saw the flock of siege engines being shepherded
across the plain he knew the siege could only end in defeat for the Trojans, and
decided on a tactical withdrawal. Aeneas took his Dardanian warriors home
with him to the hill country of Dardania, so that they could fight again another
day. It is reasonable to infer from this that many other allies of the Trojans fell
away at this point too, leaving the Trojans alone to suffer the humiliation of
capture and slaughter.

Perched in the citadel of Troy, perhaps on the parapet of one of the massive
wall-towers, perhaps from the window of his palace, Priam watched his city fall
to the invader. The old king may have been attired like the Hittite Great King.
A rock carving at Yazilikaya, a few kilometres from Hattusa, shows what King
Tudhaliyas IV, a near-contemporary of Priam's, looked like. He wore a long
robe that fell uninterrupted from his shoulders to his ankles. It had short
sleeves, leaving most of his arms bare. He wore a hemispherical skullcap or
bandanna.[1] Priam wanted to be thought a Great King – it was what all kings
aspired to – and he would doubtless have tried to look like this immensely
dignified role model. Another carving at the Yazilikaya sanctuary shows the
Hittite king enfolded in the embrace of his protector god, a huge and powerful
figure with a tall conical hat. Priam too would have made frequent and earnest

Was this Priam's palace? House M in the Trojan citadel. The South Gate is in the background to the right.

prayers to his protector god as the Mycenaeans gradually gained ground. As the end, the sack of Troy, became inevitable, Priam retreated to the Temple of Zeus in the citadel to prepare for death.

The Mycenaeans poured through the breaches in the wall and began a virtual massacre of the Trojans as they rampaged through the fallen city, fuelled by anger and frustration at the length of time it had taken to capture it, and by desire for revenge for the deaths of so many comrades. King Priam had taken refuge in the temple of Zeus; Neoptolemos found him, at the altar of Zeus Herkeios, and murdered him there. Menelaus murdered Deiphobos, who had rashly married Helen in the wake of the death of Paris. Then he found Helen herself, his polygamous wife twice-widowed within the last few days, and took her back with him across the Plain of Troy to the safety of the ships.

Cassandra tried to take sanctuary in the Temple of Athena in the Trojan citadel, clinging to the wooden statue of Athena. One of the Mycenaean warriors, Ajax son of Oileus, seized her and dragged her too down to the ships as a trophy woman. The other Mycenaean soldiers were angry with Ajax for committing this act of sacrilege. They wanted to stone him to death for it, but he returned to the city and took refuge in the Temple of Athena, where he was left alone for the time being.

The Mycenaeans killed, plundered and destroyed, setting fire to the city with their torches. Polyxena was slaughtered on the tomb of Achilles. Hector's little son, Astyanax, was also killed. Just as when they plundered the towns on the Gulf of Edremit, the Mycenaean warriors seized women as loot.

Neoptolemos took Andromache as his prize. The rest of the spoils were shared out. Demophon and Akamas found their mother Aithra and took her away with them. The wooden idol of Household Zeus from the citadel of Troy was given to Sthenelos son of Kapaneus to take home, just as the Argives later kept an ancient wooden idol of Hera that they seized as a trophy when they sacked Tiryns. Pausanias mentions the theft of the idol of Zeus as an example of a long-standing ancient practice of looting statues of gods from defeated enemies.[2]

The upper, mudbrick, parts of the walls of the city and citadel were systematically broken down. When the sack of Troy was over, the Mycenaeans struck camp nation by nation, returned to their ships, dragged them to the water's edge and, one by one, set sail for home.

The Trojans buried their dead in a cemetery just outside the southern city wall. The cemetery is unenclosed, 50m by 20m and contains 182 cremation burials in damaged jars that date from this time and *only* from this time, Troy VIh. They appear to be low status burials, and therefore probably of ordinary

The skulls of two Trojan warriors (of uncertain date) found in the ruins of Troy, still wearing their helmets. The warrior on the right was a mature man, the one on the left a delicately built young man (after Professor Virchow's reconstructions in Schliemann 1881, 508–9).

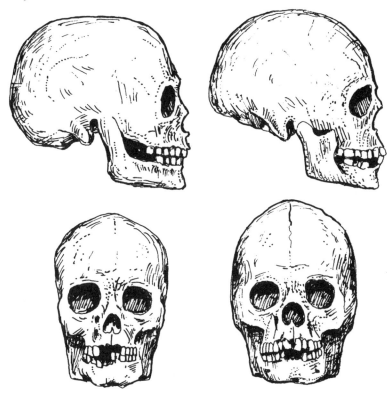

citizens – the inevitable collateral damage of any war. It seems that this was not the normal method of disposing of the dead, but rather a response to a particular emergency. The fact that no burials from any other stage at Troy have been found suggests that this was *not* the Trojans' normal way of disposing of their dead – that there were exceptional circumstances forcing them to dispose of their dead quickly. The terrible and traumatizing sack of Troy by the Mycenaeans is the simplest explanation, the most exceptional circumstance.

The archaeological evidence of the fall of Troy from the Trojan citadel itself is the destruction level prosaically referred to by archaeologists as Troy VIh. The lower walls of the citadel, made of massive masonry, were left intact. The upper walls of mudbrick were demolished. It was normal practice at that time to slight cities once a siege was over. The Greek tradition was that the Greeks deliberately demolished the walls before leaving.[3]

After the attack, and the subsequent departure of the Greeks, those Trojans who survived hastily repaired the walls of the citadel and the buildings within it, creating what archaeologists call Troy VII. They built new but smaller houses in the empty spaces. Many large earthenware jars were set into the ground in the citadel, suggesting that the Trojans were now adjusting to the idea that their city might well be attacked again. They had developed a siege mentality after the traumatic attack by the Greeks.[4] The mudbrick walls topping the citadel walls had been so severely damaged by the Greek attack that the Trojans decided to replace them in stone. For some reason they decided to use neatly squared small limestone blocks that closely resembled the mudbricks. This may have been tradition-driven, as they would certainly not have been as resistant to siege engines as the larger blocks used for the lower courses.[5]

In Troy VIIb, the city was destroyed once more, though it is not clear how. Possibly the city was taken over by another cultural group, perhaps Anatolian in origin, this time without any major structural damage.[6] By then the Trojans had already passed out of history, and out of poetic tradition. There is no Epic Cycle tradition, in either Greece or Anatolia, of 'what happened next' at Troy, except that because the dynasty of Priam was extinct – all his sons were dead – it was Aeneas, a third cousin of Hector's, who became king of Troy and king of Wilusa. Archaeology can tell us very little by way of compensation. It is as if, once the key actors in the drama departed, once the Mycenaean heroes set sail, the stage lights in the Troad were quickly dimmed to black-out and the curtain fell on Troy. No more is known. It is a salutary reminder of the fickleness of history, of the thousands of communities and hundreds of thousands of individual people whose lives are not counted.

The Mycenaeans' Voyage Home

The news of the fall of Troy was sent by beacon fires across the Aegean, so that within a very short time, perhaps even a matter of hours, the regents ruling all the mainland Mycenaean centres knew that Troy had been taken and that the great expeditionary fleet would be returning.

One of the watch-towers and beacons stood on the summit of Charvati (Mount Profitis Elias), immediately above Mycenae. It was Schliemann who noticed it first, recognizing sherds of Mycenaean pottery at the site and interpreting it as a peak sanctuary.[7] It was Captain Steffen who saw it as the signal station in the legend of Clytemnestra.[8] In 1924, excavation by Wace confirmed Schliemann's and Steffen's dating. The main building, on the summit, was a small, irregularly shaped building 20m by 15m; its surviving walls now support the platform on which the chapel stands. From it, the smoking fires of distant beacons could be seen, and it was almost certainly one of a chain of beacons transmitting key news across Greece. In Aeschylus' *Agamemnon* the last beacon fire announcing the fall of Troy is lit on what must be this mountain top, visible to the watchman on the roof of Agamemnon's palace far below, and bringing the news of the fall of Troy to Queen Clytemnestra via a string of beacons all the way from the smouldering ruins of Troy itself. Aeschylus' description is plausible in general terms, but the dramatist seems to have wanted to give his portentous news a divine send-off by putting the first beacon right over on Mount Ida. It seems likely that a lower summit on the coast close to Troy would have been the first beacon site, and most likely Beşik Tepeh, the hill directly above the Greek camp. Aeschylus was not working with a map and a ruler but from certain niceties of myth, poetry and drama.[9]

Beacons were even so the likeliest means for taking the crucial news by way of a series of intervisible summits from Troy to Lemnos, Mount Athos, Xiron and Dhirfis on Euboea, Parnon and Pateras in Attica and from there to Profitis Elias; the next beacon was probably on the Larissa at Argos. Using Aeschylus' list, which crosses the Aegean from Ida to distant Athos by way of Lemnos, Quincey has given us a possible sequence, continuing from Mount Athos via Mount Pelion, Mount Othrys, Mount Messapion and Mount Cithaeron to Mount Aigaleos and Arachnaeon and Argos. Aeschylus may have preferred Mount Messapion to the possible summits on Euboea for poetic or dramatic reasons, so that the message returns by way of Aulis, the place where the fleet had mustered ten years earlier. Homer mentions that Agamemnon's eventual arrival home by sea in the Bay of Argos was observed by 'a spy in a watch-tower' posted by Aigisthos. That watch-tower might have been on the Mycenaean acropolis at Nauplion or Tiryns, or even the Larissa at Argos. Mycenae and Tiryns are not intervisible, so Argos, visible from both, was probably routinely used as an intermediate signal station and the signal probably went from Nauplion to Argos, and then to Mycenae.

Even if Aeschylus bent history a little to make a better drama, it is likely that major news of this kind was transmitted by beacons in this way. The method was used in the Byzantine period in Turkey, and within that signalling system an upper limit of 100km between beacons was set. Aeschylus gives us a 130km stage from Ida to Lemnos, which is almost certainly too long a distance, but a stage Beşika Bay to Lemnos is only 70km.[10]

The Mycenaeans might have been expected to launch their ships at once and rush off home, but they did not. They lingered at Beşika Bay, setting off one nation at a time. They knew their kinsmen back in Greece would be expecting them to return with all kinds of treasure, and they actually had very little to show for all their efforts – and all their losses. They were ashamed at how little they had achieved.

The Mycenaeans' voyage home was fraught with difficulties. Several of the Greek royal heroes and commanders were lost, delayed or murdered, which caused serious repercussions in mainland Greece. The problems began in the Greek encampment with Agamemnon and Menelaus disagreeing with each other. Listening to some inner voice, Agamemnon decided to stay on for a time to appease the wrath of Athena. Diomedes and Nestor set sail and returned safely to their homes in Greece. The rest of the Greek fleet, including the ships of Menelaus, set sail and was scattered in a storm. Here we seem to enter the world of legend, because the distances are incredible. The storm is said to have carried Agapenor and the Arcadian fleet to Cyprus, where he founded Paphos. The storm winds carried Menelaus all the way to Egypt, which he reached with five ships, the rest being lost in the storm.[11] The storm at sea shipwrecked Locrian Ajax on the Kapherides rocks, where he was drowned.

Those following Calchas, Leontes and Polypoites travelled overland to Colophon, where Teiresias died. The ghost of Achilles appeared to those following Agamemnon as they were setting sail. It tried to stop them from continuing by prophesying future events.

Neoptolemos made his journey overland through Thrace, where he met Odysseus at Maroneia. Neoptolemos continued on his way after arranging a funeral for Phoinix, who died on the journey, and arrived in the land of the Molossoi, where he was recognized by Peleus.

Then came the safe return of Menelaus to Lacedaemon. Then came the climax of the tragedy, which the story of the Trojan War has now become – a full-blown tragedy – the murder of Agamemnon, on his arrival home at Mycenae, by Aigisthos and Clytemnestra.

The *Odyssey* tells the familiar, long-protracted story of Odysseus' voyage home.

The Fall of Mycenae
Archaeology suggests a grave weakening of the Mycenaean polity, with the Mycenaean civilization collapsing during the twelfth century BC.

At the close of the thirteenth century, barely two generations after the Trojan War, the city of Mycenae fell. The precise circumstances are shrouded in mystery. Behind the fall of Mycenae were huge tensions that were subcontinental in scale. These tensions were given ominously concrete expression a century earlier in the Battle of Kadesh. This major confrontation in Syria was a head-on clash between the armies of the two empires of Egypt and Hatti. The outcome was inconclusive. Sixteen years later Ramesses II and Hattusilis III agreed a peace that included guarantees of mutual aid in case of attack by a third power. That third power might conceivably have been the Mycenaean confederation, or neighbours to the east. But the treaty was short-lived. In 1232 BC Merneptah repulsed an invasion of Egypt by Libyans and 'northerners from all lands'. In 1191 and 1188 Ramesses III defeated invaders from both land and sea; they came from the north-east to settle in the Nile Delta.

At about this time Hattusa, the Hittite capital, was destroyed. Within the century between 1300 and 1200, the balance of power in the Near East had shifted irretrievably. The large-scale tensions experienced in Egypt, Hatti and the Levant were evidently felt by the Mycenaeans too; this was the time when the great fortification walls went up.

Various mechanisms for the collapse of the Mycenaean civilization have been suggested, such as natural disaster, economic collapse, political implosion, revolution, invasion by barbarians.[12]

One possible scenario is that a major earthquake in around 1200 BC caused the destruction at Mycenae and other centres. Great buildings collapsed at Tiryns; the survivors of the disaster built small temporary structures in the citadel, later constructing a well-planned new town outside. Pylos, the Menelaion, Zygouries, Midea and Eutresis were destroyed in 1200 BC and never rebuilt. Other centres like Mycenae and Tiryns were rebuilt and survived only to be destroyed later in the twelfth century.

An alternative possibility is that the Mycenaean centres were attacked by an enemy, one that has left little trace in the archaeological record beyond the destructions themselves. Around 1250 BC, in the aftermath of the Trojan War, there was certainly trouble, and it may have been the beginning of the final phase. Outlying houses at Mycenae were attacked and burned, possibly prompting the massive strengthening of the fortification wall; arrangements were made to ensure a supply of water inside the citadel. Tiryns and Athens expanded their defences at this time. At Pylos, so far there is no evidence for a late fortification wall, but important goods and activities were brought in closer to the centre, and access to the temple-palace was restricted in an attempt to improve security. In around 1200 BC the temple at Pylos and the citadels at Mycenae and Tiryns were all destroyed in conflagrations.

The end of Pylos came in the second generation after Nestor: 'After the end of the war against Ilium, and the death of Nestor after his return home, the expedition of the Dorians and return of the Heraclidae two generations afterwards drove out the descendants of Neleus from Messenia.'[13] If these two generations were each twenty-five years long, the overall life-span for Pylos in

Greek tradition comes to just one hundred years, which is what the archaeology also suggests – 1300–1200 BC.

Coastguards were deployed, which suggests that attack was expected to come from the sea.[14] The temple-palace at Pylos was remarkably empty of portable objects when, one March day, it was destroyed. Even the throne had been taken. Perhaps the building was systematically looted by a raiding party, who stripped it of its valuables before setting it on fire.

Who the attackers were is still a mystery. John Chadwick thought they might have been the Sea Peoples, who were a major threat to the Nile Delta from 1225 BC onwards but, since we do not know who the Sea Peoples were, the problem remains unsolved.[15] In any case inland centres like Mycenae were destroyed, suggesting that internal troubles were the cause rather than attack from the sea. Collapse may have followed in the wake of the Trojan War. Homer comments tellingly, 'Those events [of the Trojan War] were the beginning of the great wave of disaster that was rolling towards Trojans and Danaans alike.'[16] If the Epic Cycle poems give an approximation of what happened to the Mycenaean aristocracy, massive political, social and economic disruption must have ensued. The huge political and social tensions accompanying the struggles for power would have been weakening, and something of this general nature may well have led to Mycenae's fall – and Clytemnestra was not the only queen to be unfaithful during the war.[17] Diomedes' wife Aegialia was unfaithful with Cometes. Idomeneus' wife Meda was unfaithful with Leucus. Odysseus' wife Penelope was besieged by suitors who wanted to usurp the throne of Ithaca.

It is easy to imagine a political coup at a centre like Mycenae being copied at Midea, then other centres, rather like the student unrest of the 1960s. Maybe the civilization was brought down by the Mycenaean underclass, rebelling against its masters.[18] A Mycenaean fortress would have been difficult for a foreign invader to take, especially since the approach roads were watched. But the local community, who would know every inch of the building, its sally-ports, its points of weakness, the footholds on the walls that they would have learnt when playing games as children, would be in a much stronger position to penetrate the fortifications, and probably without arousing suspicion.

Chapter 13

Overview

The games were over now. The gathered armies scattered,
each man to his fast ship, and fighters turned their minds
to thoughts of food and the sweet warm grip of sleep.

(Iliad 24. 1–3)

The story of the Trojan War was a tradition that the later Greeks cherished and elaborated in their literature. On the Greek side, we can assemble a detailed narrative that includes the names of kings and princes and their genealogies, albeit with an unknown amount of poetic licence; we may for instance suspect, as discussed earlier, that the swashbuckling Piyamaradus became 'Achilles'. But the story from the Anatolian side is very different. For a long time it was assumed that no documentary evidence, no specifically Hittite history, of the struggle between Greeks and Trojans had survived. The name of the king of Troy at the time of the attack and the names of his leading military commanders were known from the Epic Cycle account, but not much more.

Recent work, in particular on the archives of the Hittite Great Kings, has shown that rather more can be pieced together about Trojan history from the fragments than was thought a hundred years ago. We now know the approximate extent of the kingdom of Troy, a kingdom called Wilusa, and even the names of three of its kings. Kukkuni and Alaksandu, for instance, are known to have been kings of Troy before the attack, around 1320 and 1280 BC respectively. Walmu was a puppet king installed by the Hittite Great King shortly after the attack, when the Trojan royal dynasty had been wiped out. The shifting relationship between Troy and the Hittite Great Kings can be traced, though very sketchily. Relations between Troy and Hattusa seem to have been unusually friendly for about a hundred years before the Trojan War, in contrast to the turbulent relationships of kingdoms further south. The fact that Wilusa lay on an important route to the west, the route from Hattusa to the Hellespont crossing into Europe, and that Troy itself was very close to that crossing, may have had something to do with it.

Work on the Hittite archive tablets has also revealed that the Mycenaeans were systematically attacking and destabilizing the cities of the west coast of Anatolia for a very long time – not for the ten years of Homer, but for a hundred years or more. Homer turns out not to have exaggerated but to have understated the scale of the war. The Mycenaeans were probing, raiding, plundering and colonizing one location after another along the whole length of the western Anatolian coastline. Both the tablets and the archaeology show this. The archive tablets also reveal that confrontation was dealt with in a fairly sophisticated way, with alternating phases of diplomacy and warfare, which is what we see again and again in the *Iliad*, in episodes such as the exchange of gifts between duellists when sundown brings battle to a close, and Priam's visit to the Greek camp to negotiate the purchase of his son Hector's body for burial.[1]

What is most startling of all is that a very great deal of what we read in the *Iliad* is consistent with the culture and customs of the mid-thirteenth century BC, and with what we now know of the geography of the area at that time. We have been conditioned to see the *Iliad* as a piece of rip-roaring blockbuster fiction from the iron age, with about as much historical accuracy as an old-style Hollywood western, whereas it comes close to being bronze age docu-drama. There are fictional elements, of course, such as the intervention of the gods, but even these passages may be telling us something true about the mindset of the combatants, who almost certainly persuaded themselves that in a very real sense the gods were with them. Ramesses, after all, at Kadesh had shouted, 'Amon is my protector and his hand is with me.'

Archaeology shows that the Trojan culture was advanced and cosmopolitan, eclectic, drawing ideas and practices from a variety of sources, but fundamentally Anatolian in complexion. By 1250 BC Troy was a great city, walled and with an imposing towered citadel, flourishing as an emporium at a major nexus of trading routes at the entrance to the Hellespont. It was by then a rich city and as such an almost inevitable target for greedy and aggressive Mycenaean raiders. Troy was on the fringe of the Hittite Empire, and the Hittite Great King's grasp on the area was uncertain. He courteously acknowledged in the decades leading up to the Mycenaean attack that Wilusa was an autonomous kingdom that from time out of mind had been on friendly terms with the Hittite Great Kings, but also reflected that its recent secession from the Hittite Empire was without precedent. It was an anomaly that, after the attack, one of his successors would rectify by putting a puppet king in place there. It may be that for him the devastating raids by the Mycenaeans on Wilusa were a proof that the Wilusans were unable on their own to manage the north-eastern border of his empire effectively, and justified *his* military intervention. He knew that Wilusa was a chariot power, the bronze age equivalent of a nuclear power, and between 1280 and 1250 the Hittite Great King may have been ready to take on trust the Wilusans' ability to defend the

Troad against invasion, but events proved that they after all needed the backing of the Great King's armies.

Archaeology, and in particular the major breakthroughs made in the course of Manfred Korfmann's Troia Project, also throws new light on the attack on Troy. The finds at Beşika Bay show that this was the likeliest location for the Mycenaean base – a small sheltered sandy bay on an otherwise exposed cliff coast. As we have seen, many other elements of the narrative as told in the Epic Cycle fall into place once this is accepted. A trial excavation in the valley connecting the Bay of Beşika and the Plain of Troy might one day reveal traces of the defensive ditch described in the *Iliad*.[2]

In ancient Greece, the Trojan War was presented as a victory for the Greeks. Troy had been overcome; Helen had been recovered and reunited with Menelaus; the House of Priam had been annihilated. But it was also presented as a very dark, bloody and destructive episode. The victory of the Greeks was a pyrrhic victory, a victory at too great a price. It took too long, too much energy, too many lives, and it strained the confederation. The leading Mycenaean commanders, Agamemnon and Achilles, were at odds with one another from the beginning. The moment Troy fell, the Mycenaeans seem to have fallen apart. The fleet under the commander-in-chief Agamemnon returned, piecemeal, to Greece. Yet even then the tragedy was not over.

Many Greek heroes were killed or prevented in some other way from returning home. Agamemnon reached the safety of his home, in the citadel at Mycenae, only to be murdered there by a usurper as soon as he arrived. For the Trojans, the destruction was on an even greater scale. King Priam was killed during the sack of Troy, all his sons were killed and the city walls were slighted. The collateral damage was also large in scale. The Trojan women were taken captive, to add degradation to the misery of their bereavement. Andromache, Hector's widow, had lost her husband, her father, her father-in-law, her son Astyanax and her seven brothers when she was taken as a prize of war by the Greeks; Andromache encapsulated the pity of war.

Troy put up far more resistance to the attack than the Greeks had expected. The towns on the Gulf of Edremit had been taken relatively easily, but Troy itself had proved very hard to capture. Even after the victory, the Greeks failed to take control of the Hellespont. They did not consolidate their victory by taking over the city of Troy and running it as a Mycenaean emporium. The war was a war of attrition and by its close both the Trojans and the Greeks were exhausted.[3]

> How blind you are,
> You tramplers down of cities! You who cast
> Temples to desolation and lay waste
> Tombs, the untrodden sanctuaries where lie
> The ancient dead – yourselves so soon to die![4]

The attack on Troy was but one in a long sequence of raids by Mycenaeans on Anatolian ports. The attack on Troy may have been remembered with a particular poignancy by the Greeks because it was the *last* of those foreign adventures. The Trojan War became inflated and highly coloured by nostalgia, because immediately afterwards the Mycenaean centres went into decline and the ruling dynasties destroyed themselves by feuding.[5]

As we have seen during the course of this book, the Trojan War can be seen as an integral part of an ambitious, large-scale Mycenaean outreach across the Aegean Sea and beyond. The Mycenaeans were making a grab for territories the Hittite kings no longer had any certainty in controlling because they were preoccupied with problems to the east. It was an episode in an interplay between Mycenaean and Hittite interests that stretched all along the intricate west coast of Anatolia. Letters from the Hittite king to the Mycenaean high king show a complicated late bronze age power struggle, with local Anatolian loyalties pulled first one way then another. Priam, Paris and Hector were perhaps little more than pawns in this larger war-game.

The Trojan War can be reconstructed on different scales. There is a notional minimal attack, which would really have been little more than a casual attack with a small force of perhaps 10 ships and 1,000 men; this would have been one opportunist raid amongst a hundred such raids on coastal towns round the Aegean. There is also a notional maximal attack, which takes the numbers given or implied in the *Iliad* at face value. This was a very large-scale enterprise involving 1,186 ships and perhaps 130,000 Mycenaean warriors. Both historians and bards in antiquity were prone to exaggeration. The army of 36,000 Hittites that the Egyptians claimed to have fought against at Kadesh may have been an exaggeration; it is thought that the force of Hittites is more likely to have numbered 20,000, and that it was met by a similar force of Egyptian and allied warriors. Troy is unlikely to have unleashed armies as large as those mustered for Kadesh. The Hittite Great King was calling up contingents from all over Anatolia to swell his army, whereas the king of Wilusa could only call on his near neighbours in north-west Anatolia for help. On balance, it seems most likely that the Greek force consisted of fifty to a hundred ships and between 5,000 and 10,000 men and that the Trojan and allied force also numbered between 5,000 and 10,000 men.

The action described in the *Iliad* races by in what might have been a matter of days. The battles are described as taking place 'end-on', one after another, and this obviously makes for good dramatic narrative (see Chapter 11). In reality, there may have been pauses between the battles lasting for days or weeks, and the physical demands of fighting might well have made these rests essential. The overall length of the core attack, as described in the *Iliad*, might have been anything between a fortnight and an entire summer.

In later antiquity, the Trojan War was seen as the most glamorous of all the military adventures. It was seen as a mark of great distinction to have one's city or kingdom associated with the war. Pausanias emphasized what a great honour it was to the Arcadians, land-locked and shipless, even many centuries after the event, to have taken part.[6] It was a part of proto-history that gave the kingdom its national identity and was a great source of pride, as well as a rich brew of other emotions. There is a strange and telling story about Pythagoras staying in Argos in the sixth century BC, and being overwhelmed with emotion when he saw, nailed to the wall of the temple at the Argive Heraion, a shield that had been brought back to Greece as part of the spoils of Troy. The Argives who were with him at the time asked him why he was weeping, and he said that he himself had carried that shield in the land of Troy, as Euphorbus. The Argives thought he was mad, but he told them that if they took down the shield from the wall they would find an inscription inside it – 'of Euphorbus'. They did, and Pythagoras was right.[7] Presumably Pythagoras was overcome by a kind of hysteria, the irrational desire to have been present at some momentous historic event before one's own lifetime. It is akin to Shakespeare's evocative re-creation of the feelings of medieval Englishmen about Agincourt. The men who fought at Agincourt were legends, and those who missed it would forever regret it.

> And gentlemen in England, now abed,
> Shall think themselves accurs'd, they were not here,
> And hold their manhoods cheap, whiles any speaks
> That fought with us upon Saint Crispin's day.[8]

There was even an Agincourt Roll of Honour, listing the names of the 1,200 gentlemen who took part; for the Troy campaign it was Homer who recorded the final Roll of Honour.[9]

The deeds of valour performed in front of the walls of Troy set a benchmark for warriors ever afterwards. The great warriors to whom these deeds were, rightly or wrongly, attributed became icons of bravery that soldiers down the ages have tried to live up to, tried and too often failed to match. The names of Ajax, Hector and Achilles have resonated down the centuries as synonyms for patriotic bravery; they became the ultimate role models for generation after generation of young men. The reckless gesture, the risking all for glory – these were the archetypes that were to become the legacy of the Trojan War. But, above all, what makes the Trojan War the father of all wars is the fact that the Mycenaeans paid too great a price for their victory. Strabo's apt comment was that 'the captors, as it happened, carried off only a Cadmean victory'.[10]

The Trojans, to judge from the poetic tradition of the Epic Cycle and from the archaeology, suffered very badly from their defeat. The city and its citadel were sacked; most of the mudbrick ramparts of the citadel were knocked down; many of the inhabitants were killed; the family of King Priam was purged out of existence. Aeneas led the Dardanians, who were the Trojans' nearest neighbours and stoutest allies, but there was no love lost between Aeneas and

Priam. Aeneas thought that, in spite of his bravery, Priam did not honour him at all.[11] This may have been a factor in Aeneas' decision to leave the Trojans to their fate as the siege closed in on them. 'Forever angered', Aeneas may have thought Priam deserved a crushing defeat. Ironically, it was, according to the Greek tradition, Aeneas who succeeded Priam as king of Troy. There were no sons of Priam left to succeed. The Priamidae were an extinct dynasty. But the grandfather of Aeneas, Assaracus, was the brother of Priam's grandfather, Ilus, so Aeneas inherited the throne of Troy. There was a later tradition that the 'Phrygians' to the east gained some sort of control over Wilusa.[12]

It would not be long before the long arm of the Hittite Great King reached out to intervene. In 1223 BC, Tudhaliyas IV wrote to the king of the Seha River Land to say that he envisaged a military expedition to install Walmu as king of Wilusa. With a puppet on the Wilusan throne, he might regain control of Wilusa. Even more significantly, this letter is the last in the Hittite royal archives to mention the Mycenaeans. From now on they were a spent force as far as Anatolia was concerned.[13]

> Muse, be near me now, and make
> A strange song for Ilion's sake,
> Till the sound of tears be about my ears
> And out of my lips a music break
> For Troy, Troy, and the end of the years
> When the wheels of the Greeks above me pressed
> And the mighty horse-hoofs beat my breast.[14]

The Trojans had lost the war in every way thinkable. Their rich and sophisticated capital city had been overrun and ransacked; their citadel had been slighted; their best warriors had been killed; their women had been taken as slaves; their aristocratic élite had been wiped out; their king and his many sons were all dead; the Priamidae were replaced by a Dardanian dynasty, shortly afterwards to be replaced by a puppet king set up by the Hittite high king. The Trojans lost and vanished. The Mycenaeans too lost and vanished. The victory of the Mycenaeans over the Trojans was the ultimate hollow victory, a multiple tragedy, and as such it became for ever after the archetype of the tragedy of war.

The Kings at the Time of the Trojan War

(NB All the dates given below are approximate.)

Hittite Great Kings: Third Hittite Dynasty

Tudhaliyas II	1460–1440
Arnuwandas I	1440–1420
Hattusilis II	1420–1400
Tudhaliyas III	1400–1380
Suppiluliumas I	1380–1334
Arnuwandas II	1334–1333
Mursilis II	1333–1308
Muwatallis	1308–1285
Urhi-Teshub (Mursilis III)	1285–1278
Hattusilis III	1278–1250
Tudhaliyas IV	1250–1220
Arnuwandas III	1220–1200
Suppiluliumas II	1200–1180

Kings of Wilusa

From Epic Cycle and Greek tradition*		Known from Hittite archives	
Teucer	1340–1320	*Kukunni*	1340–1320
Dardanus (son-in-law)	1320–1300		
Erichthonius (son)	1300–1290	*Alaksandu*	1300–1280
Tros (son)	1290–1280		
Ilus (son)	1280–1270		
Laomedon (son)	1270–1260	*Parhuitta*	1270–1260
Priam (son)	1260–1250		
Aeneas (second cousin)	1250–		
		Walmu	1223–

* Diodorus Siculus 4. 75

Kings of Mycenae

Perseus	1300–1290
Elektryon (son of Perseus)	1290–1285
Sthenelos (son of Perseus)	1285–1280
Eurystheus (son of Perseus)	1280–1275
Atreus (son of Pelops)	1275–1260
Thyestes (brother of Atreus)	1260–1250
Agamemnon (son of Atreus)	1250–1240
Aigisthos (usurper)	1240–1232
Orestes (son of Agamemnon)	1232–1220
Tisamenos (son of Orestes)	1220–1200

Note: These dates are no more than guesses; the king list is itself traditionary.

Appendix 2
The Tumuli

One of the most famous of the large tumuli around the Plain of Troy is the 'Tomb of Ajax', which originally stood on the seashore well to the north of Troy near Cape Rhoeteum. Pausanias reported that the seaward side had been eroded and the waves had exposed a human skeleton buried within. The Emperor Hadrian rescued the remains of 'Ajax' and reburied them under a huge and stately barrow, called In Tepeh, on higher ground. Hadrian raised a temple on the new barrow (Lucan, *Phars.* 9. 961–79). The statue of Ajax that Hadrian mounted on top of that had a remarkable history; it was stolen by Mark Antony, who took it to Egypt, and later brought back again to Troy by Augustus. The masonry was robbed out by the Turks, but Schliemann saw what he thought were the mutilated remains of the statue in the riverbank of the In Tepeh Asmak just below the barrow. When Schliemann excavated what remained of the original tomb, a mound by then reduced to one metre high, he found only pebbles inside.

The equally famous 'Tomb of Achilles', located symmetrically on the opposite headland, was also excavated in the nineteenth century, but before Schliemann's arrival. In the centre were found a cist grave one metre square, containing pottery, ash, charcoal and human bones. This looks full of promise as the potential burial place of a great Greek or Trojan from the late bronze age, until we read that the remains were accompanied by a sword – made of iron (Schliemann 1881, 654). The adjacent 'Tomb of Patroklos' was excavated by Frank Calvert, who found nothing in it (Schliemann 1881, 656).

Pasha Tepeh was excavated by Sophia Schliemann in 1873. She sank a shaft through the centre of the mound, reaching solid limestone only 4m below the surface. All she found was some pottery dating from after the time of the Trojan War, though possibly that represented a secondary use (Schliemann 1881, 658).

It is quite common for prehistoric barrows to contain sequences of burials and continue in use as burial places over long periods.

High on the hill to the south-west of the Plain of Troy is the 15m high mound known as Ujek Tepeh. The locals believed it was the tomb of Elijah.

When Schliemann had a shaft dug into its centre he found the bedrock 14m down. Within the mound was a rectangular tower 4.5m square and 12m high, apparently dating from the fifth century BC, though Schliemann thought it was the monument built by Caracalla in AD 215 in honour of his lover Festus. Again, the barrow may have had several uses over a long period.

The tumulus immediately to the north of the Greek camp site, Beşik Tepeh, is in many ways the most interesting of them all. It also stands about 15m high and measures 80m in diameter. It has also been named as the Tomb of Achilles. The pottery found inside the mound was not local ware. It was completely different from the pottery found at Troy, but was imported, and this is consistent with the mound being a Mycenaean monument.

Some of the tumuli had burials in them, but most seem to have been built at various times in antiquity as cenotaphs, memorials to the dead rather than actual tombs. Without more evidence it is impossible to say whether any of the barrows was raised by the Mycenaeans or Trojans to honour the dead of the Trojan War (Schliemann 1881, 648–68). Certainly commemorative mounds were raised in the late bronze age. Homer mentions that Menelaus raised a monumental mound to Agamemnon in Egypt (*Odyssey* 4. 584). Patroklos appeared to Achilles in a dream, asking that their bones should be buried together in the same mound (*Iliad* 23. 83–91). Hector too was buried in an urn that was placed under a mound (*Iliad* 24. 664–5; Schuchhardt 1891, 83–7).

It should be said, in passing, that the mound to the north of Troy traditionally identified as the Tumulus of Ilus, often referred to in the *Iliad* as a landmark on the Plain of Troy, is not a tumulus at all. Schliemann rightly pointed out that it is nothing more than a natural mound of sand, and his sketchmap clearly shows that it is part of a large sand dune that forms the site of the village of Koum Kioi; it has simply become separated from the rest of the sand dune by the Scamander, which has broken across the northern end of the dune (Schliemann 1881, 82, 83, 669). The mound immediately to the south of the city of Troy, and not far outside its Scaean Gate, has a better claim to being the Tomb of Ilus repeatedly mentioned in the *Iliad*.

The traditional Tomb of Ilus was part of a natural sand dune, and there were several other sand dunes scattered about the plain. (The dunes show up well on Spratt's map.) Although not especially high, they would have made useful vantage points, strong points for infantry that could not be overrun in a chariot charge. The Trojans would of course have known the location and individual characteristics of these hillocks well, which gave them a distinct advantage over the Greeks. The Greeks' advantage was that they greatly outnumbered the Trojans.

Notes

Chapter 1: Introduction
1. Anon 2001 Excavating Troy. http://www.iit.edu/~agunsal/truva/ exc.html.
2. It is interesting to reflect that when King Arthur lived Troy was still a living city, though only just. Arthur was defeated at the Battle of Camlan in AD 537 and died in 542 or 546, by coincidence at just the time when Troy was abandoned (Castleden 2000, 211).
3. *Iliad* 5. 744–8; Hiller 1991.
4. Hood 1995.
5. Vermeule 1986.
6. Hood 1995.
7. Byron, *Don Juan*, stanza 101.

Chapter 2: The Evidence
1. Wood 1985, 144.
2. Leaf 1915; Dörpfeld 1902.
3. A. H. Sayce, writing in 1884, quoted in Wood 1985, 92–3.
4. Blegen 1950–8; Blegen 1963.
5. Blegen and Rawson 1966; Ventris and Chadwick 1973; Chadwick 1987.
6. Castleden 2005.
7. Sperling 1991.
8. Wood 1985, 230–1 argues for 1260 BC as the date for the Trojan War. Although there is room for negotiation on the exact date, it is certainly the case that a date around 1250 BC ± 10 years creates the fewest problems.
9. e.g. Kayan 1991, 1995, 1997.

Chapter 3: Troy
1. *Iliad* 7. 90–100.
2. *Iliad* 13. 12–19.
3. *Iliad* 13. 12–19; 20. 252–3; 24. 795–820.
4. Spratt's nineteenth-century map shows a south-westward current flowing through the Hellespont with a speed of two knots; the Hellespont is, in a sense, the outfall of the River Danube.
5. Wood 1985, 234.
6. Ibid.
7. Ibid., 140.
8. 'The whole of this plain is a deposit of the rivers – I mean the plain by the sea in the front of the city; so that if the distance between the sea and the city is now twelve stadia, it must have been no more than half as great at that time' (Strabo 13. 1. 36).
9. Traill 2000, 189–90.
10. Kayan 1997.

11. Strabo 13. 1. 36. His six stadia are roughly one kilometre.
12. Kayan 1995.
13. The north coast of the Plain of Troy is fairly straight, and could not be accurately described as a bay. For the Scamander to have had its outfall in a broad bay, in either Homer's or Priam's day, the coastline must have been further south. Environmental studies suggest that in the late bronze age it was 5km further south, forming a substantial bay up to 3km wide.
14. Fields 2004, 21.
15. Ibid., 36–7.
16. Ibid., 31–3.
17. Ibid., 31–3.
18. Ibid., 40.
19. Gurney 1990, 92–3. It is impossible to tell whether the Mycenaean architects were copying the Trojans or vice versa, as Tower H at Troy and the Lion Gate bastion at Mycenae cannot be dated any more closely than 1260–1250 BC. It is more likely that both were copying the tower/bastion idea from the Hittite metropolis, Hattusa. The King's Gate at Hattusa has a single bastion projecting on one side (see the plan in Macqueen 1986, 68).
20. *Iliad* 6. 434.
21. Wood 1985, 236. Blegen's idea of a monolith as a plinth for a statue is reminiscent of the plinth for Blegen's own memorial bust outside the entrance to the Museum at Chora, near Pylos, one of a pair with Spyridon Marinatos, though I imagine Blegen would not have known this.
22. For more on the idea of continuity of sanctity at Mycenaean sites, see Castleden 2005, 176–82.
23. Fields 2004, 23–4.
24. Page 1959.
25. The absence of the Trojan élite is easily understood in contemporary bronze age terms: the men were probably killed and the women abducted.
26. The West Gate is located in survey square v11 in Korfmann 1998, w10 in Troia 1998.
27. Easton et al. 2002.
28. Mannsperger 1993.
29. Calvert 1881.
30. *Iliad* 10. 496–7.

Chapter 4: The Greeks
1. *Iliad* 2. 584–863.
2. Gurney 1990, 47.
3. *Iliad* 2. 180.
4. *Odyssey* 23. 180.
5. Taylour 1983, 152.
6. Lolos 1998, 31.
7. Mee 1988, 301–5. By 1320, the great Minoan trading operation was over (Castleden 1998, 128).
8. Kilian 1988, 149–51.
9. Cunliffe 1998, 242–3.
10. Mee 1988, 301–5.
11. Gurney 1990, 21; 42–3.
12. Most books refer to the high status building as a 'palace'. I have argued elsewhere that the so-called palaces of the Minoans and Mycenaeans were really temples (e.g. Castleden 1989, 70–95; 1990, 79–84, 145–52; 1998, 137–47; 2005, 161–82).
13. Dickinson 1994, 89.
14. Mylonas 1983, 59.
15. Dickinson 1994, 88.
16. Prag and Neave 1999, 134–5.
17. Palmer 1961, 231; Wood 1985, 218–19.

Chapter 5: The Trojans
1. Bryce 2002, 188–91.
2. Gurney 1990, 53.
3. Ibid., 54.
4. Bryce 2002, 12–25.
5. Ibid., 32–43.
6. Ibid., 38–9.
7. Gurney 1990, 68–9.
8. Bryce 2002, 51–2.
9. Gurney 1990, 99–106.
10. Latacz 2001, 67–93.
11. Bryce 2002, 73–8.
12. Ibid., 134–50. There were doubtless ceremonies surrounding the donation of such adornments as rich clothing, necklaces and other jewellery. Hecuba chooses the longest and most richly decorated dress as a gift for the goddess and goes to the Temple of Athena to present it (*Iliad* 6. 347–8). Homer may well have been describing a Mycenaean practice: it was certainly a Minoan practice and the Mycenaeans borrowed many customs from the Minoans. The temple treasure at Knossos included faience dresses, offerings of token dresses to the goddess. There is also a seal impression showing a priestess or worshipper carrying a flounced dress, perhaps as a gift for the goddess, perhaps actually to dress the wooden idol of the goddess (Castleden 1990, 116). Practices like this were part of the later, classical system too, and incredibly elaborate ceremonies surrounded the periodic presentation of new vestments to the goddess. Homer tells us that they were part of the system in the eighth century BC, or remembered through oral tradition from earlier. We know they were part of the Minoan system; so it is very likely that they were part of the Mycenaean system in between. It is also clear from the description in the *Iliad* that a seated statue was intended; you could not leave a dress on the knees of a *standing* figure. Strabo (13. 1. 41) argues the case for a seated statue of Athena well.
13. Ibid., 211–15; Macqueen 1986, 150.
14. Gurney 1990, 159–61.
15. Ibid., 27.
16. Some have suggested that Wilusa extended significantly further south, as far as the Caicos valley.
17 e.g. Starke 1996; Hawkins 1998; Korfmann 1999; Niemeier 1999; Latacz 2001; Lehmann (interviewed in *Die Welt* on 27 October 2001).
18. Leaf 1912, 165–6.
19. Wood 1985, 240.
20. Strabo 13. 1. 52–3; Leaf 1912, 176–7.
21. *Iliad* 24, 636–8.
22. Drews 1993, 106.
23. Fields 2004, 25.

Chapter 6: The Expedition Begins
1. Castleden 2005, 242–5.
2. Later Ionia was equivalent to the coastlands of the Lukka Lands and southern Arzawa, including Miletus and Ephesus.
3. Wood 1985, 167.
4. *Iliad* 20. 193.
5. *Iliad* 28. 346.
6. Wood 1985, 159.
7. Dickinson 1994, 143; Symeonoglou 1973; Castleden 2005, 102, 117.
8. Wood 1985, 248–9.
9. Wood 1985, 248.

Chapter 7: The War according to Contemporary Sources
1. This was evidently an attempt by the eighth-century poet to explain the absence of any visible trace of the defences at the time when he was writing.

2. They were all dead.
3. 'Sacred Ilium' was probably the citadel of Troy, where the city's main shrines and temples would have been located.
4. This confirms that the ships were beached near the open sea, rather than in the still waters of the Bay of Troy.
5. An earthquake? Hades was afraid that Poseidon and his earthquakes might split open the ground.
6. This suggests that the river channels were slightly entrenched.
7. This again suggests a location out on the open coast, not in the sheltered, enclosed Bay of Troy.
8. The Pergamos is another name for the citadel of Troy.
9. Castleden 2005, 245.
10. This implies that there was a more established Mycenaean settlement on Lesbos, with shrines to Mycenaean gods.
11. Castleden 2005, 246.
12. Leaf 1912, 253. There is of course an inherent weakness in this argument. The Epic Cycle poems incorporate detail that the hearer was intended to recognize, such as the ford on the Scamander, the oak tree by the gate, and so on. The story may have included these details from the bronze age, from the start, or it may be that Homer and other bards added them in for verisimilitude, to make the story more plausible (Leaf 1912, 8–9). The oak could have been standing in Hector's day, or Homer's – we have no way of knowing, and unfortunately even archaeology cannot resolve this particular puzzle.
13. This is the not the place to go over the Ahhiyawa controversy in detail. Those interested should refer to Forrer 1924, Friedrich 1929, Wood 1985, Castleden 2005. For our purposes, it is worth noting that although there are dissenters, many scholars today believe that Forrer was right, that Ahhiya (or Ahhiyawa) was Achaea (or Mycenaean Greece) and the Ahhiyans were the Mycenaeans.
14. Gurney 1990, 21–2.
15. Cline 1996.
16. Hansen 1997.
17. Sommer 1932, 275–94; Houwink ten Cate 1974, 149. The statues were probably clay idols like the ones found in the Mycenae Cult Centre; they were certainly portable enough to be transported to Hattusa.
18. That long-standing impasse could be resolved relatively easily, in fact. The technology is available to create identical replicas of the sculptures; indeed, as a goodwill gesture the British government could provide one lightweight set made in fibreglass to mount on the Parthenon and another in stone to exhibit in the museum. The Parthenon would be restored; the originals would remain safe; the issue of the original theft could be shelved; honour would be satisfied – and all for a fraction of the cost of a foreign war.
19. Gurney 1990, 38–9.
20. Wood (1985, 182) suggests that he was a royal Arzawan.
21. Gurney 1990, 40–2.
22. King Hattusilis III according to Gurney 1990, 41 and Wood 1985, 180.
23. Gurney 1990, 40–1, 43.
24. Wood 1985, 183–4.
25. Ibid., 178.
26. Macqueen 1986, 40. The hostility of the land of Arzawa is known from the tablets. King Unhazitis of Arzawa made war on Hatti in alliance with the Greeks; the Arzawan royal family had to flee to Greece when they were defeated (Wood 1985, 180).
27. Wood 1985, 179.
28. Gurney 1990, 45–6.
29. Ibid., 46.
30. Ibid., 47.
31. Wood 1985, 205.
32. Ibid., 177; Bennet 1999, 11–30.
33. The background for this account of Anatolian affairs comes from Gurney 1990, Macqueen 1986, Bryce 2002.

34. Thucydides, *History of the Peloponnesian War* 1. 9. 2, has Pelops father of Atreus originating in 'Asia'. Pindar, *Ol.* 1. 24, speaks of 'Lydian Pelops'. Pausanias 5. 1. 7 mentions 'Pelops the Lydian who crossed over from Asia'.
35. Latacz 2001.
36. Lang 1995.
37. Anderson 1995.
38. Leaf 1912.
39. Nilsson 1933, 26.
40. Wilamowitz-Moellendorf 1927.
41. MacKendrick 1962, 58.
42. Hawkins 1998.
43. Bryce 2002, 267.

Chapter 8: Arms, Armour and Tactics
1. Snodgrass 1999, 18–19; *Iliad* 10. 261–5.
2. Lorimer 1950.
3. Schliemann 1881, 473, 512–13. It is very unclear from Schliemann's account to which phase of Troy the two skeletons and the helmets they were wearing belong; they were apparently found about 8m underneath the remains of the classical Temple of Athena. Schliemann's account places them in Troy III, but possibly only because of their depth.
4. *Iliad* 13. 856–7, 869–70.
5. *Iliad* 4. 327–9.
6. *Iliad* 14. 31–103.
7. *Iliad* 14. 156–62. Diomedes made the proposal, and the other leaders agreed.
8. Papadopoulos 1979; Castleden 2005, 70–1, 72.
9. Taylour 1983, 116–18; Cunliffe 1998, 298, 301.
10. Schofield and Parkinson 1994.
11. *Iliad* 15. 783–8.
12. Mylonas 1983, 53.
13. Dickinson 1994, 99.
14. *Iliad* 4. 616; 5. 713–14; 6. 82–3; 17. 68; 17. 139–40; 22. 443.
15. Pausanias 2. 17; *Iliad* 17. 1.
16. Snodgrass 1999, 19–20.
17. Lorimer 1950.
18. *Iliad* 7. 252–8.
19. *Iliad* 15. 742.
20. *Iliad* 5. 334.
21. Snodgrass 1999, 32.
22. Lorimer 1950, 133. The shield types described in the *Iliad* could all have been used on the Plain of Troy in 1250 BC. One glaring anachronism in the *Iliad* is the reference to a bronze helmet with 'great blank hollow eyes' (*Iliad* 11. 413). No late bronze age helmet had eye-holes. This is a description of the Corinthian type of helmet, which had integral cheek-pieces sweeping forward and almost enclosing the eyes and nose, a type not made until around 750 BC at the earliest. Homer might well have known Corinthian helmets, but the heroes he was writing about could not have worn them.
23. This is one historical detail that the film *Troy* got right.
24. Hood 1978, 77.
25. Snodgrass 1999, 24.
26. Crouwel and Morel 1981.
27. Castleden 2005, 200.
28. Crouwel and Morel 1981. The young Winston Churchill, who desperately wanted to be noticed, similarly chose to ride a white horse.
29. Crouwel and Morel 1981.
30. Gurney 1990, 86.
31. Wood 1985, 248.
32. Crouwel and Morel 1981.
33. Castleden 2005, 246.

34. *Odyssey* 4. 265–74; 8. 487–520; 11. 523–32.
35. Pliny, *Historia Naturalis* 7. 202.
36. Pausanias 23.
37. *Iliad* 15. 783–8.
38. Fields 2004, 52–3.
39. Gurney 1990, 149, quoting the Akkadian text of the legend of the Siege of Urshu: 'Make a battering-ram in the Hurrian manner and let it be brought into place. Begin to heap up earth ... We will bring a tower and a battering-ram.'
40. *Iliad* 15. 783–8.
41. Schliemann 1881, 473, 512–13.
42. Gurney 1990, Plates 2 and 4. There is also a scene showing two long-haired Hittite spies being beaten by Egyptian 'skinheads' in the run-up to the Battle of Kadesh (Lehmann 1977, 239). In several places in the *Iliad*, the Greek warriors too are described as having long hair: 'long-haired Achaeans' is one of Homer's stock phrases. It looks as if both Mycenaeans and Trojans wore their hair long.
43. *Iliad* 3. 430.
44. *Iliad* 3. 393, 428–9.
45. Gurney 1990, Plates 2 and 4; Macqueen 1986, 63.
46. Macqueen 1986, 64.
47. Gurney 1990, 174, Plate 28.
48. Schliemann 1881, 605; Fields 2004, 24.
49. Schliemann 1881, 604.
50. Macqueen 1986, 59–60; Gurney 1990, 88; Schliemann 1881, 505.
51. Schliemann 1881, 603.
52. Macqueen 1986, 59–60, 126.
53. Fields 2004, 25.
54. Macqueen 1986, 153. The original text runs: *Nesas waspas, Nesas waspas / tiya-mu, tiya. / Nu-mu annas-mas katta arnut; / tiya-mu, tiya.*
55. Macqueen 1986, frontispiece.
56. Gurney 1990, Plate 3.
57. Latacz 2001.
58. Gurney 1990, 88.
59. *Iliad* 7. 395.

Chapter 9: The Landing

1. Leaf 1912, 384–9; Strabo 13. 1. 31; Pliny, *Historia Naturalis* 5. 88.
2. Kayan 1991.
3. *Iliad* 12. 140–1. Brigitte Mannsperger (1998) argues that the 'left-hand' gate was designed to accommodate returning chariots, because when horses are in flight they tend to veer to the left. Her sketch plan nevertheless shows that the 'left-hand' gate was to the horses' right as they came in from the Plain of Troy, so her argument, though intriguing, is self-defeating.
4. Sperling 1991.
5. Ibid.
6. *Iliad* 2. 552–3, 556–7.
7. Gurney 1990, 89.
8. *Iliad* 23. 126.
9. Korfmann 1985.
10. Fields 2004, 11–12.

Chapter 10: The Attack on Troy: a Minimal Reconstruction

1. Gurney 1990, 89.
2. Ibid.
3. Pausanias 2. 6. 25.
4. Gurney 1990, 145.
5. *Iliad* 7. 69, 80–1.

6. *Iliad* 5. 638–42; 14, 250–1.
7. Diodorus 4. 32. 2; Apollodorus 2. 6. 4.
8. Fields 2004, 48.
9. *Iliad* 9. 129, 271.
10. Bramston, Revd James, *The Art of Politicks*, 1729.

Chapter 11: The Attack on Troy: a Maximal Reconstruction

1. *Kypria* 41–50; Castleden 2005, 244.
2. *Ilioupersis* 21; Castleden 2005, 246.
3. Davis 1988, 54–6; Herodotus 2. 119.
4. *Kypria* 51.
5. *Kypria* 56–7.
6. Fox, T. *The Battle of Kadesh, Part II.* www.touregypt.net/featurestories/kadesh.htm.
7. Gurney 1990, 36.
8. Carpenter (1966) argued that the two expeditions described in the *Kypria* are doublets or variant narratives of a single event, re-tellings of essentially the same story, but it is easy to see that the Mycenaeans had much to gain by attacking southern Wilusa and disabling several actual and potential allies before they attacked Troy itself. Disentangling this question is difficult, because after the Mycenaean period the Greeks arrived to colonize Aeolia, the region south of the Gulf of Edremit known in Mycenaean times as the Seha River Land. Later Greek storytellers may well have confused several different expeditions from Greece across to the Anatolian coast east of Lesbos.
9. *Iliad* 2. 788; 6. 494.
10. Pausanias 8. 45. 7.
11. *Iliad* 23. 917–20.
12. *Iliad* 6. 426; 1. 369.
13. *Iliad* 6. 414–20.
14. *Iliad* 16. 153.
15. *Iliad* 23. 917–20. Achilles pulled rank in order to take the iron shot from Pelides.
16. *Iliad* 20. 219–22.
17. *Iliad* 6. 500–2.
18. *Iliad* 21. 98–100.
19. Leaf 1912, 199–200.
20. *Iliad* 9. 155.
21. Leaf 1912, 249–50.
22. *Iliad* 24. 543–5; Diodorus Siculus 5. 81. 4.
23. Mason 2004.
24. Pausanias 3. 2. 1.
25. *Iliad* 11. 735–6.
26. *Iliad* 1. 217–18.
27. *Iliad* 6. 427; 21. 78–80.
28. Leaf 1912, 267–9.
29. *Kypria* 38–9.
30. Leaf 1912, 278–96.
31. Ibid., 320–1.
32. Ibid., 322.
33. *Iliad* 23. 794.
34. *Iliad* 10. 501–3.
35. *Iliad* 21. 49–51.
36. Leaf 1912, 318.
37. *Iliad* 18. 333–7.
38. The nineteenth-century maps of the area show springs in the hills close to Beşika Bay.
39. *Iliad* 1. 57–61.
40. *Iliad* 2. 118–28.
41. Fields 2004, 17.

42. *Iliad* 2. 921–89.
43. *Iliad* 4. 340–1. Homer specifically describes a front line of chariots with infantry close behind.
44. Gurney 1990, 90.
45. Ibid., 95.
46. In the *Iliad*, the burial mound is to be developed into a defensive wall, but this would be contrary to any known practice. It is far more likely that the burial and the defence works were separate projects. The rampart is described as a stone wall, but a structure like this could not have been erected quickly; it is more likely that the ad hoc fortification consisted of an earth bank and a fronting ditch, and that this structure was built in the days before the fighting started.
47. Castleden 2005, 97–102.
48. *Iliad* 23. 267–85; 24. 919–44; Gurney 1990, 140.
49. *Iliad* 13. 154–62; Diodorus Siculus 16. 3. 2.
50. Later, when the siege was over, the gods destroyed the wall by turning against it all the united waters of the rivers running down from Ida to the sea (Rhesus, Heptarus, Caresus, Rhodius, Granicus, Aesepus, Scamander, Simois). For nine days, it was said, they flowed together at one outlet in unceasing rain before returning to their channels. This is probably an eighth-century BC attempt to explain the absence of any visible remains of the Greek defences at the expected location at that time. The flood scenario is geomorphologically impossible; this is not a description of a real event.
51. Homer developed this story of single combat to an absurd length, with Achilles chasing Hector right round the walls of Troy three times before Hector would fight him. Although individual duels probably took place, they could scarcely have taken place on this scale in the context of a battle between two armies.
52. *Iliad* 12. 180–7.

Chapter 12: The Fall of Troy and its Aftermath
1. Macqueen 1986, 128.
2. Pausanias 8. 46. 2.
3. It is mentioned in the lost *Ilioupersis*. It appeared in Euripides' *Trojan Women*, where the captive women listen to the thunderous noise of the towers of Troy being knocked down, and which Hecuba thinks sounds like an earthquake. Aeschylus too mentions the walls of Troy being 'dug down' and 'overturned'.
4. Fields 2004, 25.
5. Ibid., 37.
6. Ibid., 25.
7. Schliemann 1880, 147.
8. Steffen and Lolling 1884.
9. Quincey 1964.
10. Ibid.
11. Pausanias 8. 5. 2.
12. Castleden 2005, 218–25.
13. Pausanias 4. 3.
14. Palmer 1961; Chadwick 1987.
15. Chadwick 1976, 192.
16. *Odyssey* 8. 82–3.
17. Mylonas 1983, 249.
18. Taylour 1983, 161; Crossland and Birchall 1974, 13.

Chapter 13: Overview
1. *Iliad* 7. 344–51; 24. 382–562.
2. *Iliad* 7. 505–11.
3. Caskey 1964.
4. The collective anguish was vividly re-created by Aeschylus in *The Trojan Women*.

5. Mycenae has a destruction level dating to about 1230 BC, which may represent the climax of these domestic problems (Wood 1985, 167–8).
6. Pausanias 8. 6. 1 and 8. 45. 2.
7. Diodorus Siculus 10. 6.
8. Shakespeare, *Henry V*, Act 4, Scene 3.
9. I have to admit to feeling a certain irrational and unjustifiable pride, nearly 600 years after the event, in knowing that one of my ancestors, William Casteleyn, fought at Agincourt. In antiquity, when military glory was everything, a connection with the attack on Troy must have meant much more. Of the 5,700 Englishmen who took part in the Battle of Agincourt, the names of three-quarters of them were not recorded; this is not dissimilar to Homer's attitude to 'other ranks'.
10. Strabo 3. 2. 13. A Cadmean victory is one bought at too great a cost. The reference is to the mythical warriors who sprang from the dragon's teeth sown by Cadmus.
11. *Iliad* 13. 533–4. Aeneas was claimed as a hero by the Romans, to whom he was a founding father, and I believe a gloss was put on his behaviour at the fall of Troy. Diodorus Siculus (7. 1. 4) tells a post-Homeric version of his escape in which Aeneas heroically defended the city, survived, and was allowed by the victorious Greeks to leave with what he could take of his household goods. Aeneas chose to take his aged father, Anchises, on his back, for which the Greeks showed him great respect. But none of this is compatible with what the Epic Cycle tells us about Aeneas. Aeneas was king of Dardania, not a resident of the city of Troy, would not have had a house there and there is no reason why his aged father should have been there. In his geriatric condition the father could not possibly have gone along to join in the fighting. The story is a piece of sentimental claptrap, designed to cover up the fact that Aeneas (and doubtless many other allies of the Trojans) deserted once it was clear that the war was lost.
12. Strabo 3. 2. 13; 10. 3. 22.
13. The Millawanda or Milawata Letter.
14. Aeschylus: the Chorus in *The Trojan Women*.

Bibliography

AJA – American Journal of Archaeology   *BSA – Annual of the British School at Athens*
AS – Anatolian Studies   *JHS – Journal of Hellenic Studies*
Ant. – Antiquity

Alexander, C. 1999. Echoes of the Heroic Age. *National Geographic* 185, 54–79.

Anderson, J. K. 1970. The Trojan Horse again. *Classical Journal* 66, 22–5.

—— 1995. The Geometric Catalogue of Ships. In Carter and Morris 1995, 181–91.

Arentzen, W. 2001. Frank Calvert, Henry Austen Layard and Heinrich Schliemann. *AS* 51, 168–85.

Beckman, E. J. W. 1991. *Hittite Diplomatic Texts*. Atlanta.

Behr, H-J., Biegel, G. and Castritius, H. (eds) 2002. *Troia: Ein Mythos in Geschichte und Rezeption*. Braunschweig. 8–40.

Bennet, J. 1999. Re-u-ko-to-ro za-we-te: Leuktron as a secondary capital in the Pylos region? In Bennet, J. and Driessen, J. (eds), *A-na-qo-ta: Studies Presented to J. T. Killen*, 11–30.

Blegen, C. 1950–58. The Palace of Nestor excavations. Annual reports in successive issues of *AJA*.

—— 1963. *Troy and the Trojans*. London: Thames and Hudson.

Blegen, C., Caskey, J. L. and Rawson, M. 1953. *Troy: Excavations Conducted by the University of Cincinnati*, Vol 3. Princeton: Princeton University Press.

Blegen, C. and Rawson, M. 1966. *The Palace of Nestor at Pylos in Western Messenia: I. the Buildings and their Contents*. Princeton: Princeton University Press.

Boedeker, D. (ed.) 1997. *The World of Troy: Homer, Schliemann, and the Treasures of Priam*. Washington DC: Society for the Preservation of Greek Heritage.

Bowra, C. M. 1960. Homeric epithets for Troy. *JHS* 80, 16–23.

Bryce, T. R. 1989. Ahhiyawans and Mycenaeans – an Anatolian viewpoint. *Oxford Journal of Archaeology* 8, 297–310.

—— 2002. *Life and Society in the Hittite World*. Oxford: Oxford University Press.

Calvert, F. 1881. Thymbra, Hanai Tepeh. In Schliemann 1881, 706–20.

Carpenter, R. 1966. *Discontinuity in Greek Civilization*. Cambridge: Cambridge University Press.

Carter, J. B. and Morris, S. P. (eds) 1995. *The Ages of Homer: a Tribute to Emily Townsend Vermeule*. Austin: University of Texas Press.

Caskey, J. L. 1964. Archaeology and the Trojan War. In Finley (ed.), *The Trojan War*, 9–11.

Castleden, R. 1989. *The Knossos Labyrinth: a New View of the 'Palace of Minos' at Knossos*. London: Routledge.

—— 1990. *Minoans: Life in Bronze Age Crete*. London: Routledge.

—— 1998. *Atlantis Destroyed*. London: Routledge.

—— 2000. *King Arthur: the Truth Behind the Legend*. London: Routledge.

—— 2005. *Mycenaeans*. London: Routledge.

Chadwick, J. 1976. *The Mycenaean World*. Cambridge: Cambridge University Press.

—— 1987. *Linear B and Related Scripts*. London: British Museum Publications.

—— 1990. *The Decipherment of Linear B*. Cambridge: Cambridge University Press.

Cline, E. H. 1996. Assuwa and the Achaeans: the 'Myceanean' sword at Hattusa and its possible implications. *BSA* 91, 137–51.

Crossland, R. A. and Birchall, A. (eds) 1974. *Bronze Age Migrations in the Aegean: Archaeological and Linguistic Problems in Greek Prehistory*. Park Ridge: Noyes Press.

Crouwel, J. H. and Morel, J. 1981. *Chariots and Other Means of Land Transport in Bronze Age Greece*. Amsterdam: Allard Pierson Museum.

Cunliffe, B. 1998. *Prehistoric Europe: an Illustrated History*. Oxford and New York: Oxford University Press.

Davis, J. L. 1998. *Sandy Pylos: an Archaeological History from Nestor to Navarino*. Austin: University of Texas Press.

Dickinson, O. 1994. *The Aegean Bronze Age*. Cambridge: Cambridge University Press.

Dörpfeld, W. 1902. *Troja und Ilion*. Athens: Barth and von Hirst.

Drews, R. 1993. *The End of the Bronze Age: Changes in Warfare and the Catastrophe c.1200 BC*. Princeton: Princeton University Press.

Easton, D. F. 1985. Has the Trojan War been found? *Ant.* 59, 188–96.

—— 1997. *The Quest for Troy*. London: Weidenfeld and Nicolson.

Easton, D. F., Hawkins, J. D., Sherratt, A. S. and Sherratt, E. S. 2002. Troy in recent perspective. *AS* 52, 75–109.

Fagles, R. 1991. *Homer: the Iliad*. London: Penguin.

Fields, N. 2004. *Troy c.1700–1250 BC*. Oxford: Osprey Publishing.

Finley, M. I. 1964. The Trojan War. *JHS* 84, 1–20.

—— 1986. *The World of Odysseus*. London: Penguin.

—— (ed.) 1991. *Aspects of Antiquity: Discoveries and Controversies*. London: Penguin.

Foltiny, S. 1967. The ivory horse bits of Homer and the bone horse bits of reality. *Bonner Jahrbücher* 167, 11–37.

Forrer, E. O. 1924. Vorhomerische Griechen in den Keilschrifttexten von Boghaz-koi. *Mitteilungen der Deutschen Orientgesellschaft Literaturzeitung*, 113–18.

Foxhall, L. and Davies, D. K. (eds) 1984. *The Trojan War: its Historicity and Context – Papers of the First Greenbank Colloquium, Liverpool, 1981*. Bristol: Bristol Classical Press.

French, E. and Wardle, K. (eds) 1988. *Problems in Greek Prehistory*. Bristol: Bristol Classical Press.

Friedrich, J. 1929. Werden in den hethitischen Keilschrifttexten die Griechen erwähnt? *Kleinasiatische Forschungen* 1, 87–107.

Garstang, J. and Gurney, O. R. 1959. *The Geography of the Hittite Empire*. London: British Institute of Archaeology at Ankara.

Gurney, O. R. 1990. *The Hittites*. London: Penguin.

—— 1997. The annals of Hattusilis III. *AS* 47, 127–39.

Guterbock, H. G. 1983. The Hittites and the Aegean World: I. The Ahhiyawa problem reconsidered. *AJA* 87, 133–8.

Hansen, O. 1997. KUB XXIII 13: a possible contemporary bronze age source for the sack of Troy/Hisarlik. *BSA* 92, 165–7.

Hawkins, J. D. 1998. Tarkasnawa King of Mira. 'Tarkondemos', Boghazkoy, sealings and Karabel. *AS* 48, 1–31.

Hertel, D. 2001. *Troia: Archäologie, Geschichte, Mythos*. Munich: C. H. Beck.

—— 2003. *Die Mauern von Troja: Mythos und Geschichte im antiken Ilion*. Munich: C. H. Beck.

Hiller, S. 1991. Two Trojan Wars? On the destruction of Troy VIh and VIIa. *Troia* 1, 145–9.

Hood, S. 1978. *The Arts in Prehistoric Greece*. Harmondsworth: Penguin Books.

—— 1995. The bronze age context of Homer. In Carter and Morris 1995, 25–32.

Houwink ten Cate, H. J. 1974. Contact between the Aegean region and Anatolia in the second millennium BC. In Crosland and Birchall 1974, 141–61.

Hunter, L. W. and Handford, S. A. 1927. *Aeneas Tacticus on Siegecraft*. Oxford: Oxford University Press.

James, A. (trans.) 2004. *Quintus of Smyrna: the Trojan Epic Posthomerica*. Baltimore: Johns Hopkins University Press.

Kayan, I. 1991. Holocene geomorphic evolution of the Besik Plain and changing environment of ancient man. *Troia* 1, 79–92.

—— 1995. The Troia Bay and supposed harbour sites in the bronze age. *Troia* 5, 211–35.

—— 1997. Geomorphic evolution of the Ciplak valley. *Troia* 7, 489–507.

Kilian, K. 1988. Mycenaeans up to date: trends and changes in recent research. In French and Wardle 1988, 115–52.

Kolb, F. 2002. Vor Troia sinken alle Fiktionen in den Staub. *Süddeutsche Zeitung*, 8 January 2002.

Korfmann, M. 1985. Beşik-Tepeh, 1984. *AS* 35, 182–3.

—— 1987. Beşik-Tepeh, 1986. *AS* 37, 180–1.

—— 1990. Altes und Neues aus Troia. *Das Altertum* 36, 230–40.

—— 1992. Troia Ausgrabungen 1990 und 1991. *Studia Troica* 2, 1–41.

—— 1993. Troia Ausgrabungen 1992. *Studia Troica* 3, 1–38.

—— 1994. Troia Ausgrabungen 1993. *Studia Troica* 4, 1–50.

—— 1996. Troia Ausgrabungen 1994. *Studia Troica* 6, 1–64.

—— 1997. Troia Ausgrabungen 1996. *Studia Troica* 7, 1–72.

—— 1998. Troia Ausgrabungen 1997. *Studia Troica* 8, 1–70.

—— 1999. Troia Ausgrabungen 1998. *Studia Troica* 9, 1–34.

—— 2000. Troia Ausgrabungen 1999. *Studia Troica* 10, 1–52.

—— 2001a. Troia Ausgrabungen 2000. *Studia Troica* 11, 1–50.

—— 2001b. Troia als Drehscheibe des Handels in 2. und 3. vorchristlichen Jahrtausend. In Latacz et al. 2001, 355–68.

Korfmann, M. and Mannsperger, D. 1998. *Troia: ein historischer Überblick und Rundgang*. Stuttgart: Theiss.

Koşak, S. 1981. Western neighbours of the Hittites. *Eretz-Israel* 15, 12–6.

Lang, M. 1995. War story into wrath story. In Carter and Morris 1995, 149–62.

Latacz, J. 2001. *Troia-Wilusa-Wilios: drei Namen für ein Territorium*. Basle.

—— 2004. *Troy and Homer: Towards a Solution of an Old Problem*. Oxford: Oxford University Press.

Latacz, J., Blome, P., Luckhardt, J., Brunner, H., Korfmann, M. and Biegel, G. (eds) 2001. *Troia: Traum und Wirklichkeit*. Stuttgart: Theiss.

Leaf. W. 1912. *A Study in Homeric Landscape*. London: Macmillan.

—— 1915. *Homer and History*. London: Macmillan.

Lehmann, J. 1977. *The Hittites: People of a Thousand Gods*. London: Collins.

Littäuer, M. A. 1972. The military use of the Mycenaean chariot. *AJA* 76, 145–57.

Lolos, Y. G. 1998. *The Capital of Nestor and its Environs*. Athens: Oionos.

Lorimer, H. L. 1950. *Homer and the Monuments*. London: Macmillan.

Lurz, N. 1994. *Der Einfluss Ägyptens, Vorderasiens und Kretas auf die Mykenischen Fresken*. Frankfurt am Main: Peter Lang.

MacKendrick, P. 1962. *The Greek Stones Speak*. London: Methuen.

Macqueen, J. G. 1986. *The Hittites and their Contemporaries in Asia Minor*. London: Thames and Hudson.

Mannsperger, B. 1993. Das Dardanische Tor in der Ilia. *Troia* 3, 193–9.

—— 1998. Die Mauer am Schiffslager der Achaier. *Troia* 8, 287–304.

Mason, H. 2004. *Looking for the Aeolian Migration*. www.apaclassics.org/AnnualMeeting/04mtg/abstracts/mason.html [31/08/04]

Matthieson, S. 1999. *How Important was Trade to Troy?* www.met.ed.ac.uk/~stephan/en/archaeo/handel-troja.html [04/01/05]

Mee, C. 1988. A Mycenaean thalassocracy in the Eastern Aegean? In French and Wardle 1988, 301–6.

Mellink, M. J. (ed.) 1986. *Troy and the Trojan War*. Bryn Mawr.

Mountjoy, P. A. 1998. The East Aegean–West Anatolian interface in the Late Bronze Age. Mycenaeans and the kingdom of Ahhiyawa. *AS* 48, 33–67.

Mylonas, G. 1983. *Mycenae Rich in Gold*. Athens: Ektotike Athenon.

Niemeier, W.-D. 1999. Mycenaeans and Hittites at war in Western Asia Minor. *Aegaeum* 19, 141–55.

Nilsson, M. P. 1933. *Homer and Mycenae*. London: Methuen.

Page, D. 1959. *History and the Homeric Iliad*. Berkeley: University of California Press.

Page, D. L. 1964. Homer and the Trojan War. In Finley 1964, 17–20.

Palmer, L. R. 1961. *Mycenaeans and Minoans: Aegean Prehistory in the Light of the Linear B Tablets*. London: Faber and Faber.

Papadopoulos, T. J. 1979. *Mycenaean Achaea*. Göteborg: Paul Åströms Forlag.

Prag, J. and Neave, R. 1999. *Making Faces*. London: British Museum Press.

Quincey, J. H. 1964. The beacon-sites in the Agamemnon. *JHS* 83, 118–32.

Schliemann, H. 1880. *Mycenae*. New York: Charles Scribner's Sons.

—— 1881. *Ilios, the City and the Country of the Trojans*. New York: Charles Scribner's Sons.

Schofield, L. and Parkinson, R. B. 1994. Of helmets and heretics: a possible Egyptian representation of Mycenaean warriors on a papyrus from El-Amarna. *BSA* 89, 157–70.

Schuchhardt, C. 1891. *Schliemann's Excavations: an Archaeological and Historical Study*. London and New York: Macmillan.

Seeher, J. 2002. *Hattusha Guide*. Istanbul: Yayinlari.

Snodgrass, A. M. 1999. *Arms and Armour of the Greeks*. Baltimore: Johns Hopkins University Press.

Sommer, F. 1932. Die Ahhijava-Urkunden. *Abhandlungen der Bayrischen Akademie der Wissenschaften*. Neue Folge 9.

Sperling, J. 1991. The last phase of Troy VI and Mycenaean expansion. *Troia* 1, 155–8.

Starke, F. 2001. Troia im Machtgefüge des zweiten Jahrtausends vor Christus. In Latacz et al. 2001, 34–45.

Steffen, H. and Lolling, H. 1884. *Karten von Mykenai*. Berlin: Dietrich Reimer.

Symeonoglou, S. 1985. *Topography of Thebes from the Bronze Age to Modern Times*. Princeton: Princeton University Press.

Symington, D. 1991. Late bronze age writing-boards and their uses: textual evidence from Anatolia and Syria. *AS* 41, 111–23.

Taylour, W. 1983. *The Mycenaeans*. London: Thames and Hudson.

Traill, D. D. A. 2000. Priam's Treasure clearly a composite. *AS* 50, 17–35.

Ventris, M. and Chadwick, J. 1973. *Documents in Mycenaean Greek*. Cambridge: Cambridge University Press.

Vermeule, E. T. 1986. Priam's castle blazing: a thousand years of Trojan memories. In Mellink 1986, 77–92.

Walter, U. 2001. Winning Helen – myth, history or invention? *Frankfurter Allgemeine Zeitung*, 26 July 2001.

Wilamowitz-Moellendorf, U. 1927. *Die Heimkehr des Odysseus*.

Wood, M. 1985. *In Search of the Trojan War*. London: BBC.

Index